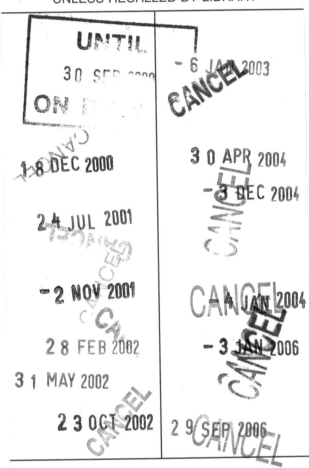

Implementing Evidence-based Changes in Healthcare

Edited by

David Evans

R&D Dissemination Facilitator,
NHS Executive London

and

Andrew Haines

Professor of Primary Health Care,
Royal Free and University College Medical School

Forewords by

Jenny Simpson

Chief Executive, The British Association
of Medical Managers

and

Trisha Greenhalgh

Senior Lecturer in General Practice,
Royal Free and University College Medical School

Radcliffe Medical Press

©2000 David Evans and Andrew Haines

Radcliffe Medical Press Ltd
18 Marcham Road, Abingdon, Oxon OX14 1AA

British Library Cataloguing in Publication Data

A catalogue record for this book is available from the British Library.

ISBN 1 85775 382 8

Typeset by Advance Typesetting Ltd, Oxfordshire
Printed and bound by TJ International Ltd, Padstow, Cornwall

Contents

Foreword

I believe that this is an important book. For too long the NHS has relied on dedicated and committed individuals to drive forward clinical change, with little or no support from their organisations.

As we move into the world of clinical governance it becomes critically important to understand how to help clinical change projects to succeed. NHS managers, particularly clinical managers, need to be able to systematically support such change; within a framework of evidence.

The book is a collaboration between the programme evaluators and the individual projects. Both are to be congratulated. The evaluators have found some of the common themes and threads, but have still allowed the individual tales of the projects to be told. The projects for their part have been direct and honest, not only about their successes, but about their failures.

What are the key messages? In the end they're very simple. Any clinical change will involve a wide range of stakeholders: from consultants to GPs, from nurses to social workers and from individual patients to patient groups. All must be involved in a proper and timely fashion.

Project managers need support, particularly from senior management, in a consistent and continued manner.

Finally, change takes time!

This is a book to dip into, it has many exciting insights, enjoy it.

Jenny Simpson
January 2000

Foreword

A 79-year-old woman falls in the street and fractures her hip. She is rushed to the local hospital, but the casualty department is chaotic and she spends seven hours on a trolley. Her emergency operation is delayed for 36 hours. She develops a post-operative thrombosis.

A 19-year-old student visits the nurse practitioner at his local surgery on a Friday evening with a sore throat. The nurse is concerned that if she does not give an antibiotic, the student may call out the doctor over the weekend. She prescribes a seven-day course of amoxycillin.

A 49-year-old British Pakistani man presents to his general practitioner with 'stomach pains'. He is told he has an ulcer and is given ranitidine. His symptoms quickly settle, but recur after a few weeks. He continues taking the tablets, assuming that his doctor can do no more for him. A year later he collapses at work and, when admitted to hospital, is found to have inoperable gastric cancer.

These cases raise many questions about best clinical practice and how to achieve it. What is the nature of the evidence supporting (or discrediting) the clinicians' actions in each case? How would we find such evidence? When we had found it, how would we check if it was trustworthy and relevant to the situation described? Does all the evidence point in the same direction, or is there a genuinely equivocal 'clinical bottom line'? What influence should the values and preferences of the patient have on the management decision, and how, on a practical level, can these be incorporated?

All these are difficult questions, but even once they have been answered, there are many more rivers to cross before the goal of effective clinical practice is reached. If the evidence says something *should happen*, how can we ensure that it *will happen* – not just to this patient on this occasion, but to all patients or potential patients in a similar situation on every occasion? This question can be addressed at many different levels.

First, from the perspective of the clinicians and administrators at the coal face: who will take the blood test, sign the X-ray form, explain the alternatives to the patient, administer the drug, do the operation, and so on – and who will record that the task has been done?

Second, from the perspective of the team: how can we distill these recommendations for best practice into a guideline or protocol, and how can we absorb it into our everyday work? What skills, tools and support do the members of our team need in order to follow the protocol? What interfaces for communication and shared responsibility does our protocol create with other individuals, teams and organisations?

Third, from the perspective of the organisation: what is the overall level of need in this clinical area, what structures and systems do we need to deliver this and other relevant protocols, and how will we know if our systems are working?

Finally, from the perspective of policymakers: how can we ensure that locally developed protocols and systems for addressing clinical needs are both affordable from our limited resources, and congruent with national and international recommendations for best practice?

Somerset Maugham famously said that a good short story needs a mystery, a religion, an aristocrat and sex. This unique collection, in which individuals, teams and organisations have shared their attempts to deliver best practice, conveys a sense of all these. The many 'rate-limiting steps' are variously identified in terms of stakeholders, personalities, resources, relationships, information, beliefs, cultures, policies, systems and a long list of unknowns. The changes, and failures to change, at these different levels make tough but compelling reading. Some lessons – such as the need to 'mainstream' new practices, engage key stakeholders, provide appropriate IT support and be realistic about evaluation – are very obvious from the case studies. Others – such as the widely differing views which different people and groups may have about the same project, the degree of 'flak' that individual project workers may sometimes experience and the fact that we will readily change our behaviour when X asks us to but not when Y does – are less easily understood or measured.

David Evans and Andy Haines encouraged the authors of these stories to 'tell it as it really happened'. One gets the feeling that some accounts have been sanitised and that others are incomplete, but there are some brave admissions and the views of the external evaluators provide a valuable perspective. As a result this is probably the best attempt yet to capture on paper the nitty-gritty of the evidence-into-practice agenda in UK healthcare. I hope you find it a ripping good read.

Trisha Greenhalgh
January 2000

Preface

Success and failure are present in this book in almost equal measure. Its chapters describe in detail the numerous minor, and occasionally major, achievements, disappointments, elations and frustrations of research implementation. We believe that the authors have described their experience with a degree of candour rarely found when people write of their own work. The book is a tribute to the contributors' desire to share with colleagues the lessons they have learned, both positive and negative.

We believe that the chapters which follow graphically reinforce the contention that implementing changes in clinical practice and health services is complex, challenging and not resource-neutral, as some may imagine. The expectation that the emergence of research evidence automatically results in timely and appropriate changes in care and service provision is naïve, and examples demonstrating this range from the earliest records of science in medicine to the present day. Our hope is that these frank descriptions of practical, proactive work on research implementation in the NHS will not only contribute to readers' individual perspectives of this subject, but also add to the wider debate about the legitimacy and importance of research implementation as an activity in its own right. It is our conviction that this debate is essential, and that it will be a major determinant of the ultimate success or failure of the NHS Research & Development (R&D) Programme, and of other initiatives such as the National Institute for Clinical Excellence, which aim to promote changes in practice.

The Programme, which is funded from a levy raised from the NHS itself, will in the long run be judged not by academic criteria such as publications, citations or prizes, but by the difference it makes to the health and health services provided for the people who have paid for it. The unique place of the NHS in the public's affection sometimes protects its institutions from the rigours of performance-oriented scrutiny which is normal elsewhere. For the NHS R&D Programme, however, taxpayers' loyalty to the NHS could prove to be a double-edged sword, which could quickly be turned against the Programme if, at the inevitable time of reckoning, it is perceived as having failed to provide benefits commensurate with its opportunity costs. The unique, unprecedented chance to direct R&D towards the most important issues for a nation's health, which the Programme has provided, must not be squandered for want of the final effort to ensure that research evidence leads to improved health and healthcare. We hope that this book will play a small part in ensuring that this eventuality is avoided, through sharing real-life experiences of research implementation in the NHS.

David Evans
Andrew Haines
January 2000

List of contributors

John Aldous	Consultant in Public Health, Hillingdon Health Authority
Mark Ansell	Effectiveness Facilitator, Barking & Havering Health Authority
Sue Collett	Clinical Guidelines Facilitator, Redbridge & Waltham Forest Health Authority
Mark Dancy	Consultant Cardiologist, Central Middlesex Hospital NHS Trust
Sarah Davies	Information Facilitator, Ealing, Hammersmith & Hounslow Health Authority
Chris Deeming	Clinical Effectiveness Project Manager, Hillingdon Health Authority
Peter Elliot	Medical Adviser, Redbridge & Waltham Forest Health Authority
Julie Ferguson	Pharmacist Audit Facilitator, Camden & Islington Health Authority
Mike Gogarty	Consultant in Public Health, South Essex Health Authority
Sally Gooch	Assistant Nursing Director, Tower Hamlets Health Care NHS Trust
Angela Haigh	Research Assistant, Central Middlesex Hospital NHS Trust
Anna Hansell	Specialist Registrar in Public Health, South Essex Health Authority
Sonja Hood	Senior Research and Policy Officer, Kensington, Chelsea & Westminster Health Authority
Alison Hopkins	Clinical Nurse Specialist (Tissue Viability), Tower Hamlets Health Care NHS Trust
Raymond Jankowski	Consultant in Public Health, Ealing, Hammersmith & Hounslow Health Authority
John McClenahan	Fellow, King's Fund

Francesca Scott	Clinical Nurse Specialist (Tissue Viability), Tower Hamlets Health Care NHS Trust
Peter Sheridan	Deputy Director of Public Health, Enfield & Haringey Health Authority
Lizzi Shires	Primary Care Education and Audit Co-ordinator, South Essex Health Authority
Alaganandan Sivakumar	Consultant in A&E, Brent & Harrow Health Authority
Lesley Smith	Researcher, King's Fund
Suzanne Smith	Commissioning Manager, Ealing, Hammersmith & Hounslow Health Authority
Stephanie Taylor	Senior Registrar in Public Health, Kensington, Chelsea & Westminster Health Authority
Chris Watts	Director of Public Health, Barking & Havering Health Authority

Job titles as at the time of the projects.

Acknowledgements

In addition to the contributing authors, and the many people involved in the projects, we would specifically like to thank the following people for their help, patience and support in producing this book: Sue Andrew, Penny Bateman, Sally Davies, Shak Hajat, Gillian Nineham, Chris Owen, Paula Moran, Peter Richardson, Steve Whitlam and Wendy Zhou.

We are particularly indebted to John McClenahan and Lesley Smith for their insightful commentaries from an external perspective on each of the projects, which appear as supplements to each chapter.

Introduction

Context

The length of time taken for emerging research evidence to bring about appropriate changes in healthcare has been highlighted as a problem in recent years, and a growing literature has starkly exposed the cost of such delays in terms of avoidable suffering.[1] Recognition that the traditional approach of 'passive diffusion' is inadequate to ensure that research findings influence clinical practice has led the NHS to fund initiatives such as the NHS Centre for Reviews and Dissemination, national programmes for Health Technology Assessment and the study of Methods to Promote the Implementation of Research Findings in the NHS. From the launch of the NHS R&D Programme, the North East Thames (and later North Thames) Region recognised that its locally funded portfolio of R&D projects should include work to develop understanding and experience of turning research evidence into changes in service provision and clinical practice. Accordingly an Implementation Group was established (in 1993), with a budget for the commissioning of R&D implementation projects, and reporting to the Regional R&D Committee.

In addition to calling for research proposals in the usual 'open' way, it was decided that projects which fitted into the current model of separate purchaser and provider functions would be tested. Accordingly, participation in a project testing the feasibility of implementing the results of research through evidence-based medicine was offered to all trusts in the Region*, and a parallel initiative aimed at purchasers was also initiated; namely the Purchaser-Led Implementation Projects. The work described in the chapters of this volume arose from these projects.

The approach to purchasers (health authorities) followed the appointment of a Research Implementation Facilitator at the region, whose early work had included discussions with directors of public health and others from health authorities to determine why these organisations had either been uninterested or had failed to achieve funding in successive service-wide calls for R&D implementation project proposals. At the time (1995) there was considerable emphasis on the role of the health authorities in managing the healthcare resources for local populations through effective commissioning.

---

*This project was called the 'Front Line Evidence Based Medicine Project', and a report is available as a downloadable PDF file from the London Region R&D Website: http://www.doh.gov.uk/ntrd/rd/reimplem/coma1.htm

The apparent failure of these organisations to take advantage of opportunities to implement and evaluate changes in care, based on research evidence offered by the calls for implementation projects, had been disappointing. In establishing the health authority (or purchaser-)-led implementation projects, the North Thames R&D Implementation Group took account of the reasons the health authorities had given for their lack of interest or success in attracting R&D resources in the past and this resulted in the following ground rules being established.

- The new initiative would be open *only* to health authorities. They would be encouraged to work *with* other NHS organisations, and would be able to devolve management of projects if they so wished. However, the topics selected, accountability and funding would be via the health authority, and applications from other organisations would not be considered. (This was intended to allay specific fears expressed by several health authorities relative to their perceived disadvantage in competing with academic departments or NHS trusts for research resources.)
- Each health authority in the region would be funded up to *the same* maximum amount (£50 000), subject to meeting the quality criteria for their projects. Authorities would be able to focus on one project or could choose to have two or more. However, only £50 000 would be available, regardless of the number of projects. (This was intended to meet some authorities' fears that they were disadvantaged compared with others, and that if there was competition *between* health authorities, some would attract more funds at the expense of others.)
- Steps would be taken to 'de-jargonise' and simplify the process of applying for funding. It had been noted that the language and culture of research had been perceived to be a barrier to applying for previous R&D implementation funds by individuals at health authorities. The wording, tone and style of the 'standard' research application form clearly reflected research culture and this had excluded people without experience and fluency in that vocabulary, which was felt to have adversely affected previous applications. For the purposes of R&D implementation projects, which would be led by health authorities and externally evaluated, it was recognised that project applicants' ability to demonstrate conversance with research terminology and methodologies would be much less important than their ability to influence change in their organisations.
- There would be certainty of funding, subject only to project applications meeting two criteria relating to the subjects chosen and the project plan. This was to address the fact that the time spent (or 'wasted' as it was often regarded) on previous unsuccessful applications had been cited as a reason for the health authorities' reluctance to respond to recent calls. It was felt that while organisations such as academic departments were able to set

aside staff time for working on research proposals, and could plan for an acceptable rate of failure of applications, health authority personnel would be likely to work on proposals as additional work, over and above their normal duties. The idea that a large proportion of applications would be unsuccessful in achieving funding was therefore far less acceptable to the health authorities. This was not only because the work involved was likely to have been undertaken in personnel's own time, but because the high risk that such effort might prove fruitless was at odds with a management culture where strenuous effort would normally be expected to be rewarded with positive results.

Project approval

Health authority chief executives and directors of public health were first invited to submit simple, two-page expressions of interest, detailing the implementation topic and why it had been selected. Feedback and guidance were provided by a subgroup drawn from the Implementation Group, who dissuaded a small number of project ideas, encouraged others and made suggestions as to ways in which ideas might be developed or reinforced in order to make them supportable. In the latter cases, authorities were asked to develop firmer proposals, and when ideas were thought unsuitable, they were asked to reconsider and submit alternative ideas.

Two basic criteria were applied to both expressions of interest and the firmer proposals when these were considered at a later stage (by a subgroup of the Implementation Committee). These were that projects should be based on robust research evidence, i.e. that the quality and level of acceptance of research findings was such that there was little possibility of a project being undermined by having a weak basis in research; and that projects should have a realistic plan, with specified objectives which stood a reasonable chance of being achieved. With the benefit of hindsight it is clear that while the first of these criteria was applied reasonably successfully (no project failed because research 'evidence' was refuted), the second was far less well applied. This may be a reflection of a widepread weakness at the time in visualising the essential component parts and a realistic scale for a research implementation project (something which it is hoped that programmes such as this, and the National PACE* initiative have begun to address).

---

*PACE (Promoting Action for Clinical Effectiveness) was a national programme of projects aimed at implementing changes based on research evidence, which began shortly after the North Thames initiative.

Origins of this book, what it includes and omits, and how to use it

This book contains 12 chapters, and 11 of these (Chapters 2–12) were written by people who led Health Authority-led Research and Development Implementation Projects in the North Thames Region of the NHS in the period 1996–98. Chapter 1 was written by the external evaluators of the programme, Lesley Smith and John McClenahan of the King's Fund.

The origins of the book are that in 1998, when final reports from the projects were due, the editors had the idea of gathering together material from all of the projects, enabling rapid and widespread dissemination of the lessons learned. It was agreed that, subject to there being sufficient enthusiasm among the project participants, their experiences and the lessons from the projects would be presented as chapters of a book (chapters being accepted as an alternative to the mandatory final reports required by the NHS Executive Regional Office). The project leaders were consulted, and from the 15 projects in the programme, 11 signed up to each produce a chapter* following a format which would include sections on *lessons learned* and *things we would do differently if we were starting tomorrow*, which were included with the specific purpose of eliciting critical information. We have also endeavoured to explain technical terms in order to make this book accessible to readers from a wide range of backgounds.

The external evaluators of the programme were also enthusiastic and agreed to contribute a chapter on the overall programme (Chapter 1). In addition, they have also written short commentaries on individual projects, included after each chapter, providing an evaluator's view of each project, which readers will find helpful for getting the most from the book. This is not because the authors of individual chapters have sought deliberately to portray their work in a favourable light (in fact understatement of achievement was far more common), but because they were personally very 'close' to the projects, whereas the evaluators had a more distant vantage point.

When the idea of a book was first proposed, it was our intention that it should be *used* by readers to compare how colleagues in different contexts had tackled implementation problems, enabling readers to benefit from the lessons learned and the clear messages of what project leaders would do differently if they could start again from scratch. We hope that this has been achieved by the consistent presentation of *lessons learned* and *things we would do differently*,

---

*Although four of the 15 projects have not participated directly in the compilation of this book, they were included in the external evaluation of the programme, and lessons observed from this perspective are incorporated into Chapter 1. A full list of all 15 projects, identifying those with a chapter, is included on pp xx–xxi.

as well as the index, which will enable readers to 'dip' into relevant parts of the book. However, having read all of the material in detail ourselves, and come to appreciate the richness of the experience it contains, we hope that readers will also read it through (as well as using it for guidance on specific issues). Reading the chapters all together will provide a particularly comprehensive insight into attempting to implement changes based on research evidence across a broad range of settings in the NHS.

What this book is not, and how to avoid being misled by it

This book is not about research. It does not present 'evidence' of the kind described in academic publications on the subject of implementing change. The reader should at all times be aware that despite the fact that the *raisons d'être* of each project lies in research evidence, this book is much more about peoples' experience of trying to make things happen and stimulating change than about evidence-based practice. We do not apologise for this, as one of the main reasons for producing the book was to address the imbalance between the growing volume of literature on the theory of evidence-based practice and the lack of material on implementation, based on real-world experience. In any case, we suspect that most readers will be well aware of the literature on evidence, and for those who are not, we have included a short selection of recommended texts and sources of evidence at the end of the book.

Nevertheless, readers should not be misled, for example by uncritically trusting the references provided by the authors. References included are for the most part those which the projects *actually used* when they tackled particular aspects of their projects, and they should not necessarily be regarded as the 'best' sources of evidence. Indeed in some cases, because the work may have been undertaken up to three years ago, papers cited may now be out of date. We therefore suggest that all aspects of the book are considered with a critical eye, and that readers should remember that these chapters reflect what *actually* happened, rather than what we might *wish* to have happened in an ideal world. (In particular, we would suggest that readers do not take statistics quoted, such as numbers needed to treat (NNT), at face value, but seek out the best *current* values themselves, being mindful of the limitations of these statistics and using them with due caution.)

Similarly, inconsistencies between messages in different chapters have not been removed to produce a smooth finish or to fit a convenient theory. As editors, our priority has been to respect the frankness of the authors, and while we recognise that a lack of internal consistency may be the price paid, we think that the authenticity of the book, which is complex and sometimes apparently contradictory, justifies the approach. Notwithstanding the 'uncut' approach to reporting and the gritty reality of the projects, for the most part the experiences described in this book are consistent with the findings of recent studies on implementation, both in terms of the barriers identified and in confirming the advantage of multifaceted approaches in overcoming them.

Although the NHS has changed substantially since these projects were initiated, the desire to promote evidence-based change in practice remains central to many of the NHS developments in recent years. The focus of the drive for change has shifted to clinical governance at the level of primary care groups or hospital trusts, however, many of the issues described in this book are without doubt of continuing relevance. We hope that by exposing the range of barriers which clinicians and managers in the NHS face when they seek to implement changes based on research evidence, the North Thames projects will contribute to a process of sharing good practice that the National Service Frameworks, National Institute for Clinical Excellence (NICE) and Commission for Health Improvement (CHI) will be driving in the months and years ahead. We hope that colleagues in the wider health service community will benefit, through the dissemination of this book, from the 20+ person-years' work which was invested in the North Thames projects, and will be inspired to use these lessons in their own workplaces to unlock the potential of research evidence to the benefit of all who are served by the NHS.

Lessons learned

- People consistently underestimated the time necessary to undertake a project to implement changes in services or clinical practice based on research evidence.
- Project participants were generally positive about opportunities they were given to learn from each other at facilitated workshops.
- The health authorities that experienced the most difficulties with their projects were not the same as those that had been less confident about competing in an 'open' way for R&D resources before the projects began.
- Most of the projects generated a large amount of activity, but ability to measure impact has been limited. Nevertheless, in terms of widening the ownership of R&D, the fact that the projects were able to engage many people who had no previous involvement in R&D was important.
- No health authority attempted to rely only on the leverage of commissioning to implement changes in service provision or clinical practice based on research evidence. The projects that were most successful in achieving changes in services and clinical care were those that involved winning broad support and *enabling* change, and it was notable that no project attempted to bring about change by 'tightening up' the specifications of what would be 'purchased'.

continued overleaf

- Where health authorities used the initiative to support several projects rather than one, their energy was dissipated to the point where projects failed to get started or stalled (this happened with abortive projects in Brent & Harrow and Kensington, Chelsea & Westminster, and a failed project in East London & The City).
- In the one case where major organisational change occurred after the projects had been established (in Hertfordshire where one health authority was divided into two), it proved impossible to facilitate two projects, despite additional resources being made available.

Things we would do differently if we were starting tomorrow

- Be firm in allowing only one project per authority.
- Dissuade applicants from overambitious aspirations.
- Establish and enforce commitment to a minimum standard of project management by involving someone with experience of leading a similar project to provide advice to project leaders at the planning stage.
- Ensure that projects have the capacity and intention to gather baseline data relevant to the influence of their project. Encourage the timely and accurate use of audit to measure the influence of projects over as broad a range of dimensions as possible.
- Plan for the dissemination of lessons learned from an earlier stage, and establish a method of capturing lessons as they are learned during the lifetime of projects.
- Involve those mechanisms being developed by primary care groups and trusts to promote clinical governance, linking continuing education, clinical audit and risk management.

References

1 Haines A and Donald A (eds) (1998) *Getting Research Findings into Practice*. BMJ Books, London.

2 Smeeth L, Haines A and Ebrahim S (1999) Numbers needed to treat derived from meta analysis – sometimes informative, usually misleading. *BMJ*. **318**: 1548–51.

Full list of approved health authority-led Research & Development Implementation Projects in North Thames

Projects in **bold** are chapters in this book

Health authority	Project	Lead manager	Chapter	Page
Barking & Havering	**Coronary heart disease and obstetrics and gynaecology**	**Director of Public Health Chris Watts**	**2**	17
Barnet	Low back pain, diabetic retinopathy, *Helicobacter pylori*		–	–
Brent & Harrow	**Protocols in A&E**	**Consultant in A&E Alaganandan Sivakumar**	**3**	39
Brent & Harrow	**Non-invasive cardiac assessment**	**Consultant Cardiologist Mark Dancy**	**4**	67
Brent & Harrow (did not start)	Schizophrenia		–	–
Camden & Islington	*Helicobacter pylori*	**Prescribing Facilitator Amalin Dutt**	**5**	89
Ealing, Hounslow & Hammersmith	**Diabetes register**	**Consultant in Public Health Raymond Jankowski**	**6**	113
East London & The City	Cardiac intervention		–	–
East London & The City	**Leg ulcers**	**Assistant Nursing Director Sally Gooch**	**7**	133
Enfield & Haringey	**GP learning sets**	**Consultant in Public Health Peter Sheridan**	**8**	177
Hillingdon	*Helicobacter pylori* **Leg ulcers Coronary heart disease**	**Consultant in Public Health John Aldous**	**9**	193
Kensington, Chelsea & Westminster (did not start)	Dyspepsia		–	–

Health authority	Project	Lead manager	Chapter	Page
Kensington, Chelsea & Westminister	**ECG & ACE inhibitors in chronic heart failure**	**Senior Registrar in Public Health Stephanie Taylor**	10	211
North Essex	Cancer services		–	–
Redbridge & Waltham Forest	**Diabetes, asthma and hypertension**	**Director of Public Health Lucy Moore**	11	235
South Essex	**Hypertension in the elderly**	**Consultant in Public Health Mike Gogarty**	12	257
West Hertfordshire	Anticoagulation		–	–

Editors' note

All author royalties due to the editors of this book will be used to resource the Effective Healthcare CHAIN* Network for healthcare professionals interested in research and evidence-based practice. For further information on CHAIN visit the website:

http://www.doh.gov.uk/ntrd/chain/chain.htm

or write to:

David Evans
Research and Development
NHS Executive (London)
40 Eastbourne Terrace
London W2 3QR.

*Contacts, Help, Advice and Information Network

1

Evaluation of the Purchaser-led Implementation Programme

Lesley Smith and John McClenahan

Introduction

When putting evidence into practice, people hope the implementation process will be as clear-cut, well-defined and linear as the clinical trials themselves sometimes appear to be. What they discover is that it is messy, time-consuming, expensive and circuitous.[1]

Our aim in this chapter is to help professionals identify what would be worth doing. Specifically, where and how could they set up an implementation project that would make a tangible improvement in professional education, service development and, ultimately, patient outcomes? Through examples from the 17 projects, we will give readers ideas of key points to think about.

Evaluation

Background

In October 1996, North Thames Research & Development commissioned the King's Fund to carry out an evaluation of the Purchaser-led Implementation Programme. We were asked to identify the elements that led to success and the outcomes a 'successful' implementation project could hope to deliver.

Approach

In looking at ways of carrying out the evaluation, we decided on a developmental evaluation model. This approach is especially helpful when the item for evaluation changes while the evaluation is being carried out and/or when it is poorly defined.[2]

We chose this approach for three main reasons:

1   It encourages participants to set their own objectives, reflect on what they have learned and change course as necessary.
2   It allows for changes in the evaluation methodology as and when needed.
3   It allowed us to move from detached observation to action research. We wanted to do what we could to encourage these projects to work, without losing our independence as evaluators. This is a fine line to tread and needs to be constantly renegotiated.

We broke the evaluation down into three parts: (a) setting objectives and planning evaluation, (b) barriers to change and strategies to overcome them and (c) sustainability. Our task was to identify the general lessons coming out of the projects in these three areas and to feed them back to both the projects and the funders, North Thames R&D.

Timescale

The timescale for the projects and for the evaluation shifted considerably. North Thames originally funded 17 projects for 18 months, but nine had already done some work prior to receiving this money. Only three (GP learning sets, Camden & Islington *Helicobacter pylori* and cancer services) ran for 18 months and then effectively stopped, although one lost to follow-up (East London & The City cardiac) may no longer be continuing as the project worker has left. The other 13 have gone on for longer with extra funding coming from other sources. As the projects have taken longer than expected, so has the evaluation – originally planned for 18 months, it stretched to two-and-a-half years.

Methods

Workshop for external experts

In April 1997, we asked 15 professionals with experience in implementation to a workshop. Eight attended, including a medical director, GP, voluntary organisation director, health authority chief executive, senior nursing lecturer, academic, representative from the Centre for Reviews and Dissemination (CRD) and the Implementation Facilitator for North Thames R&D.

We wanted to involve people from outside because we felt that they had a great deal of collective knowledge on how to make change happen which would be useful for the projects. With this experience, they would be more realistic about what projects could be achieved in 18 months.

We asked them to define 'success', which they did as either:

1   A project which meets all of its objectives.
2   A project that does not meet its objectives, but individuals and the organisation analyse why and learn from it.

They also identified a set of nine elements of 'successful' implementation projects against which the projects could be assessed.[3] They were:

- undertaking **groundwork** thoroughly
- involving **users** (defined as local professionals as well as patients)
- **facilitating the change** before meeting resistance
- **avoiding hindrances** where possible
- choosing a good **leader**
- creating the right **environment** within the organisation
- **overcoming barriers** after meeting resistance
- incorporating **evaluation**
- encouraging **sustainability**.

Workshops for project teams

In the summer of 1997, we met with project teams in the first of a series of workshops. The topic was 'setting objectives and evaluation'. Fifteen projects were represented. By this time, one of the projects had been cancelled (schizophrenia) and so we were now evaluating 16 rather than 17.

The second series, covering levers, barriers and strategies for change, took place in the winter of 1997. We also looked at local professionals' acceptance of the evidence. Again, all but one of the 16 projects were represented.

The third series took place a year later in the winter of 1998, when North Thames funding had officially finished for all of the projects. Using a self-assessment questionnaire based on *Features likely to lead to success* drawn up from the workshop with the expert group,[3] we asked project teams to rate their own strengths and weaknesses as well as assess where the project was in meeting its objectives. The resulting discussion was the focus for this workshop series.

We met with teams from ten of the projects at the workshops, and had individual meetings with another three project teams. Two of the projects dropped out from the evaluation (East London & The City cardiac and Brent & Harrow cardiac) after we contacted them numerous times and they did not respond. One further project (Kensington, Chelsea & Westminster dyspepsia) had been cancelled between the second and third series of workshops.

Telephone surveys

In the second workshop, we asked project teams to draw stakeholder maps. They identified local people who might have some perspective on the project's success, whether as colleagues of the project team or as practitioners in the wider world. We wanted to talk with a sample of them to confirm our impressions from the workshops.

Project teams supplied anywhere from three to nine names. We do not know if project teams picked only those who they thought would be positive. Nonetheless, even the most positive respondents gave some information about their concerns.

We chose three to six names for each project. Our selection of whom to include depended a great deal on what we knew of each project. For projects with a primary and secondary care interface, we contacted both hospital staff and community specialists. For community-based projects we talked with primary care staff and one or two health authority colleagues. For hospital projects, we talked to staff from a range of disciplines and levels within the trust.

Four projects were excluded: two because it was too early to get information, one because contact names and numbers arrived too late and one because no candidate responded after numerous attempts to contact.

We included 49 potential candidates. We got information on 12 projects from 36 people while the survey was conducted from January to March 1998. Respondents were asked about their understanding of the project's goals, the chances of meeting those goals, strengths and weaknesses, and sustainability. Abridged versions of the survey summaries appear in the second interim report.[4]

We carried out a second survey of local participants from February to June 1999. The questions for this survey covered the project's success, strengths and weaknesses, long-term sustainability and potential for replicability elsewhere.

Fifty-six candidates were invited to take part. We got information on 11 projects from 48 people. Fourteen of the second survey respondents had participated in the previous survey. Four projects were not included: two because they were dormant at the time we wanted contact names and two others because they had dropped out of the evaluation.

Data quality

Information at the 12 workshops was recorded by hand by two researchers, then written up and sent back to participants to check for accuracy. For one workshop, we took notes and used a tape recorder because one researcher was ill. The record of this workshop was written up from notes, then checked with the tape. Interestingly, the tape and researcher's notes concurred well, the only difference being that the tape offered further clarification.

Information from the telephone interviews was harder to validate. If one or more interviewees brought up the same point, or mentioned something that had been discussed in the workshops by the project teams, we believed the point was valid. If something major was brought up by one of the interviewees which was not confirmed by other respondents, we would discuss it with the project teams in informal telephone conversations. For the first survey, a collated sheet of A4 with anonymised results was sent back to all project teams.

Data analysis

At the end of the evaluation, we had a great deal of information for each project including: interim and final reports (or book chapters), the results from the two telephone surveys (between three and eight interviews per project), workshop notes, notes from telephone conversations and self-assessment questionnaires.

We divided the analysis into two parts: outcomes and processes. We devised one model for outcomes and one for processes. For outcomes, projects were analysed on the basis of 12 elements (*see* Figure 1.1). The process model included elements specified in the *Features likely to lead to success* document. Two researchers analysed each project independently and the results were compared.

We had not completed the analysis stage at the time of writing this chapter, but we can discuss a number of preliminary findings.

Results

Identifying a 'successful' implementation

Figuring out which projects are 'successful' and having the evidence to back up that claim is difficult. Only one project team (hypertension in elderly people) was able to carry out a complete, reliable evaluation looking at the impact their work had on changing clinical practice. Several other teams looked at process measures (e.g. number of GPs attending events) or proxy

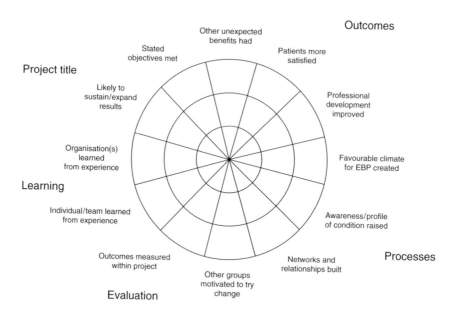

Figure 1.1   Outcomes and processes.

measures (e.g. 'Prescribing Analysis and CosT' (PACT) data). Although these measures are useful in gauging if any change is happening, and are the best most could do within the time and money available, they are not very satisfactory in helping others learn what really does work.

Another difficulty is that these projects are in no way static. A project that looks very promising at one point of the evaluation could falter and stall a few months later. Throughout the analysis stage, we continued to have contact with the teams, which affected our assessment of their success. For example, when we last met the primary care guidelines team in January, sustainability looked very good. Five months later, both the project manager and worker left and so its future, for the time being, is not so clear. Giving these projects a definite rating of 'successful' is difficult because, with a couple of exceptions, they are constantly evolving.

A further difficulty in identifying 'successful' implementation projects is that the definitions of success given by the external stakeholder group (meeting objectives and learning from the project) were not all that helpful in singling out those projects which had made a bigger impact. Objectives in implementation work are continually revised in light of what becomes feasible. Measuring success against objectives becomes meaningless because objectives can be changed so the project can always be defined as successful. Similarly, if just one person has learned something from the experience, then even the most ineffectual of projects can be called a success. Since every project team has learned a great deal, all the projects were successful in this sense. But not all of them made an impact in changing practice.

So, without quantifiable indicators or a good working definition of success, we devised an alternative definition. **The more successful projects are the ones in which the evidence is integrated into routine practice to the point that people could not envisage working in the old ways**.

What does a successful implementation project look like?

The projects that have made the patchiest progress towards routine practice are those that used a purely educational approach. This approach was usually based on one-off training events, audit and/or guideline development. They made the least impact in terms of breadth (i.e. number of people now acting in accordance with the evidence) and depth (i.e. how firmly rooted in daily practice). An exception was the GP learning sets project, which was based on regular educational meetings, but still failed to make significant changes in clinical behaviour. The reasons for this are discussed in its commentary.

Repeatedly, project teams and survey participants stated that educational initiatives alone would not change practice. One project manager said:

> 'They know, they **know** the knowledge. We often start from the assumption that people need to be told all this stuff, that they need to have it reinforced. But it isn't about that. It isn't about more guidelines; it's about getting that behaviour changed.'

So although the majority of these projects have made some progress in initiating change, they need more time, energy, funding and strategic thinking before they can make a bigger impact.

For embedded change to happen, a further step is needed. Education cannot be a one-off event. It needs to be systematically incorporated into staff's professional development, either through regular team audit meetings or visits by the project team.

What's more, along with continuing education, **the ways in which practitioners work need to be substantially reorganised** so the new evidence-based way becomes the best option. As Ferlie, Wood and Fitzgerald (1998) term it, project teams or practitioners themselves need to *translate* the evidence into the practitioners' particular circumstances, so they can compare their performance against agreed standards.[5] As one survey respondent put it:

> 'It's not a knowledge gap with practitioners – they know it all – but they have problems in how to organise it.'

In some projects, this meant establishing a new service. For others, it meant reconfiguring existing services. Even at practice level in projects that overall were not firmly embedded, we found that GP practices within the project area which had significantly reorganised their ways of working had made dramatic progress. The pitfall of this approach is that it is very labour-intensive for both project teams and practitioners.

New services or ways of working, coupled with education, mean that it is much easier for practitioners to adopt the evidence-based route. But for some projects the problem is that although the evidence-based way may be the best option, the former ways of working still exist so the new practice is not routine. So, for example with the open-access cardiac services, GPs can still refer to outpatients if they choose. There is an 'escape route'.

Another obstacle to becoming a routine practice is that the financial future is still uncertain for several of these projects. For example, the future of the new Barnet clinics (physiotherapy and diabetes retinopathy) and Kensington, Chelsea & Westminster open-access services depends on the results of internal evaluations. Nevertheless, projects that have come this far have made great strides in the past two-and-a-half years and have very promising outlooks in terms of becoming part of routine practice.

We found there were two projects (A&E protocols and nurse-led anti-coagulation) which are now so much a part of routine practice that practitioners could not revert to the old ways. As well as continually updating staff's knowledge and reconfiguring old services or establishing new ones, these two projects have gone one step further. **The old service or ways of working no longer exist – they have been totally replaced by the new ones**. So, clinicians have no choice but to practise in the evidence-based way. For example, in the A&E department, staff have to use computer-generated protocols because there is no other documentation available.

When projects reach or are near to this level of progress, another benefit comes in – patient satisfaction. Not only do these projects contribute to improving the quality of care and regularly updating professionals' education, but patients are reported to be happier.

Why have some projects become more embedded than others?

This provides a useful description of successful implementation projects and characterises the approaches that have led them to becoming successful. But at this stage of the analysis, without looking at process elements more closely, it is difficult to determine exactly *why* certain project teams are better able to reach every project's goal of becoming a part of routine practice.

What we can say is that six of the eight projects based in primary care have found it much harder. This is unsurprising.

Organisations in primary care are much more diffuse. So, instead of having to influence just one department with a limited number of staff, like the purely secondary care projects of A&E and nurse-led anticoagulation, project teams in primary care have to work extensively with professionals from dozens of different organisations, each with their own idiosyncratic ways of working. This is not to say that implementation projects based in primary care are a waste of time – far from it. It is just that the effort needed to make an impact is much greater since project teams need to help reconfigure many more individual organisations.

Experience

The gardening metaphor

Working towards embedding change is difficult, draining, surprising and rewarding. Creating a garden is a useful analogy for getting a sense of what implementation feels like.

Initially, project teams started with the belief that managing an implementation project *ought* to be like a feng shui garden, with clear, orderly lines and few weeds. They wanted to set SMART objectives (**S**pecific, **M**easurable, **A**chievable, **R**esourced, **T**ime-bound), develop and apply useful strategies, circumvent obstacles and finally collect quantifiable information that shows their actions have made a difference. After Step 1 comes Step 2 and so on until the project is finished. **This linear model did not work for any of them**.

Project teams *would like* managing an implementation project to be like this mature garden with lots of beautiful, flourishing plants. The initial project would develop into a self-sustaining, integrated system. In time, professionals will base their decisions on the best evidence available. As an evidence-based approach becomes the normal way of working, there will be an improvement in patient satisfaction and ultimately a quantifiable benefit in patient outcomes.

This is beginning to happen for three projects (A&E protocols, nurse-led anticoagulation, leg ulcers), although none can yet show a quantifiable improvement in patient outcomes. All three have been so successful they are now being taken on by other departments within the organisation (leg ulcers) or have actually been adopted by completely separate organisations (nurse-led anticoagulation and A&E).

In practice, managing an implementation project can be a lot like ploughing up a stony, stump-covered hill with an old horse. It is hard, you are never quite sure what the next obstacle will be and it takes a great deal of work before anything measurable is achieved.

Although not all of the project teams found their experience quite this gruelling, all of them faced more difficulties than they had imagined. There was general agreement with the comment, 'even though I knew there would be resistance, I didn't expect this much'.

Three general points on the gardening metaphor

A garden is never finished

The gardening analogy works in other ways. A garden is never 'finished', nor is implementation work. It just changes and adapts as new circumstances arise. Project teams found that even if they conclude one piece of work, they then go back to it several times. In practice, they revisited almost all aspects of their work.

One good example is objectives. For all but one of the projects, objectives were changed. As we tracked objectives in the first 18 months, five projects modified their objectives once, eight revised them twice, one project did three times and for one this information is not known.[3]

This happened when the original bids were scaled down to something more manageable, as key project participants left or joined, after external circumstances such as local reorganisations or changes in governmental policies, or when objectives were no longer achievable. One participant coined the phrase, 'objectives are a moving target'. If we were to come back to project teams five years from now, the objectives would have changed many more times in the interim.

Stalls in momentum

Another similarity with gardening is that momentum rises and falls. Sometimes you have more work than at others; sometimes you know there is a lot to do but other activities take priority; sometimes you don't have enough energy; and sometimes you are waiting for previous actions to bear results.

The frenetic pace of change in the NHS does not help. It is difficult to sustain enthusiasm in the face of constant reorganisations and changes in key personnel.[6] Six of the projects have been based in trusts or health authorities undergoing a reorganisation; two of the project teams have had a new chief executive or director of public health; and one project team has had all three. During these periods of intense change, the work is unofficially suspended as the team waits to learn whether the project will continue.

It takes lots of time

One gardener wrote, 'be prepared to wait for results: gardening is not about quick fixes'.[7] Nor is implementation. A project worker commented that it takes three times as long as you expect to get anything done. Early on, project teams recognised that making any substantial measurable changes in 18 months would be very difficult.

One reason is that it takes time to convince enough people that change is needed. Before anything concrete can be done, people need to:

- be aware that there is a possibility of change
- recognise that change is needed
- make an emotional commitment to change
- make a rational commitment to change by clarifying and diagnosing the problem.[8]

This is very time-consuming. What's more, the project teams stressed that this work is best done on an informal, individual basis – which means it takes even longer.

Lessons learned

Implementation work has a steep learning curve. Just abandoning the linear model, as typified by the Feng Shui garden, is a major adjustment. Project teams have adopted a different mindset as they see their earlier expectations not working. This has not been easy.

They have had to experience what Smale (1996) calls the 'managing change fallacies' first hand.[9] For example, the primary care guidelines team learned that the cascade principle does *not* work in letting GPs know about new guidelines. The team working on secondary prevention of coronary heart disease found that people *do* want to reinvent the wheel by devising completely new guidelines rather than adapting ones from other sources. And the GP learning sets team learned that 'more of the same' has not been successful in trying to extend the learning set approach from a geographical subset of practices where it had been successful, to the whole health authority.

Since so much has been learned, focusing on ten key points is difficult. Having said that, project teams often came back to the same lessons. In an attempt to break out of the linear model, they are in no particular order. However, those marked by an asterisk need to be worked out early on.

*Finding organisations and individuals that are ready

The A&E project is an example where the environment is almost ideal. The hospital has been using protocols for several years and approximately 95% of their surgical cases are currently protocol-driven. The A&E department is relatively non-hierarchical with excellent multidisciplinary working between different disciplines ('nurses refer on to doctors and doctors take the nurses' assessments seriously'). An inquisitive, open culture is also present ([protocols are] 'good because it makes us question things and our way of doing things.')

In contrast, conditions for the East London & City Health Authority (ELCHA) cardiac project could not have been worse, despite a keen project worker and good support from local academics and librarians. Consultants experienced the

continued overleaf

project as a serious threat, voicing concerns about nurses having 'unfair access' to computer terminals and junior doctors 'bypassing' senior ones.[10] One cardiologist stated in a departmental debate open to all professionals that '[Evidence-based medicine is] public health doctors trying to tell clinicians how to practice (sic)'.[11] Needless to say, this project did not take off.

* Picking a good topic

Picking a 'good' topic means choosing one that meets the following criteria:

- able to generate widespread enthusiasm for change
- locally relevant
- sound evidence
- leads to early tangible benefits for patients (improved patient care) or staff (professional or service development).

The Kensington, Chelsea & Westminster cardiac project met all of these criteria. Although it was conceived and managed by the health authority, the cardiac audit and open-access echo service quickly picked up enthusiasts in both primary and secondary care. It was also a popular choice at the health authority as morbidity and mortality from heart disease is high. The evidence was uncontested by clinicians. And their support increases, as they see positive benefits for their patients, who are receiving tests much earlier, and for themselves since they are learning about the differences between cardiac and respiratory diseases.

* Picking the right project worker and 'ring-fencing' time

A good project worker is essential. Almost all of the six survey respondents for the primary care guidelines project mentioned the drive, personality, motivation, enthusiasm and/or non-threatening style of the project worker as being a key factor to the project's success. Her genuinely empathetic style helped 'get the trust of the practices', which is in itself a major success.

Two projects, Kensington, Chelsea & Westminster dyspepsia and nurse-led anticoagulation, had difficulties as the project workers had other work going on at the same time. In the case of the dyspepsia project, this was a contributing factor to its cancellation. Project teams without a designated project worker, such as hypertension in the elderly, also found it difficult to get the work done.

In looking at all of the North Thames projects, because project workers have such insecure employment positions, it is difficult to believe that hosting organisations genuinely value clinical effectiveness work. Thirteen of the 14 project workers started out on temporary contracts. Two-and-a-half years later, only four of them are better off with permanent contracts, including one with a promotion to Assistant Director of Public Health.

But for the other nine, three left when no further funding could be found. Even more surprising, three left even *with* further funding. Two others remain on temporary contracts. Having invested heavily in these individuals, who now have a wealth of information on how to manage implementation projects, it is

continued

a great shame that this expertise is regularly lost to the organisations that stand to benefit the most.

*Locating the project within the sphere you want to influence

The primary care guidelines team were housed initially at the Multi-professional Audit Advisory Group (MAAG)* and later at a local surgery. They feel this contributed to their success in getting GPs on board as they were not seen as being from the health authority.

In contrast, the Camden & Islington *Helicobacter pylori*, secondary prevention of coronary heart disease and diabetes register projects, all of which were primary care-based and located in the health authority, were subject to extra suspicion from GPs. As Gill Musson found in her evaluation of the *Facts* programme, independence from statutory bodies and drug companies can be central to why GPs choose to take part.[12]

Incorporating evaluation from the start

Ten of the 15 projects had some sort of internal evaluation. It is extremely difficult to measure a clear impact on changing practice, especially within the tight timescale of 18 months, but these teams were able to demonstrate that some sort of change was happening, even if they could not show irrefutably that the change was a result of the project.

The project teams that didn't incorporate evaluation were in a tricky position. A good example is the leg ulcers project. On the one hand, the team had anecdotal reports from staff and patients that the new system was an improvement. But without either qualitative or quantitative data from before the intervention, they cannot prove to more critical professionals that the new service has made a difference. Early on they believed they had a choice of getting the intervention underway or carrying out a proper baseline evaluation which would be time-consuming. They chose the former and with hindsight wish that they had collected even superficial baseline data.

Building on existing mechanisms

Many teams found it useful to plug into existing mechanisms rather than create their own events. Examples include carrying out educational seminars through the existing education and audit programme (Brent & Harrow cardiac, hypertension in elderly people, Hillingdon *H. pylori*) and getting the MAAG on board in looking at uptake of the guidelines (primary care guidelines).

Getting the genuine commitment and involvement of key people

Getting key people involved is absolutely essential. But the enthusiasm and commitment needed is wider than a handful of locally respected, vocal clinicians. Key people include a much broader spectrum. The back pain project worker

continued overleaf

---

*These groups were formerly known as 'Medical Audit Advisory Groups', a title that remained in use in some other health authorities.

identified a huge number of potential allies in her stakeholder map, including those often forgotten about, such as pharmaceutical company representatives, neighbouring trust and health authority staff and a local group set up to review local hospital services. The Kensington, Chelsea & Westminster cardiac project team made sure that practice managers, practice nurses and receptionists were all on board.

Project teams that do not look at the widest possible spectrum may flounder. The cancer services project team was particularly badly hit by not mapping out potential people clearly enough at the beginning. Covering two trusts, several secondary care specialities, primary care, dozens of disciplines from all levels *and* health authority staff, they had a monumental task in finding all the right people and engaging their enthusiasm. Two years after they started, one project team member commented that they were just now becoming clear on who needed to be involved.

Engaging in a constant process of review

The diabetes register project team was unusual in that it carried out regular, systematic project review. Other projects tended to review in an ad hoc manner, mainly when problems arose. This was not always the best approach. A project worker commented:

> *'Even though it can be boring, it's important to constantly go back to the project plan.'*

He wished he had done this more often, as he believed he would have identified problems earlier.

Smale (1996) suggests using a problem-solving approach with four key questions: What's the problem? What needs to change? What needs to stay the same? Has the problem been solved yet? By continually asking these questions, the reasons for changing practice are kept in the forefront of the team's mind and teams avoid changing more than what is necessary. Other helpful questions to add may be: What worked? What didn't? What did we learn? Where do we go now? Is the project still manageable? If we do X, what are the wider implications? If we do Y, where will the power shift?

Tailoring your approach

A project worker commented:

> *'The flexibility and versatility of these projects are their strengths.'*

In practice this meant:

- breaking up the work into manageable pieces
- offering as much help as you can
- using marketing techniques, where possible
- designing user-friendly formats
- trying more than one way.

continued

The Camden & Islington *H. pylori* project team became masters in adapting their approach. To get the attention of practitioners, they commissioned a graphic designer to design a user-friendly flowchart for the guidelines. When practices said that the audit was too much work, they broke it down into stages so practices could do as much or as little as they wanted. When practices said it was still too much work, the Audit Facilitator offered an extra pair of hands and the team came up with some money to pay practices who did carry out the audit.

Getting a team together

Adopting a team approach, with at least two key enthusiasts who can carry on the project on their own temporarily, may keep a project going.

Six of the projects became low priorities after their original bid writers left for new posts. One of these, GP learning sets, suffered massively. The original bid writer was keen, but she took that enthusiasm with her when she left. Nearly a year later, a public health consultant eventually took over the work, but he saw it as 'one more thing to do', and was not nearly as motivated as he wanted to be.

Knowing when to delegate work to others is also helpful. The back pain project worker makes sure that the GP leaders on her team do most of the work with other GPs as she is non-clinical and subject to suspicions of 'you're not one of us'.

Handing on the work to someone else at the appropriate time is important. The nurse-led anticoagulation project worker found his position increasingly uncomfortable after Hertfordshire Health Authority split into two. He was based in West Hertfordshire HA, but the anticoagulation clinics were in the East & North Hertfordshire HA area. With hindsight, he believes he and the project leader should have passed the project to East & North Hertfordshire HA.

Conclusion

Although project teams learned a tremendous amount, the ten lessons that they went back to were:

- finding organisations and individuals that are ready
- picking a good topic
- picking the right project worker and ring-fencing time
- locating the project in the sphere you want to influence
- incorporating evaluation from the start
- building on existing mechanisms
- getting the genuine commitment and involvement of key people
- engaging in a constant process of review
- tailoring your approach.

References

1 Dunning M, Abi-Aad G, Gilbert D, Hutton H and Brown C (1998) *Experience, Evidence and Everyday Practice.* King's Fund, London.

2 Øvretveit J (1998) *Evaluating Health Interventions: an introduction to the evaluation of health treatments, services, policies and organisational interventions.* Open University Press, Buckingham.

3 Smith L and McClenahan J (1997) *Putting Practitioners through the Paces: initial findings in our evaluation of putting evidence into practice.* King's Fund, London.

4 Smith L and McClenahan J (1998) *Snakes and Ladders: levers, obstacles and solutions to putting evidence into practice.* King's Fund, London.

5 Ferlie E, Wood M and Fitzgerald L (1998) *Achieving Change in Clinical Practice: scientific, organisational and behavioural processes.* Centre for Corporate Strategy and Change, Warwick Business School, Warwick.

6 Dobson S, Gabbay J, Law S and Locock L (1997) *Interim Report: evaluation of the PACE programme.* Templeton College and Wessex Institute for Health Research and Development, Oxford and Southampton.

7 Pearson D (1999) By the book. *The Sunday Times.* 17 January.

8 Prochaska J and DiClementi C (1984) *The Trans-Theoretical Approach.* Krieger Publishing, London.

9 Smale G (1996) *Mapping Change and Innovation.* HMSO, London.

10 Standing H and Holti R (1998) *Evidence Based Practice at the London Chest Hospital.* Tavistock Institute, London.

11 Bannerjee S (1998) *Final Report: cardiac intervention, North Thames Purchaser-led Implementation Project, East London and the City.* ELCHA, London.

12 Musson G (1996) *Interim Report: qualitative evaluation of the facts aspirin programme.* Sheffield Business School, Sheffield.

2

Promoting the secondary prevention of coronary heart disease through clinical guidelines in primary care in Barking & Havering

Mark Ansell and *Chris Watts*

Introduction

This chapter describes the development, dissemination and implementation of guidelines for the secondary prevention of coronary heart disease (CHD) in primary care in Barking & Havering, a health authority in East London. The project was initiated by the public health directorate of the health authority, following discussions with local GP representatives. This topic was selected in response to concerns about the local prevalence of CHD, and the rise in the mortality rate after 1994 in particular.[1] The acknowledgement by local GPs of growing professional consensus with regard to the role of the primary healthcare team in delivering effective care in CHD further reinforced the selection of this topic as the Health Authority-led R&D Implementation Project for Barking & Havering.[2]

Objectives

The project had two aims: a clear primary objective with a relatively narrow focus, and a more general secondary aim. The primary objective was to increase the provision of clinically effective interventions* in patients with known

---

*Clinically effective interventions in this case being defined as care and treatment which has been shown to reduce coronary events and death in patients with known CHD.

CHD. The secondary objective was to generate, through the work, expertise in influencing the behaviour of health professionals, which could be applied at a later stage to a range of other contexts where changes in practice are considered desirable. The extent to which these objectives have been achieved is discussed in the light of a prospective audit undertaken in collaborating practices, and changes in prescribing observed from analysis of 'PACTLINE' (prescribing) data.* Discussion of these data is informed by reference to a project diary maintained by the project facilitator.

Development, dissemination and implementation of the guideline

A team comprising the project facilitator, two GPs, the chairman of the GP Education Board and the health authority director of public health was assembled at the outset to steer and manage the project. The process followed in developing, disseminating and implementing the guideline was suggested by three systematic reviews of the literature regarding effective methods of changing the clinical practice of health professionals.[3–5] Further information was sought from similar projects working in general practice, specifically the FACTS project in Sheffield[6] and the East London Guidelines Project.[7]

Development of the guideline

Evidence, content and format

The project team accepted the advice of Grimshaw *et al.*[4] that the resources required to undertake a rigorous, systematic review would be beyond the means of most local groups. We therefore chose to use a highly commended systematic review of the evidence regarding the effective management of CHD in primary care as the basis for the guideline.[8–10] The guideline was written to meet the critical appraisal criteria suggested for clinical guidelines.[11,12]

- Evidence was provided to support each recommendation.
- Evidence and recommendations were graded in accordance with the scheme developed by the US Preventive Services Task Force.[13]
- Effectiveness was quantified in terms of the number needed to treat.[14]

---

*The 'PACTLINE' system is managed by the Prescription Pricing Authority and gives monthly data regarding the cost and number of items of specific medications or classes of medication prescribed by individual practices.

- In addition to clinical recommendations, the guideline contained advice regarding the organisation of effective care for patients with known CHD in general practice and information on how to conduct an audit to evaluate current practice.

Supporting materials

In addition to the guideline itself, two further related products were produced to support implementation:

- a laminated A4 sheet summarising the key recommendations
- a prompt card, to be placed in the casenotes of patients with CHD, which would serve as both an *aide-mémoire* and a record for treatment and care.

Peer review of the guideline

The draft guideline was reviewed by a small panel of local health professionals comprising two cardiologists, two GPs with clinical assistant posts in cardiology, a health promotion specialist and a dietician. The aim of the review process was threefold. First, to check for errors, omissions or misinterpretation of the evidence. Second, to gain the endorsement of local experts. Third, to identify any barriers which might hinder or prevent use of the guideline. Members of the project team discussed the guideline with the health professionals from the review group individually. This way of working was designed to enable the individuals on the review group to voice their own views frankly, without fear of embarrassment or conflict with their peers or other professionals. The guideline was approved by the review group in March/April 1997, and was endorsed by an independent standing group, the Guidelines Sub-Group of the GP Forum in July 1997.

Dissemination – the *marketing* of the guideline

The guideline was presented four times in total, on two occasions at postgraduate education meetings at each of the two academic centres within the district. The aim of the first pair of presentations (May 1997) was to generate interest among GPs and to involve a wider group of health professionals in discussion of the evidence for the effective secondary prevention of CHD.

The following was stressed:

- the reliability of the evidence underpinning the guideline (with emphasis on its foundations in systematic reviews or large randomised controlled trials)

- the likely effectiveness of the recommended interventions in terms of reduction in deaths and/or coronary events (i.e. which would be achievable if all GPs were to adhere to the guideline)
- the endorsement of the guideline by the review team
- the district-wide nature of the project and the notion that secondary prevention should be an issue for general practice
- that the project team would offer practical assistance to practices
- that the objective of the project was to improve the care provided to patients, *not* to identify poor performance *nor* to limit the clinical freedom of health professionals.

The round of second presentations (July 1997) was used as an opportunity to recruit GPs to the project. The results of two audits were presented: the first undertaken in four local practices, and the second at the local acute hospital. Details of how the guideline might be implemented in individual practices were presented and evidence from a number of audits undertaken elsewhere in the country was also reported, demonstrating that local practice was not untypical but similar to that observed elsewhere.

A copy of the guideline was sent to each practice within the district ($n = 100$) in September 1997, together with the A4 laminated sheet summarising the major recommendations. In addition, various short articles were included in publications circulated in primary care by the education board and the health authority. Wherever possible, members of the project team also made use of informal personal contacts with local GPs to promote active implementation of the guideline.

The recommended implementation strategy

The project team suggested that practices interested in implementing the guideline should adopt the following process:

- develop a register of patients with CHD and/or left ventricular failure
- undertake an audit of the care provided to a sample of these patients
- hold a practice meeting to discuss the results of the audit and develop an action plan
- place prompt cards in the notes of patients with CHD as a minimum response (these would act as a reminder to the GP that the patient should be considered for secondary prevention; would prompt the appropriate care as set out in the guideline; and would provide a record of relevant care given)
- re-audit six months later.

Practices were also asked to consider the practicability of establishing a regular clinic for patients with CHD as it seemed that the care recommended in the guideline would be more likely to be provided in this context rather than during a routine GP consultation.[15] It was also suggested that the following information sources could be used, either singly or in combination, to develop a disease register:

- the practice's own computer system, to identify patients with a diagnosis of CHD and/or heart failure and/or patients who had received a prescription for nitrates
- a list of their patients admitted to hospital over the last two years with a diagnosis of CHD or heart failure (which the project team was able to provide)
- the personal knowledge of individual members of the practice team with regard to individual patients.

A recommended audit methodology was contained within the guideline, and the project team offered to facilitate post-audit practice meetings. These would be aimed at developing practice action plans to address issues revealed by the audit which the practice considered to be significant and capable of being resolved.

The implementation strategy in practice

Seventeen practices were recruited to implement the guideline, and there was considerable variation between them in terms of size, resources and their level of computerisation. The proposed implementation strategy was explained to each, and most were concerned about the staff time that implementation would require, to the extent that they were prepared to implement the guideline only on condition that the project team agreed to undertake the majority of the work. In these practices, the project team developed the disease register and conducted the audit, supported by reception staff who contributed by finding the notes required for the audit and placing the prompt cards in the notes of patients on the disease register.

Each of the (17) practices involved, without exception, has acknowledged that the audit showed that their own practice had been inconsistent. All recognised that they had both reasons and scope for improvement. Two of the practices chose to develop a nurse-led, protocol-driven CHD clinic, but the other 15 elected to pursue improvements in the care provided to patients with CHD through opportunistic* contacts. All participating practices aimed to

---

*In the context of our project the term *opportunistic contacts* was used to describe doctor–patient encounters initiated by the patient, and these frequently involved a visit to the GP for a different, perhaps unrelated, health reason.

maintain a register of patients with CHD using either paper-based records or their practice computer systems.

Did the project work?

Five practices (14 GPs) were recruited to pilot the implementation of the guideline, four of which included one partner who was already involved, either as part of the review team or the Guidelines Sub-Group of the GP Forum. The pilot was conducted in summer 1997 with the aim of bringing to light any problems with the implementation strategy, so that these could be ironed out prior to widespread dissemination of the guideline. In fact, the pilot did not identify any real problems with the guideline itself. However, it did point to the fact that the main barrier to implementation would be likely to be the time involved in the implementation process. Later in the summer of 1997, when the project was rolled out, a further 12 practices (18 GPs) requested the support of the practice team, ten of these responding to the second pair of presentations made by the project team and two to a public health advice sheet sent to all practices in the district. A further 20 practices (26 GPs) requested supplies of the CHD prompt cards in response to a circular put out by the project team to all local practices. Around a third of the district's population was covered by practices expressing interest in implementing the guideline a year after the project was launched.

Did practice change in line with the guideline?

Relevant prescribing data and records of non-pharmacological interventions have been audited to provide an indication of the impact of the project. At the time of writing, eight of the 17 practices participating had completed a cycle of audit/re-audit, and our analysis is confined to these sites. The interval between baseline and re-audit was 6–8 months. The data are presented in Tables 2.1 and 2.2. Each table gives the average proportion of patients in receipt of the recommended care across all eight practices, and a subanalysis which gives the average across practices adopting *a similar implementation strategy*. Of the eight practices whose data is analysed, one had set up a nurse-run clinic and five used the prompt cards to mark patients' notes; the remaining two practices were 'paperless' in that only the practice computer system was used to access patient records during the course of consultations. (In these 'paperless' practices the prompt cards were of no use, but the practices never-theless claimed to be attempting to improve care on an opportunistic basis.)

Table 2.1   Pharmacological interventions – the observed change in prescribing behaviour at baseline and re-audit

Implementation strategy		Baseline	Re-audit
Aspirin			
Audit alone	%	62	75
	Number	155	166
	Change	13% (95% C.I. 3%, 23%)	
Prompt cards and audit	%	71	83
	Number	230	230
	Change	12% (95% C.I. 5%, 20%)	
Clinic, prompt cards, audit	%	57	96
	Number	37	45
	Change	39% (95% C.I. 22%, 56%)	
All eight audited practices	%	66	82
	Number	422	441
	Change	16% (95% C.I. 10%, 22%), $p < 0.0001$	
ACE inhibitor			
Audit alone	%	65	74
	Number	23	27
	Change	9% (95% C.I. −17%, 34%)	
Prompt cards and audit	%	68	91
	Number	59	32
	Change	23% (95% C.I. 7%, 38%)	
Clinic, prompt cards, audit	%	88	100
	Number	8	9
	Change	13% (95% C.I. −10%, 35%)	
All eight audited practices	%	69	85
	Number	90	68
	Change	16% (95% C.I. 4%, 29%), $p = 0.02$	
Statin			
Audit alone	%	29	59
	Number	34	34
	Change	30% (95 C.I. 7%, 52%)	
Prompt cards and audit	%	48	58
	Number	42	60
	Change	11% (95% C.I. −9%, 30%)	
Clinic, prompt cards, audit	%	40	85
	Number	10	13
	Change	45% (95% C.I. 8%, 81%)	
All eight audited practices	%	40	62
	Number	86	107
	Change	22% (95% C.I. 8%, 36%), $p = 0.002$	

Number = total sample size.

Tables indicated patients receiving recommended intervention.

All patients who have ischaemic heart disease (IHD) and no specific contra-indication to have a record of aspirin prescription/record of recommendation that patient should buy their own/record that patient refused treatment.

All patients with a history of left ventricular failure and no specific contra-indication to have a record of ACE inhibitor prescription/record that patient had refused treatment.

All patients aged under 70 years with IHD and a recorded total cholesterol greater than 5.5 mmol/l to have a record of statin prescription/or record that patient had refused treatment.

Statistical test used was the chi-squared test.

Table 2.2   Non-pharmacological interventions – the observed change in the provision of preventive interventions recorded in patient records at baseline and re-audit

		Implementation strategy							
*Patients receiving recommended intervention***		*Audit alone*		*Prompt cards and audit*		*Clinic, prompt cards, audit*		*All eight audited practices*	
		%	No*	%	No*	%	No*	%	No*	*Change***
Blood pressure	Baseline	63	155	81	230	92	37	75	422	3% (–3%, 9%),
	Re-audit	57	166	90	230	96	45	78	441	p = 0.3
Blood/urine glucose	Baseline	27	155	38	230	68	37	36	422	15% (8%, 22%),
	Re-audit	42	166	53	230	71	45	51	441	p < 0.0001
Weight	Baseline	33	155	49	230	41	37	42	422	10% (3%, 17%),
	Re-audit	37	166	56	230	91	45	52	441	p = 0.003
Dietary advice	Baseline	23	155	25	230	51	37	27	422	10% (4%, 16%),
	Re-audit	23	166	37	230	84	45	37	441	p = 0002
Exercise advice	Baseline	19	155	13	230	35	37	17	422	14% (8%, 20%),
	Re-audit	20	166	29	230	87	45	31	441	p < 0.0001
Smoking status	Baseline	92	155	80	230	97	37	86	442	9% (5%, 13%),
	Re-audit	96	166	94	230	98	45	95	441	p < 0.001

*Total sample size.

**All patients who have IHD to have a record of blood pressure, a blood or urine sugar check and weight in previous 15 months. All patients with IHD to have a record of having been advised about diet and exercise in the preceding 15 months. All patients with IHD to have a record of smoking habit. All smokers to have a record of having been advised to quit in preceding 15 months.

***Figures in brackets indicate 95% confidence interval.

NB: We have not given CIs for all comparisons because this would make the table unwieldy.

Corroborating evidence regarding the change in statin prescribing was provided by an analysis of PACTLINE data. Over the period, prescribing of these drugs across the health authority had increased by a greater amount than the regional average, and prescribing in the participating practices had increased even further. The increase in the rate of prescribing of statins locally coincided with the first presentations of the guideline in spring/summer 1997. Given these data, and setting aside the possibility of unknown confounding factors, it would seem reasonable that these changes in prescribing behaviour were the result of the guideline project and the associated implementation strategy. At the very least, the differences in levels of prescribing certainly reflect changes in practice in line with the guideline, and the timing is consistent with the guideline implementation. However, we recognise the risk in making inferences from a project of this nature, which involved small numbers in an uncontrolled environment. We therefore accept that it is not possible to estimate accurately the extent to which changes in practice can be attributed to the influence of the project. A considerably more robust trial design would be necessary to be able to quantify the impact of interventions such as ours, and this would have required resources far beyond our limited budget.

These data suggest that overall there was a modest increase in the recording/monitoring of risk factors and provision of advice. The observation that blood pressure and smoking were most effectively recorded is not surprising given the strength of evidence for the importance of these two risk factors. However, it is less encouraging that at re-audit significant numbers of patients were still not receiving the recommended advice.

Reflections on the experience of the CHD guidelines project

Developing the guideline

Getting the format right

The guideline contained a considerable amount of evidence regarding the effectiveness of secondary prevention interventions. When it was presented, few GPs expressed any uncertainty about the effectiveness of secondary prevention. It is therefore doubtful whether the supporting evidence was crucial in persuading many GPs to implement the guideline. With hindsight we feel that we may have succumbed to the temptation to produce an impressive document at the expense of the main objective: changing practice. While a comprehensive review of the literature may appeal to the evidence-based medicine enthusiast, it may actually be off-putting to a GP whose need is for a clear, concise statement of best practice, from a reliable source. In retrospect, we think that greater practitioner involvement in the development of the guideline may have helped us to focus on producing a document containing just the level of supporting evidence with which most GPs would feel comfortable.

The importance of local ownership

Grimshaw et al.[4] suggested that limiting the involvement of local clinicians in the development of guidelines may reduce the likelihood that a guideline will subsequently be used. Eve et al.,[6] working with GPs in Sheffield, reported that a sense of local ownership could be generated by effective marketing post development. In our project only a small number of clinicians were involved in the development of the guideline, an approach taken because we feared that development through a consensus process would be excessively time-consuming and might lead to a dilution of the underlying evidence. Our experience was probably more consistent with Eve's analysis. However, we have recognised that greater GP involvement might have led to a more *GP-friendly* guideline, but this would have been for reasons of presentation rather than ownership.

The dissemination process

Formal presentations

The four formal presentations made by the project team reached around 50% of local GPs. Although they were not particularly effective in terms of recruitment to the project (only eight enquiries resulted directly from these events), they did provide an opportunity to expose the project to a large number of GPs and may have encouraged some to respond later (i.e. to written circulars). We thought it advantageous to use an existing programme of presentations given that GPs have little or no uncommitted time, and the experience of the project has confirmed our belief in this approach.

Written documents

We took the view that because GPs receive a large amount of mail, they are unlikely to read unsolicited guidelines, particularly if they appear bulky. We thought that higher response rates might be achieved if documents were kept short and addressed to other members of the practice team who are less inundated with post. We accepted that written materials will have a low success rate in terms of the numbers of people whose practice changes as a result of postal dissemination, however, we considered that the relative ease of preparation justified the approach. We also thought that the widespread commercial use of unsolicited mailings was an indication that despite being derided as 'junk mail', a proportion of material disseminated in this way must 'hit the spot', or companies (whose acumen in marketing is surely far greater than ours) would not persist with it.

Personal contacts: establishing a relationship with GPs

Eve *et al.*[6] suggested that change in primary care can best be promoted by informal contacts between individuals. This is consistent with our experience, as eight of the 17 practices recruited to fully implement the guideline were also involved in either the guideline development or other projects involving the Health Authority Public Health Directorate. However, the location of the project within the health authority may have had a counterproductive aspect. Some GPs were clearly wary of what was perceived to be 'allowing the health authority the opportunity to monitor their clinical practice'. One important implication of this point was that the local Medical Advisory Audit Group (MAAG) declined to support the project, partly because members were reluctant to give a signal which could cast doubt on the independence of the MAAG from the health authority. We thought that suspicion of the health authority was also reflected in the relatively small response to the four presentations and two circulars offering *hands-on* assistance from the project team (12 practices from a total of 100 in Barking & Havering).

Interestingly, a single circular offering a supply of the prompt cards with 'no strings' (i.e. no health authority presence at the practice) produced 20 responses. With hindsight, we consider that a systematic assessment of the networks within primary care should have been made before deciding on the location of the project. Our assumption that the health authority would be able to utilise established networks such as the MAAG, as and when it wished, was mistaken. In future, primary care groups (PCGs)[16] are likely to provide a network through which more effective care might be promoted. It would seem sensible for health authorities to consider how they might help PCGs to fulfil this function in a way which would be acceptable to individual GPs. Our view is that this may involve providing the requisite resources in terms of finance and skills, but devolving to the PCGs themselves the lead role for implementing changes in clinical practice.

Local opinion leaders

The review team (two GPs holding clinical assistant posts in cardiology and cardiologists at both local trusts) was chosen on the basis that members were considered to be local opinion leaders. They participated in the presentations of the guideline and spoke in support of the recommendations made. Use of opinion leaders to promote change has been shown to be effective in the United States,[17] however, the positive experience in the US may not be transferable to the UK, where the organisation of health services is markedly different, and the research evidence on this point is weak.[18] The factors which make opinion leaders effective change agents in the US are less significant or even absent in the UK.* GPs in the UK may be more isolated and less influenced by the opinions of colleagues, however, they may be encouraged to join a project if a critical mass of their peers is involved.[19] We think, therefore, that rather than involving specific individuals (i.e. supposed opinion leaders) the

---

*For example, in the US, doctors in primary care have admitting rights at local hospitals and thus have greater contact with their colleagues in secondary care. Within secondary care, the hierarchy in specialisms may result in a relatively small number of clinicians leading the practice of many others.

key to the successful implementation of guidelines in UK primary care may lie in recruiting sufficient practices to give a project the necessary momentum in its early stages. With regard to getting people involved, our experience is again consistent with Eve *et al.* [6] in that one-to-one, personal contacts may be the most reliable means of recruiting. Even though our project did not entail *systematic* one-to-one contacts as described by Eve, it was clear that a disproportionately large group of the practices involved included practitioners who had been exposed at an early stage to personal contact with members of the project team. (Sometimes in an *opportunistic* way, in that they were involved with the health authority for *other* reasons.)

The implementation strategy

Appropriateness

If we ask ourselves whether the suggested implementation strategy was appropriate for all practices, the honest answer is no. It fell down where practices maintained patient records through systems that were either wholly paper-based or wholly electronic (paperless), and this undoubtedly reduced the incentive for such practices to get involved. The highly computerised, paperless practices needed computerised prompts, but neither the project team nor the practices themselves had the required expertise to develop them (or alternatively, the resources to purchase them). The fact that practices used a variety of different systems (or editions of the same system) further complicated the issue. We think that if local groups do develop computerised prompts it would be sensible if they were accessible to others to enable sharing rather than reinvention. A co-ordinated, central register of prompts would be a great help in this respect. At the other extreme, the paper-only practices had little incentive to get involved because of the scale of the task of developing a disease register. Thankfully, paper-only practices now form only a small proportion of the total, and for practical reasons it would therefore be unwise to invest in an alternative implementation strategy for this group. Our view is that it would be better to devote any available resources to encouraging such practices to acquire and use appropriate computerised prompting systems.

Support for practices

It had been our hope that most practices would require advice rather than 'hands-on' support to implement the guideline. However, from the experience of the project, time pressure and the scarcity of auditing skills in general practice made this expectation unrealistic in the majority of cases. (Most of the GPs involved in our project said that they had no time to implement the guideline.) Some suggested that they might be able to participate if they were to be reimbursed for the additional staff time that guideline implementation would require, and it was agreed that GPs could seek payment from the education board for locum cover if they undertook the work themselves. (However, no GP actually made a claim of this nature.) It can be argued that rather than trying to work with overstretched GPs, implementation might reasonably have been delegated to practice nurses. However, the education board would have been unable to provide reimbursement for practice nurses' time, and even if resources had been available from another source, in many cases there was actually little or no scope to increase practice nurse input. This is because in our district many nurses work part time or share their time between two practices. In this context, additional (financial) resources may not be enough because practice nurses may simply be unwilling or unable to work for the necessary additional hours.

Aside from the issue of time, the lack of computer skills was a further barrier to implementation in many practices. Most did not have the skills 'in-house' for computerised audit of current practice, nor did they have the ability to 'flag' the computerised records of patients with CHD. Some computerised practices were consequently unable to develop a disease register using their computer. Disease registers developed with the assistance of the project team differed markedly in size, ranging from 1.5–4.5% of the total practice population. It is probable that much of this difference can be attributed to the *way* that individual practices enter data on to their systems, and factors such as the length of time a practice has been computerised. Our view is that in future it would seem sensible for PCGs to be encouraged to ensure that all of their constituent practices have a common level of basic computer skills.

Opportunistic versus systematic implementation

The suggested implementation strategy was designed to promote opportunistic interventions. This approach has obvious attractions because little or no additional resource is needed, nor is practice reorganisation necessary. The approach also appears at first sight to offer plenty of scope for interventions. Calnan [20] reported that 65% of men and 76% of women consult their GP in any one year, and 90% of people consult their doctor within a five-year period. Logically we expected still higher consultation rates in older people with existing CHD, however, this was not measured. The project evaluation suggested that improvements in prescribing can be made on an opportunistic basis. This was expected, given that the implementation strategy employed a number of techniques which have been shown to increase compliance with guidelines. [3] The *subanalysis*, which divides the practices into three groups reflecting the level of implementation activity in which they engaged (*see* Table 2.2), supports the view that patient-specific prompts are a simple but effective means of promoting opportunistic intervention and hence changes in clinical behaviour. It appeared that the practice initiating a clinic had made greatest progress, at least on those topics where recording was low at the outset, while the highly computerised, 'paperless' practices (where the prompt cards could not be used) had made the least progress.

The change in prescribing of statins at district level was unexpected, given that the dissemination of unsolicited guidelines and public presentations alone have previously been shown to be relatively ineffective as a means of changing clinical practice[5,21,] and we are therefore particularly cautious about attributing the observed changes to the impact of the project. Additionally, we know that during the period under observation other external factors would have added to pressure in promoting the increased use of statins. Few GPs could have been unaware of the evidence regarding the effectiveness of these drugs given the large number of papers in the scientific journals,[2,22,23] professional publications[24,25] and statements from the NHS,[26] which coincided with the project. In addition, GPs would have been exposed to the extensive promotion of the use of statins from advertisements in the 'GP press' and from drug company representatives. Although a number of GPs had been wary of increasing statin prescribing because of the costs involved, a health authority recommendation on the use of these drugs on the grounds of clinical effectiveness may have reduced such worries and promoted prescribing. Our view, based on the experience of the project, is that while the opportunistic approach was effective in respect of prescribing, its value in health promotion activity is less clear. Stott and Davis[27] suggest that there is scope to undertake opportunistic health promotion in primary care and our baseline audit revealed high rates of blood pressure measurement (which may be attributable, as Calnan and Williams[15] suggest, to opportunistic intervention). However, the recording of blood pressure *did not* improve between audit and re-audit. Given that most other indicators *did* improve, it may be that the baseline performance (i.e. 75% of patients having a record of a blood pressure reading being taken in the preceding 15 months) represents the best that can be achieved opportunistically. Modest improvements were observed with regard to the provision of advice about diet and exercise, however, performance remained poor relative to other interventions. We can think of two possible explanations for this. On the one hand, it may simply be that the whole health promotion package cannot be delivered opportunistically in a 5–10-minute GP consultation (which by definition is likely to have another, perhaps unrelated purpose). Alternatively, GPs may be unconvinced of the effectiveness of giving advice as a means of inducing change in the behaviour of patients. (Calnan and Williams[15] reported that many GPs have doubts about the effectiveness and/ or appropriateness of health promotion, particularly around diet and exercise.)

In our project we noted a substantial increase in the provision of advice to smokers about giving up from 34% to 60% (CIs 9%–45%, highly significant), although this was based on small numbers of observations ($n = 65$ at baseline and $n = 48$ on re-audit). This may be different from other preventive interventions because GPs have a more positive view of the efficacy of advice about smoking cessation, particularly when linked to the patient's presenting problem (e.g. CHD).[28] There is also convincing evidence that brief advice from GPs can have a significant, although small, effect on smoking behaviour.[29]

There is a growing body of literature suggesting an association between practice organisation and the comprehensive provision of secondary prevention interventions.[30–32] In simple terms, in the current context, this means that a systematic approach (as opposed to an opportunistic one) will lead to greater benefit. Our audit data from the one practice that had been able to establish a CHD clinic are consistent with this connection. GPs may not, however, be easily convinced that investment in such clinics is appropriate. Hulscher *et al.*[33] reported on a survey of GPs in the Netherlands, which found that over half felt they were not responsible for health promotion, and a similar proportion thought that proactive preventive interventions were unacceptable to patients, although secondary prevention may well be more widely acceptable.

Even when advice is given, whether by opportunistic or systematic route, there remains doubt about the effectiveness of 'lifestyle' advice as a health intervention, and recent systematic reviews[34,35] have demonstrated the weakness of evidence relating to the value of doctors' advice on dietary change. Our project contributes little to the resolution of these debates, however, the rewarding finding from the audits to date is that (as with prescribing) the changes observed in the participating practices have been in the right direction.

Lessons learned

- Ensure the 'group' developing the guideline is acceptable to the majority of the target health professionals.
- Where possible, use pre-existing, evidence-based guidelines or systematic reviews as the basis for local statements. Consider distributing external guidelines if local clinicians are in agreement.
- Develop communication networks in primary care. Health authorities may facilitate this process by involving different GPs in the projects it undertakes, rather than always relying on the same GP representatives.
- Ensure that practices are actively encouraged to receive training in the use of their computer systems. At least one agency within the district should maintain sufficient computer expertise to assist with the implementation of projects in general practice.

continued overleaf

- Implementation schemes should acknowledge that better practice organisation and/or different models of providing care may be the key to providing better clinical care.
- Be realistic in setting goals and milestones. Progress is likely to be slow at first while relationships and trust are established between the project team and health professionals.
- GPs should be encouraged to provide only those interventions which are known or very likely to yield significant benefits, in particular secondary prevention. Any incentives available, e.g. health promotion payments, should be employed to reinforce this message.
- Investment plans to meet the challenge of CHD, e.g. as part of a local Health Improvement Programme,[16] should address practice organisation and the establishment of CHD clinics where appropriate to facilitate the provision of effective interventions, such as aspirin, ACE inhibitors and statins.

Things we would we do differently if we were starting the project tomorrow

- negotiate the attachment of the project facilitator to the MAAG or education board
- use an 'off-the-peg' guideline
- develop (or find existing) computerised prompts to support implementation of the guideline
- modify our message to GPs, emphasising the advantages of developing clinics to support the delivery of effective care
- seek additional funding to support the establishment of clinics.

References

1   Watts C (1998) *The Annual Report of the Director of Public Health: 1997.* Barking & Havering Health Authority, London.

2   Moher M, Schofield T, Weston S and Fullard E (1997) Managing established coronary heart disease: general practice is ideally placed to provide co-ordinated preventive care. *BMJ.* **315**: 69–70.

3   Oxman AD, Thomson MA, Davis DA and Hayes RB (1995) No magic bullets: a systematic review of 102 trials of interventions to improve professional practice. *Can Med Assoc J.* **153(10)**: 1423–30.

4   Grimshaw J, Freemantle N, Wallace S, Russell I, Hurwitz B, Watt I, Long A and Sheldon T (1995) Developing and implementing clinical practice guidelines. *Quality in Health Care.* **4**: 55–64.

5   Davis DA, Thompson MA, Oxman AD and Haynes RB (1995) Changing physician performance. A systematic review of the effect of continuing medical education strategies. *JAMA.* **274**: 700.

6   Eve R, Golton I, Hodgkin P, Munro J and Musson G (1997) *Learning from FACTS – lessons from the framework for appropriate care throughout Sheffield (FACTS) project.* Occasional Paper No. 97/3. SCHARR, University of Sheffield, Sheffield.

7   Feder G, Griffiths C, Highton C, Elderidge S, Spence M and Southgate L (1995) Do clinical guidelines introduced with practice-based education improve care of asthmatic and diabetic patients? A randomised controlled trial in general practices in East London. *BMJ.* **311**: 1473–8.

8   PACE (1995) *Digest of Research Evidence.* King's Fund, London.

9   Anon (1995) *Bandolier.* **13**: 7.

10   Moher M (1995) *Evidence of effectiveness of interventions for the secondary prevention and treatment of coronary heart disease in primary care. A review of the literature.* Anglia and Oxford RHA, Oxford.

11   Cluzeau F, Littlejohns P, Grimshaw J and Feder G (1995) Draft appraisal instrument for clinical guidelines. In: *Report from General Practice 26: the development of implementation of clinical guidelines.* Royal College of General Practitioners, Exeter.

12   Hayward RS, Wilson MC, Tunis SR, Bass EB and Guyatt G (1995) User's guides to the medical literature VIII. How to use clinical practice guidelines. A: Are the recommendations valid? The evidence-based medicine working group. *JAMA.* **274(7)**: 570–4.

13   US Preventive Services Tack Force (1989) *Guide to Clinical Preventive Services. An assessment of the effectiveness of 169 interventions.* Williams and Wilkins, Baltimore, USA.

14   Cook RJ and Sackett DL (1995) The number needed to treat: a clinically useful measure of treatment effect. *BMJ.* **310**: 452–4.

15   Calnan M and Williams S (1993) Policies and practices for the assessment and management of risk factors for coronary heart disease prevention: the perspective of the general practitioner. *Euro J Pub Health.* **3**: 274–80.

16   Department of Health (1998) *The New NHS: modern, dependable.* Department of Health, London.

17   Lomas J, Enkin M, Anderson GM *et al.* (1991) Opinion leaders vs audit and feedback to implement practice guidelines: delivery after previous Caesarean section. *JAMA.* **265**: 2202–7.

18   Eve R (1995) *Implementing Clinical Change: learning from the US experience.* FACTS Project, Sheffield.

19   Haines A and Jones R (1994) Implementing the findings of research. *BMJ.* **308**: 1488–92.

20   Calnan M (1991) *CHD Prevention: prospects, politics and policies.* HMSO, London.

21   Freemantle N, Harvey EL, Grimshaw JM *et al.* (1996) The effectiveness of printed educational materials in changing the behaviour of healthcare professionals. In: *The Cochrane Database of Systematic Reviews* [updated 6 June 1996]. The Cochrane Collaboration; Issue 3. Update Software, Oxford.

22   Byrne C and Wild SH (1996) Lipids and secondary prevention of ischaemic heart disease. *BMJ.* **313**: 1273–4.

23   van der Weijden T and Grol R (1998) Preventing recurrent coronary heart disease: we need to attend more to implementing evidence-based practice. *BMJ.* **316**: 1400–1.

24   Schofield T (1996) Cholesterol: a rational approach. *The Practitioner.* **240**: 364–8.

25   Anon (1996) Management of hyperlipidaemia. *Drugs and Therapeutics Bulletin.* **34(12)**: 89–92.

26   Standing Medical Advisory Committee (1997) *The Use of Statins.* Department of Health, London.

27   Stott NCH and Davis RH (1979) The exceptional potential in each primary care consultation. *J Royal College Gen Pract.* **29**: 201–5.

28   Coleman T and Wilson A (1996) Anti-smoking advice in general practice consultations: general practitioners' attitudes, reported practice and perceived problems. *Br J Gen Pract.* **46**: 87–91.

29   Silagy C and Ketteridge S (1997) The effectiveness of physician advice to aid smoking cessation. In: T Lancaster, C Silagy and D Fullerton (eds) Tobacco addiction module of the *Cochrane Database of Systematic Reviews* [updated 3 July 1997]. The Cochrane Collaboration, Issue 3. Update Software, Oxford.

30   Fullard E, Fowler G and Gray M (1987) Promoting prevention in primary care: controlled trial of low technology, low-cost approach. *BMJ.* **294**: 1080–2.

31   Campbell NC, Thain J, Deans HG, Ritchie LD, Rawles JM and Squair JL (1998) Secondary prevention clinics for coronary heart disease: randomised trial of effect on health. *BMJ.* **316**: 1334–7.

32   van Drenth BB, Hulscher M, van der Wouden JC, Mokkink H, van Weel C and Grol R (1998) Relationship between practice organisation and cardiovascular risk factor recording in general practice. *Br J Gen Pract.* **48**: 1054–8.

33   Hulscher M, van Drenth BB, Mokkink H, van der Wouden J and Grol R (1997) Barriers to preventive care in general practice: the role of organisational and attitudinal factors. *Br J Gen Pract.* **47**: 711–14.

34   Tang JL, Armitage JM, Lancaster T, Silagy CA, Fowler GH and Neil HAW (1998) Systematic review of dietary intervention trials to lower blood total cholesterol in free living subjects. *BMJ.* **316**: 1213–20.

35   Ebrahim S and Davey Smith G (1997) Systematic review of randomised controlled trials of multiple risk factor interventions for preventing coronary heart disease. *BMJ.* **314**: 1666–74.

Secondary prevention of coronary heart disease

When the project worker came into post in October 1996, he faced a number of difficulties.

The original bid was ambitious and largely unachievable, with the long-term aim of introducing effectiveness into commissioning. There were no stated objectives and no plans for evaluation. After meeting with various people who had worked on effectiveness projects before, the project worker was able to set feasible objectives and get ideas about evaluation. He made the project more manageable.

A second problem ran throughout the project. The original bid writer, a consultant in public health who was keen on effectiveness, left before the project worker started. When he went, he took his network of contacts along with him and no-one was quite sure what had been agreed. The project then fell under the auspices of the Director of Public Health, who was interested, but busy and unable to commit much time.

Fortunately, the project worker linked up with the GP Education Board, which is very active in the area. Two non-local GPs, who were funded by London Initiative Zone money to provide locum cover, were keen to work on the guidelines. So, for the period of guideline development there was a team. During the implementation phase, these GPs moved on and the project worker was once again without much support.

Time was a third problem. Even though the objectives were much more realistic, the project worker realised that he would not be able to show an impact in 18 months. One of his first tasks was to make a case for extending his contract, which he did successfully. He was not the only project worker who did this; all of the project teams commented that more than 18 months is needed to show that change has occurred.

Despite these difficulties, this project has been successful in a number of ways. They took too long over the first set of guidelines but learned from the experience, and successive guidelines are produced much more quickly. More importantly, the public health department of the health authority has learned a great deal about what works and what doesn't in changing clinical practice. An added bonus is that the public health department has strengthened its relationship with (some) local GPs and learned that top-down approaches don't work. This more partnership-oriented approach, which is reflected in the tone of the Health Improvement Programme, is timely with the coming of primary care groups (PCGs).

Their implementation strategy, a combination of audit, feedback and reminders, goes on the premise that 'to know is to act differently' (Smale, 1996). What this project shows is that knowing is just the first step. The GP and practice nurse with a CHD clinic had to make a series of steps in which they regularly reconsidered their commitment to patients with CHD. They moved from:

1   We know what we are supposed to do and we are willing to audit to see if we're doing it.
2   Audit shows we're not doing it. Do we drop it or make changes?
3   Some changes made. Let's re-audit.
4   Audit shows we're still not doing it. Do we drop it or make much bigger organisational changes?
5   Much bigger organisational changes made. Let's re-audit.
6   Audit shows an improvement, for example 10–12 previously undiagnosed hypertensives now on treatment (out of about 60 cases).
7   Let's keep this up and continue to re-audit.

The energy and enthusiasm of these practitioners had to be very high before they saw a clear, demonstrable improvement. The question for project teams becomes: How can we help clinicians reaffirm their commitment at every step so that they too can achieve real change?

Not many practices chose to re-commit their energies to CHD work after the initial audit. Nonetheless, there was some discernible improvement in appropriate prescribing, as shown by PACT data. With the coming of PCGs, the possibility of positive changes in clinical practice looks more promising. As one interviewee commented:

'The PCG has a definite agenda to deliver on this and it will come up early on. Aspirin is easy to deliver on and PCG boards want results ... The vast majority of GPs are not that interested. It's not a knowledge gap with practitioners – they know it all. But they have problems in how to organise it.'

Hopefully, having a model from the practices with a CHD clinic will help. What's more, public health department staff have become convinced that this type of effectiveness initiative is worthwhile. They have commited further resources by funding CHD clinics and taking the project worker on board in a more secure post.

A great deal of good work has come out of the initial £50 000. Our only concern is that this learning is not lost, as it seems to be stored so much in one individual, the project worker. It would be a shame if there was a repeat of the loss of momentum and confusion which occurred after the original bid writer left. With the high turnover in the NHS, more than one person needs to be truly committed to keep this type of work going.

3

Implementing evidence-based practice (or best possible practice) through protocols in an Accident and Emergency Department in Brent & Harrow

Alaganandan Sivakumar and
Angela Haigh

Introduction

Although a large body of evidence exists and a number of consensus-based guidelines are available, there has been no research to quantify the extent of evidence-based practice in an accident and emergency (A&E) setting. Sackett *et al.* (1995)[1] found that 82% of patient management in a general medical environment is evidence based and concluded that previous pessimism as to extent of evidence-based practice in current practice is misplaced. Most A&E departments disseminate information regarding evidence or consensus statements in one form or another, but it is difficult to ensure that this advice is followed and to evaluate the effect on outcome. By using protocols to implement evidence-based practice, Central Middlesex Hospital has sought to improve systematically the consistency with which evidence is incorporated into daily practice in a busy A&E department.

Background and project aims

Central Middlesex Hospital is a district general hospital with a catchment of 250 000 people. The A&E Department treats 56 000 new patients annually. As in most A&E departments, junior doctors who are on six-monthly rotation are responsible for a large proportion of the daily workload. These doctors have a steep learning curve when they start and often leave just as they are becoming familiar with the work. The management of minor injuries and illnesses is largely the role of specially trained emergency nurse practitioners. A principle concern in the department has been to ensure that practice is up to date, consistent and makes use of the best available research evidence. The turnover of medical staff and the volume of work makes this objective hard to achieve.

In collaboration with Brent & Harrow Health Authority (in the context of the Health Authority-led Implementation Project), Central Middlesex A&E embarked in 1996 on a project intended to help to embed evidence-based practice in the department. We had experience of using protocols (with nurse practitioners) as a means of implementing evidence-based practice and were interested to find out if similar methods could be used with the doctors. We interviewed doctors informally and using a semi-structured technique to try to understand why several sets of guidelines (which had been available to them) had not been well used. One surprising conclusion drawn from the interviews was that doctors did not follow guidelines because they were not aware of them! We also noted that in the normal course of events doctors would not think of looking for guidelines, and attributed this partly to pressure of work and partly to the influence of medical culture, which stresses the value of independence of thought. Furthermore, when we looked closely at the issue of guidelines and their applicability to our workplace, more obstacles became apparent. A&E medicine is characterised by a broad mix of clinical problems, experienced in the first instance as symptoms. Existing guidelines were typically disease-based (i.e. beginning at a point after diagnosis), which renders them ineffective at the start of the clinician–patient encounter. The sheer volume of disease-based guidelines which would be required in an A&E department was also thought to have discouraged their use. The view that '... there simply isn't time ...' was commonly held.

Traditionally, in the majority of A&E departments, clinical notes (clerking) are taken on casualty cards. The cards are documents with space for patient details on the front, followed by unstructured pages for clinical notes. When guidelines for patient management have been promoted in A&E they have traditionally been displayed on wall posters, on notice boards or as booklets. We felt that combining guidelines with the patient documentation (clinical notes) would provide an opportunity to ensure that guidelines were available each time the clinician–patient encounter takes place. Relevant evidence could be set out on the patient documentation in a manner designed to be helpful in an A&E context, and which would lend itself to the doctor–patient consultation far better than books or wall posters. It was from this assessment of the status quo and our ideas for overcoming the barriers to evidence-based guidelines in A&E that the nature of the project developed. We identified a set of objectives:

- to develop a series of evidence-based protocols for use in A&E
- to develop a system to enhance the use of these protocols
- to evaluate the use and maximise the impact of the protocols
- to promote the long-term sustainability of using protocols by:
  - developing a culture of evidence-based practice
  - developing a system which is easy to keep up to date.

What we mean by 'protocol'

We found it impossible to find a universally acceptable definition of a protocol. The terms *protocol, guideline* and *clinical pathway* are often used interchangeably. However, they are sometimes distinguished on the basis of the degree of structure or the amount of freedom allowed, with guidelines perceived to be more flexible than protocols. We found the definition of guidelines cited by Layton and Morgan[3] helpful: 'systematically developed statements to assist practitioner and patient decisions about appropriate healthcare for specific clinical circumstances'. Brian Hurwitz in his review on clinical guidelines (1994)[2] described other related terms, such as protocols, as 'transformed versions of guideline statements', for use in specific contexts. We wanted to combine guidelines applicable to A&E with the patient documentation, and we regarded that process as the 'transformation' which would define our documents as *protocols*. We wanted them to be 'active' guidelines, which would follow the patient, informing and recording their care during their time in hospital. We took the view that any robust information which could potentially contribute to the patient–clinician encounter should be considered for inclusion in the protocols. This included nationally agreed standards, published evidence from trials and reviews, and risk management strategies.

Central Middlesex Hospital has considerable experience in the use of protocols,[3-6] mostly in the context of inpatient care. The hospital has been using them to guide patient management since the early 1990s, and staff generally have a positive attitude towards protocol use. Until we began our project, however, only a limited number of the protocols in use around the hospital had been tried in A&E, and in these cases use had been inconsistent and had accounted for only a small proportion of the workload. As already mentioned, the fact that protocols tend to be *diagnosis-* rather than *symptom*-based* made their application in A&E problematic, as patients nearly always present with symptoms rather than diagnosed problems. We felt that to overcome this mismatch, and enable protocols to have an impact from the outset of the clinician–patient encounter, we would need to reconfigure them as symptom-based documents.

The precursor to the main project was the introduction of a comprehensive system of protocols guiding the work of the emergency nurse practitioners. The prime motivation for this initiative was to manage closely the delegation of clinical responsibility (i.e. from doctors to nurses). These early A&E protocols were symptom- or complaint-based, and were aimed at maximising the thoroughness of the examination and supporting nurse-led care up to the boundaries of permitted decision making. The wider project (which formed the Health Authority-led Implementation Project) drew from the experience of this earlier work with the emergency nurse practitioner protocols, but had the more ambitious objective of expanding the system of protocols so that they would be available (and *used*) by nurses *and* doctors, for *all* clinical care in the department.

Protocol design

We wanted to ensure that we would have protocols to cover the majority of our work. In the case of major trauma, and in other circumstances where risks are high, we had a very clear understanding of the types of symptoms that protocols needed to cover. In order to ensure that we also had comprehensive coverage of minor injuries, we conducted a survey to analyse the range of common symptom groups attending the minor injury unit in the A&E department. We established that over 90% of patients with minor injuries attended with a single predominant symptom rather than multiple symptoms. We decided to aim at developing a range of *symptom-specific* protocols which would cover the majority of cases, with a *general* protocol for patients who had a less common problem or multiple symptoms.

---

*An example was the cardiac pain protocol. Even though this appeared to be symptom-based, it begins at a point where a particular subtype of pain has been identified (cardiac as opposed to pleuritic or non-specific). As a consequence its value in the immediate assessment of patients presenting with undiagnosed chest pain was minimal. Similarly the protocols for diabetic ketoacidosis and miscarriage, though well developed, and focusing on subjects relevant to work in A&E, also started at a point after an initial diagnosis had been made, greatly reducing their value in A&E.

The layout of the protocols underwent several revisions. Our experience, derived from drafting the protocols for nurse practitioners, reflected the wishes of the staff concerned that they should be tightly controlled, with clinical responsibilities and pathways precisely defined. The nurse practitioners had wanted a clear structure, not least because they saw the protocol as important for their own legal protection, and senior medical staff were keen to influence and define nurse practitioner activity. As a consequence these early protocols followed a strict 'check-list' format (*see* Box 3.1) and had a prescriptive tone. This had reassured consultants that their advice would be closely followed, and helped nursing staff to feel comfortable and firmly supported in new, decision-making capacities. As experience led to confidence, in both nurse practitioners and the senior medical staff, the style of the protocols was adjusted to a more information-based, less prescriptive format which took account of the growing expertise of nurse practitioners (*see* Box 3.2). We recognised that this more flexible format was likely to be more acceptable to medical staff, who tended to object to prescriptive guidance, when we considered extending the use of protocols to cover all consultations.

In the first instance, however, we were unable to produce a wide range of new documents, so the doctors were encouraged to use the check-list style nurse practitioner protocols, with the suggestion that they could write notes on traditional casualty cards or on the back of the protocol sheets. From audit we found that in only a third of cases were the doctors' notes being made on the appropriate protocols. We tried to identify the reasons for this through informal interviews, staff appraisals and audit meetings (these are set out in Table 3.1).

When we set about designing new protocols we found that a format based on a yes/no algorithm was too simplistic and unhelpful for the majority of work in A&E. This was because in A&E one of the main tasks is to *identify* the problem, and yes/no choices rarely fitted the composite nature of the necessary decisions. Nevertheless, we recognise that algorithm-driven protocols may be useful in defining care pathways (guiding the initial investigations and treatment of a patient) *following* the identification of the essential problem.

We wanted the protocols to be reasonably short (we attempted to keep our protocols to within two to three A4 sheets) but recognised that short protocols could not cover every eventuality. A pragmatic solution was to ensure that the basic framework of each protocol focused on common or high-risk situations. We thought that it was vitally important for the user to be able to deviate from the advice given in the protocol at any stage. This was clinically desirable (as it is not possible to anticipate *every* situation) and legally essential to preserve mutual clinical responsibility. Nevertheless, we wanted the protocols to be sufficiently robust to be followed in the majority of cases, and so that deviation from the protocol would be the exception

Box 3.1 Checklist format

Trauma (isolated eye injury)

Name: **Episode no:** **Date:** **Time:**

Occupation: **Side:** R/L/Both

History: _____

Past history: Eye problems Other:

Mechanism: Penetrating (go to Box 1)/Blunt (go to Box 2)

VA: R = L = If reduced check with pin hole: R = L =

Other injuries:

Use appropriate protocols or exclude.

Box 1 Penetrating injury Refer Eye Dr/Stat [ ]/Time:

Eyelids: Laceration/Bruise/Swelling/Perforation

Conjunctiva: Congested/Laceration/Perforation/Haemorrhage/
Can't examine

Cornea: Cloudy/Opaque/FB/Perforated/Can't examine

Pupils: Perl/Can't see/Oval/Irregular/Unequal

Side: R = L =

Other:

Box 2 Blunt trauma

	Eye clinic	*Eye department*
Pain	No/Mild	Significant
VA	Normal	Decreased
Eyelid	NAD/Bruised but eye visible	Laceration to lid margin/ Eye not visible
Eye movement	Full/No diplopia	Restricted/Diplopia
Conjunctiva	NAD/Congested	Haemorrhage
Cornea	NAD	Glazed/Cloudy/Hyphaema
Fluorescein stain	NAD	Stain/Ulcer present
Pupil	Normal	Unequal/Abnormal
Fundus	Normal	Abnormal/Can't focus

Orbital margin: Tender/Swelling/Infra orbital numbness/NAD

Side: R/L/B Teleconsult if abnormal. May need facial bones X-ray.

If significant blunt trauma: send to eye department.

Box 3.1   *continued*

Any ocular foreign body seen: Yes/No
If Yes, use eye FB protocol in addition. Attach to current protocol.

Additional notes: _____

Treatment

Analgesia: Not needed/Advise paracetamol/Codydramol See protocol

Drug: **Signature:**

Discharge steps

Disposal: Eye clinic routine/Eye clinic stat/Admit/Discharge/GP/Other

Date/time of appt:

Letter: To GP/Eye clinic/Other

'Dr to see' or teleconsult features in protocol checked: [ ]

Advice: [ ]

Variation from protocol	*Reason*

Signature:

rather than the norm. A 'variation box' was provided to document deviations from the guidelines. The clinician using the protocol was required to state explicitly each 'variance' from the guidance given and the reason for it. Variances could then be examined to ascertain whether the protocol required amendment, whether the practitioner was capable or whether some other change was desirable.

Each protocol ends with some essential prompts to facilitate safe discharge (*see* Box 3.3). This *risk management* element is a key component of A&E work, where often the most difficult decisions can be about whether or not to send patients home. The current layout incorporates essential guidelines in the first part of the protocol, followed by a documentation section which is essentially space for free text, with a few strategic prompts to ensure that essential information is captured.

Box 3.2   Information-based format   **Protocol Code AP/898**

Ocular Trauma & Foreign Body

Patient Name: _____   **Episode Number:** _____

Seen by (print name): _____   **Date/Time:** _____

Urgent	Refer to eye team if penetrating injury Pupil/visual acuity abnormal: refer Dr Stat

Eye team involvement:	X-ray positive, Penetrating FB, Evidence of intra-ocular injury (Fundus abnormal/can't focus, Restricted movement/Diplopia, Glazed/cloudy cornea, Hypheama, Reduced visual acuity) Refer to eye clinic: Conjunctival haemorrhage, FB sensation, Fluorescein stain/ulcer present, Significant pain
Blunt trauma:	Indications for #: Tenderness of orbital margin, Numbness maxillary area, Diplopia Routine X-ray if: Significant trauma to globe, Clinical feature indicating # = Facial bone view Examine X-rays for #, opaque sinus and tear drop sign. Check orbital and sinus margins
FB:	X-ray if high-velocity trauma (Drilling/chipping): Routine orbital X-ray of eye looking up and down. Remove with benoxinate. Eye pad. Chloromycetin ointment 2 hrly if not allergic. Residual FB/rust ring/corneal abrasion – over pupil – eye clinic. Otherwise consultant review If FB sensation but none found, consider conjunctivitis/iritis (*see* Ocular Non-Trauma Protocol)
Laceration:	Complex laceration or eyelid/tarsal plate involvement – refer Eye/Max facial Dept. Give adequate analgesia. Ensure laceration clean/adequately debrided before closure. Suture if full thickness/widely gaping wound. If suture use 6/0 non-absorbable Compound wounds – Flucloxicillin and amoxycillin Animal/human bites – augmentin
If discharged:	Give advice re driving. If no follow-up advise review if symptomatic 4 days

Box 3.2   *continued*

History/Examination Indicate source of history if not patient. Describe lacerations, wounds, bruising, etc.

Date/time injury: _____

Side: _____

Site: _____

Occupation: _____

Mechanism:

Allergies: None/

Contact lenses: Yes/No

VA right: _____

VA left: _____
If VA reduced, check with pinhole. If abnormality describe.

Is this a problem?
Upper sac   Yes/No
Lower sac   Yes/No
Conjunctiva   Yes/No
Cornea   Yes/No
FB   Yes/No
Arc eye   Yes/No
Iris prolapse   Yes/No
Fluorescein stain   Yes/No/Not done
LA (*Benoxinate might make examination easier. Caution if conjunctivitis*)

Investigations/Findings If X-rays give side and site
Examine X-rays for #, opaque sinus and tear drop sign. Check orbital and sinus margins

Findings on X-ray: _____

Clinical diagnosis: _____

Box 3.2 *continued*

Treatment

Analgesia   None/Drug & Dose _____   Sign _____
Tetanus status   Not relevant/Covered/Treatment: Advice leaflet +
                                                      explanation Yes/No

Disposal
Refer/Admit   Yes/No   Destination/Team: _____
Discharge   Yes/No   Check ability to cope at home, especially elderly
                          Follow-up: None/GP/Eye clinic/Consultant review

_____
          Variation from protocol   *Reason for variation*
_____

_____

Signature: _____   **Position:** _____

Protocol content

The content of each protocol was established partly by a pragmatic process of reference to the evidence where we were able to find it, and consensus on best practice where we were not. We were well aware that many guidelines in circulation are actually consensus-based rather than evidence-based, and that

Table 3.1   Reasons for not following protocols

Reasons given for not using the protocol	*Solutions tried*
Unawareness or unfamiliarity with protocols	New doctors were sent protocols before they started in the department and were assessed on their content
Not liking the design	Protocol design was changed from a check list to knowledge-oriented format to suit doctors. Effort was made to make forms user-friendly designs. Continuous updating based on audit
Loss of clinical freedom	Variation concept reinforced early. Emphasised that clinical freedom can be exercised meaningfully only on the basis of information/knowledge
Inappropriate starting point for protocols	Move from disease-based to symptom-based protocols
Too many protocols making choice difficult	Focusing on high-risk/high-volume conditions. Computer storage/generation simplified selection and aquisition of correct protocols
Patients arriving at A&E do not fit into simple categories*	The 'general' protocol was included as part of the system for cases which genuinely could not be assigned to specific protocols. However, the general protocol had to be made via a menu which included *all* protocols. This helped to ensure that selection of the general protocol would be an *active* decision, and would not become an *alternative* to following the system, or a lazy habit!
Use of casualty card for documentation	The casualty card was eliminated, making a protocol the *only* document for record-taking

*We regard this as a popular misconception. From our own analysis we found that 90% of minor injuries/illnesses (and approximately 60% of patients with major problems) present with a single set of clear symptoms.

sometimes that was because the necessary evidence is simply not available. We were also conscious that searching for the available evidence requires considerable resources, and that it would be virtually impossible to undertake systematic reviews in the context of a district general hospital.

Nevertheless, we wanted to promote a culture of evidence-based practice, and sought a way of accommodating this with our aim of introducing a comprehensive set of protocols for A&E (not *all* of which could be evidence-based, at least at first). In order to get the project off the ground we established a number of searches using Medline to look for existing guidelines,

---

Box 3.3   Essential prompts to facilitate safe discharge

Treatment

Only discharge if you can answer yes to ALL of the following:

Remains alert	Yes/No
Responsible carer for 24 hours	Yes/No
No amnesia to current event > 5 mins	Yes/No
No vomiting > 3 times	Yes/No
No indication # (Clinical/X-ray)	Yes/No

Analgesia   None/Drug & Dose _____   Sign _____

Tetanus status: Not relevant/Covered/Treatment:

Advice leaflet
+ explanation: Yes/No

---

meta-analyses, systematic reviews and other relevant publications. We took the view that it would be important to attain a critical mass at an early stage (i.e. to develop protocols for a significant proportion of the workload) because this would lead to faster progress towards achieving fully comprehensive protocols. We considered that attaining *full* coverage of the department's work by protocol should rank as a higher priority than striving to introduce a small number of 'gold standard' evidence-based protocols which would relate to only a small fraction of our work. Our strategy was to shift *working routines* to protocol use first, and focus on improving the evidence bases of the least robust protocols later. We regarded this pragmatic approach as being critically important for success.

Medline was made available in the department and individual doctors and nurse practitioners were encouraged to work on specific protocols that interested them most. Doctors were encouraged to review the literature to answer queries raised from case presentations, and formal training in critical appraisal skills was provided. Many of our reviews proved to be easier than we had anticipated because of the limited number of relevant publications and the consistency of results in published research. Existing reviews of nationally and internationally commended guidelines were initially accepted at face value (e.g. the British Thoracic Society asthma guideline and Harrogate criteria for skull X-rays). We found that problems with these documents, which usually related to doctors having difficulty in following the *structure* of existing protocols (rather than there being problems with the *content*), usually came to light as a result of audit, and that these could be addressed as part of the audit cycle. In the case of new protocols, changes to key clinical decisions were made by analysing adverse incidents and complaints, or because of the interest of individual staff members in particular problems.

Obviously our method ran the risk of bias and so it was important to develop a consistent way of analysing and presenting evidence from literature review. The methodology described by Guyatt, Sackett *et al.*[7–11] provided a useful framework which we attempted to use to describe the quality of evidence. This uses key elements – study design, confidence intervals, numbers needed to treat and the concept of heterogeneity – to weight research papers.

Even when literature reviews produce definitive conclusions about a therapy, decisions still need to be made with regard to the level of risk or outcome necessary to warrant a change in practice. Gains in outcome need to be weighed against resource implications (and any increases in the level of adverse outcomes) and these are decisions which, though best *informed* by evidence, are seldom completely 'evidence-based'. In our field, A&E, *acceptable risk* is often the key to decision making. Individual clinicians may not agree on what constitutes an acceptable risk for a particular clinical situation; the acceptability of risk is, after all, a personal value judgement. Our experience has been that the incremental accumulation of evidence over a period of time, based on small reviews of local practice, can play an important part in informing clinicians' assessment of acceptable risk. In the real-life context of a busy A&E clinic this can very effectively complement the evidence from large-scale systematic reviews (such as those undertaken by the *Cochrane Collaboration*). We recognise that on their own, smaller, local reviews lack power and risk missing valuable evidence, but we have found that if we encourage clinicians to undertake local reviews *in tandem* with using 'gold standard' evidence from systematic reviews where available, the effect has been very positive, both in terms of building up the culture of evidence-based practice and promoting informed, effective risk management.

Protocol use

Although people often acknowledge the desirability of changing practice, doing something 'the way we always do it' is usually more comfortable, quicker and often feels more efficient in a pressurised situation. This latent conservatism in the workplace has often been regarded as a barrier to the implementation of new, evidence-based practices. We thought that if the power of habit in the workplace could be turned around, so that it became a force *for* using research evidence rather than a *barrier* to it, our project would stand a much better chance of making an impact. We therefore focused considerable effort on making the use of protocols a 'work habit' in the department. We found that a number of issues impacted on how successful we were at introducing protocols for mainstream use.

- If protocols were available for only a limited range of conditions, a doctor would be less likely to look for them, particularly in a busy environment such as an A&E department. We found that protocols were far more likely to be used when clinicians were aware that there was a comprehensive system of protocols which would cover *all* cases (*see* Boxes 3.4 and 3.5)
- A protocol was also more likely to be used if one *had* to be chosen each time a patient was 'clerked' (even if the choice was the general protocol). We felt strongly that making protocols the *only* source of documentation would be a key step to achieving their widespread, routine use.

Box 3.4   Protocols for minor problems

Protocol

General Minor
Insect Bites/Allergic Reaction
Burns
Isolated Minor Chest Wall Injury
Ear Problems including Lacerations
Elbow
ENT Foreign Body
Epistaxis
Facial/Nasal Injury
Foot/Ankle/Tibia/Fibula Trauma
Minor Head Injury
Knee Trauma
Laceration & Skin Foreign Body
Limb Non-Trauma
Ocular Non-Trauma
Ocular Trauma & Foreign Body
Post Coital Pill
Sharps & Inoculation Injuries
Shoulder
Skin Non-Trauma
Thorax Non-Trauma
Upper Limb Trauma
Walking Neck Injuries
Wrist

Box 3.5   Protocols for major problems

Protocol

General Adult Majors
Paediatric Assessment
Abdominal Pain
Asthma
Chest Pain
Difficulty in Breathing
Calf Pain and ?DVT
Overdose
Painful Hip > 65
Adult Sickle Cell
PV Bleed

Ownership

At the start of the project we thought that ownership of protocols by the end-users would be crucial. However, during the course of the work we came to change this view. We found that rather than wanting to have a say in the content of a protocol, doctors were more interested in whether protocols were well-designed, easy to use and helped them to manage their cases. Obviously the information on the protocols had to be credible, either through having a strong evidence base or being founded on a reputable statement of consensus. With hindsight, we feel that in the past too much emphasis had been placed on ownership of the *details*. In our experience, ownership of the *process* of protocol use was far more important. This may be particularly relevant to A&E and other departments where there is a rapid turnover of staff. We found that new members would often accept the existing system, taking their lead from senior staff, and had no wish to exert personal influence over the content of protocols. Our view is neither wholly consistent nor inconsistent with research evidence on this subject. Baker and Fraser (1997)[12] in their study on use of protocols by GPs, concluded that ownership was not necessarily more important than scientific credibility and/or perceived utility. However Clemmer and Sphuler (1998)[13] placed a significant emphasis on ownership, expressing the view that the process of protocol development was more important than the resulting document. Our experience was probably most closely aligned to the review by Duff *et al.* (1996),[14] which stressed the importance of strategies for implementation when assessing the overall impact of guidelines. We recognise that our observations are likely to be related to the relative inexperience of the doctors and the rapid (six-monthly) turnover of staff, and may therefore not be representative of the wider community of hospital doctors.

Accessibility

The protocols needed to be easily accessible and consistently available. We were aware that having large piles of paper protocols stored on shelves would at the very least add to confusion, and at worst lead to chaos. We were keen to avoid the possibility of running out of a particular protocol at any point (there could be logistical difficulties in ensuring a consistent supply of high-quality photocopies 24 hours a day in a busy A&E department). These worries were overcome by storing the protocols as data sheets on computers in the department, which could be selected from a menu and printed out as required. Setting up this simple, computerised system to generate protocols on demand was an important part of the project, and acquisition of the computers and printers accounted for a significant proportion of the project costs. Basic training in the use of the computer system has been provided and users have been encouraged to discuss any ideas they may have for improvements. The significance of having a simple system to ensure easy access to any protocol at any time cannot be overstated.

We felt that it was important that senior staff showed enthusiasm towards the system and were receptive to suggestions for change or improvements. Regular audits on the use and appropriateness of protocol selection were a way of demonstrating this commitment to implement and continuously improve the system of protocol use.

Evaluating the use and impact of the protocols

Our primary aim was to establish a system which facilitated the use of evidence where possible, and best practice throughout, not to test whether using evidence improves outcomes. We contented ourselves that if the protocols we used were based on the best available evidence (or credible consensus where evidence was unavailable), then improved outcomes would surely result. A systematic review by Grimshaw and Russell (1993)[15] identified 11 studies of guidelines which had assessed patient outcomes, nine of which reported significant improvements, and a subsequent *Effective Health Care* bulletin concluded that: 'the introduction of guidelines can change clinical practice and affect patient outcome'.[16] Despite this assurance, we recognised that given the proliferation in guideline and protocol usage, the evidence base for improvements in outcomes from protocol use is perhaps not as robust as we might have wished. However, our view was that this may be more of a reflection of the difficulties of outcome *measurement* than an indictment of protocols as a lever for improved outcomes. We were aware that getting involved in attempting to measure outcomes would be beyond the scope of our project, and therefore focused our attention on evaluating protocol usage rates, the appropriateness of protocol selection, and adherence to the standards defined in the protocol.

Protocol usage

At the time of writing we have 35 protocols. The overall rate of use has given a good indication of the acceptability of the protocols, and during the course of the project this has been used to highlight practical problems with the design, content, storage and retrieval of protocols. The pattern of usage of individual protocols has given valuable feedback on the perceived usefulness of each. In particular, consistent use of the *general* protocol in preference to an appropriate, specific protocol, by a number of different practitioners, has been indicative of faults in the design of that specific protocol.

An example of an instance where the general protocol was often chosen where a specific protocol was available, was in relation to ankle, foot and lower leg injuries. Initially, these were covered by three separate protocols, however, the overlapping nature of injuries in this part of the body made appropriate selection problematic, and consequently there was overuse of the general protocol. By merging the three protocols into a 'foot, ankle and lower leg' protocol we were able to produce a (reasonably) specific protocol which was much more helpful to clinicians and, as a consequence, used far more commonly.

Having a 'general' protocol was worthwhile in another key respect. This was in the infrequent cases where a member of staff objected on principle to the idea of following protocols. In this context the 'general' protocol provided a 'safety valve' in that it offered a way of complying with the departmental policy of universal protocol use without requiring adherence to a detailed, specific protocol. While we considered that the use of the latter was entirely justified, the existence of the general protocol form (which required only minimal effort to follow) provided a way to avoid alienating the small number of colleagues who remained unconvinced of the value of extending the use of protocols. This 'latitude' was particularly helpful given that *clinical freedom* is an important point of principle to some doctors, and the option to use the general protocol undoubtedly provided a way of pre-empting potential confrontation in this respect.

Occasionally, the protocol chosen proved not to be the most appropriate selection for the clinical problem of the patient. In some cases this was attributable to the limitations of the clinicians involved, but more frequently it occurred when there was uncertainty about the symptoms. We have found this difficult to avoid. However, in such cases we have found that adherence to protocols, even though not the most appropriate, has led to important information being elicited and recorded, and has not been a cause for major concern.

Adherence to the standards in protocols

We have developed a scoring system for protocol use which we will be applying to each of the protocols in turn. At the time of writing we have used this system to examine the use of the protocols for asthma and head injury, and in both cases we have noted a substantial increase in adherence to the protocols since their introduction. We recognise that *using* a protocol is not the same as *following* a protocol. A key finding from our evaluation of adherence to the guidance in the protocols was that appropriate action was taken on indications for investigations more commonly in cases where the 'check-list' type of protocols had been used (as opposed to the 'general information' format). For example, the Ottawa decision rules for ankle X-rays[15] were followed better when the indications were set out as a checklist (*see* Boxes 3.6 and 3.7). As stated earlier, the move away from the check-list approach had been an expedient measure aimed at making protocol use more acceptable to doctors. We think that the task of 're-educating' doctors in our department to use protocols has now been largely achieved, so we may in future look for an effective way of incorporating *some* check lists into the protocols. The objective would be to reach an acceptable balance between the advantages of the check-list approach in terms of adherence to sound guidance and a system that will be embraced wholeheartedly by medics.

Long-term sustainability

As discussed earlier, the project aimed to develop a culture of evidence-based (or best available) practice, and we recognised that the keys to sustaining that culture would be establishing a system which would be easy to keep up to date. We identified two aspects to achieving this aim:

- maintaining constant surveillance of the literature
- regular updating of protocols reflecting changes in research evidence and clinical practice.

The former is a daunting task in a district general hospital, and as with other aspects of the project our solution has been pragmatic rather than ideal. The

Box 3.6   Ottawa decision rules for ankle X-rays I   **Protocol Code A1/0299**

Foot/Ankle/Tibia/Fibula Trauma

Patient Name: _____   **Episode Number:** _____

Seen by (print name): _____   **Date/Time:** _____

Ankle Dislocation	Requires urgent reduction then back slab and X-ray (not toes). Check neurovascular status pre and post reduction. YOU (Not orthopods) must reduce the dislocated ankle NOW. Just pull it straight (Give entonox). Do not wait for X-rays. GET HELP if unsure. Return to trauma clinic.

Indications for X-ray	• Bone deformity
	• Tendon injury to check bone avulsion fragment
	• Swelling/bruising over bone *and* associated loss of function (inability to weight bear soon after trauma and/or in A&E)
	• Pain/tenderness: – over posterior surface or tip of either malleolus – ankle X-ray
	              – over 5th metatarsal base – X-ray of foot not routine ankle
	              – over navicular bone
	Note: Isolated tenderness over the outer surface of the malleolus is a poor predictor of #
	       Tibia & fibula – include knee and ankle on X-ray
	• Open #, neurovascular damage, displaced #

Refer orthos	• Complex lacerations, complete tear ligament/tendon
Displaced fracture	• **Get help**. Refer ortho
Undisplaced fracture	• Tibia AK POP, splint, POP check, trauma clinic • Lower fibula/ankle POP back slab BK, NWB, crutches, trauma clinic • Avulsion # Treat as sprain (small stable avulsion #) • Metatarsal Tubigrip, advice, walking aid. If multiple # POP, trauma clinic. If very displaced refer orthos • Toes Adjacent strap, advice

Box 3.6   *continued*

Sprain/soft tissue injury	**Archilles tendon rupture:** Feel for gap on tendon. Does the foot move on squeezing the calf? Tubigrip/walking aid/analgesia/advice. Follow up at review clinic if significant swelling/stiffness/pain.

Consider POP if very painful/swollen.

Pretibial laceration   Do not use sutures – use steristrip to uncurl flap, dressing as laceration protocol.
Trauma clinic if #; unless minor metatarsal/tiny avulsion fractures only. Otherwise review clinic.

Disposal

History/Examination Indicate source of history if not patient. Describe lacerations, wounds, bruising, etc.

If fall from height check calcaneus, knee, spine/back pain, arm injury, neck injury. Check for compartment syndrome.

Date/time injury: _____

Side: _____

Site: _____

Occupation: _____

Mechanism: _____

Age: _____

Stability: _____

Test by rocking talus within the tibiofibulae matrix

Allergies: None/

lead clinician for the project has taken overall responsibility for *horizon scanning*, however, all clinical staff have been encouraged to participate in the process, and the same principle which we used to implement the project (i.e. dividing small parts of the whole task between individual members of staff) has been applied to the task of looking out for emerging new (or more robust) evidence. The breadth of work undertaken in A&E makes keeping up with new evidence particularly challenging. We have found it helpful to foster a wide range of contacts, both within the A&E community and more widely, linking into other related specialities and organisations. We have found that networking in this way has been a very effective method of picking up relevant emerging

Box 3.7   Ottawa decision rules for ankle X-rays II

Ankle injuries protocol

Name: _____   Episode No: _____

Name of DR/ENP: **Date/Time:**

History: (Include side)   **Allergies:**

Pain over malleolus: YES/NO

Exclusions to protocol: Major trauma/Multiple trauma.
Use other protocols as appropriate (if skin wound, laceration protocol)
Number of protocols used:

Clinical features	No	Yes	Notes/site	Action/Guidelines
Deformity	No	Yes		If dislocated/badly deformed reduce immed prior to X-ray, under Entonox/IV sedation back slab and X-ray. Check nerve/circulation.
Compromised circulation Check cap, refil, colour, temp	No	Yes		Correct deformity urgently, release constrictions, get help.
Tenderness over malleoli	No	Yes	If yes, indicate which part of which malleolus:	X-ray needed only if tender over posterior surface or tip of either malleoli. Routine X-ray not needed if tender only over lat/medial surface.
Tender 5th mt base	No	Yes	Any swelling?	X-ray of foot not routine ankle.
Can't wt bear soon after trauma	No	Yes		X-ray of associated ankle pain/injury.
Can't wt bear in A&E	No	Yes		X-ray if associated ankle pain/injury.

Additional notes: (If fall from height examine calcaneus, rest of leg, spine.
Routinely check foot and tibia/fibula fully)
Checked: [ ] ---

Box 3.7   *continued*

X-ray: side and site:
X-ray findings:
Final diagnoses:

☐1 **No BI**   ☐2 Tubigrip   ☐3 Advice leaflet   ☐4 Analgesia
                                                  & explanation   if req

                      ☐5 Walking aid   ☐6 Review clinic if very painful/marked
                          if req   swelling/poor mobility. Routine
                                                  follow-up not needed

☐7 **Displaced #**   ☐8 Refer ortho team. Consider analgesia
(Tib/Fib/Ankle/Foot)

☐9 **Undisplaced #** ☐10 BK Pop slab   ☐11 Crutches NWB   ☐12 Trauma clinic
(Foot/malleoli)

                      ☐13 Analgesia if req   ☐14 Review clinic (if # MT/tiny
                                                  avulsion fractures)

Disposal   ☐15 Admit
☐16 Discharged: ☐17 No follow-up   ☐18 GP   ☐19 Review clinic

                                                                  0 Trauma
                                                                       ☐2
                                                                  1 Advice

☐0 Analgesia   Drug & Dose _____ **Sign** _____

☐0 Letter   ☐0 DN   ☐0 GP   ☐0 CPN

Variation from protocol   *Reason for variation*

Signature: _____

evidence quickly.* Nevertheless we accept that this type of informal networking is insufficiently systematic to be relied upon as the sole means of keeping up to date, and we have sought to supplement this with a systematic attempt to keep abreast of robust and relevant new research evidence.**

Changing the individual protocols is not actually an arduous task because the protocols are based in computer files to be printed off when needed, rather than held in volume storage as hard copy. Once the initial development work has been done we have found that making changes to protocols has been relatively easy. The majority of our protocols have undergone two or three major changes and a number of minor changes since their introduction.

Summary

The project concept, that evidence-based (or best available) practice could be promoted by the use of protocols, was accepted by the majority of participants from the outset, and backed by senior hospital staff. We did not struggle to achieve acceptance of the *idea* of using protocols to guide care, but we found most problems to be practical and resource-based. Much of the energy in the project was devoted to changing clinicians' work habits, but we regarded this as primarily a practical rather than intellectual or philosophical challenge. Overcoming the logistical problems of keeping stocks of unused paper protocols was critical, and we have overcome the problem of retaining a large volume of *completed* documents by using an optical storage system*** which scans notes on to optical discs which can be retrieved by computer as required.

Throughout the project we have followed a pragmatic 'solve-the-problems as-you-go-along' approach. We feel that by celebrating each step forward, however small, the project gained momentum and a favourable reputation, which in turn encouraged further participation and support. We began with the philosophy that ultimately change is achieved in steps rather than leaps, and although our position changed on several issues in the course of the work, we remain committed to the tenet of *incremental* progress. We view the fact

---

*A recent example of the value of networking in this way involves the administration of the post-coital pill. New research evidence has contradicted the previously held assumption that efficacy was unaffected by the timing of taking the drug, provided that it was taken within 72 hours of intercourse. We were notified of the new findings by the public health department at the health authority and were quickly able to alter the relevant A&E protocol.

**The trust librarian has been recruited to monitor relevant *new* additions to the Cochrane Database of Systematic Reviews.

***The optical storage system was funded by the trust on the basis of efficiency savings, and did not involve project funds. We regard taking advantage of any opportunities to link into other sources of funding in this way as an essential part of consolidating the progress achieved in an implementation project, and a crucial aspect of ensuring sustainability.

that changes achieved have been modest rather than momentous as likely to be advantageous in terms of long-term sustainability.

Furthermore we attribute the fact that participation in the project has been widely regarded as a positive experience by clinicians as confirmation that the step-wise, pragmatic way of bringing about changes in practice was the right one for our environment.

Lessons learned

- Doctors may not like the idea of working with protocols which use a checklist format, however, this format maximised adherence to guidance.
- Ownership of guideline *contents* is not critical to their acceptability to users.
- Protocols must be perceived to be useful and should address common concerns.
- Protocols cannot cover all eventualities, therefore they should be flexible and clearly provide clinicians with the freedom to follow different courses of action when circumstances and their judgement make this advisable.
- Recording deviations from protocol guidance is a valuable source of information, both for improving the protocols and assessing the competencies of clinical staff.
- Access to protocols at all stages is an important consideration, from the time a protocol is first needed to its final storage.
- Even with a system designed to minimise the possibility of clinicians having difficulties accessing protocols, simple problems can cause major disruption. For example printer paper running out will surely lead to neglect of protocol use!

Things we would do differently if we were starting tomorrow

- think again about how we used the resources available for the project. We put the majority of resources into computers (which have only a limited lifetime). It might be better to put a smaller proportion of resource into technology and use some to finance a research assistant or other extra person devoted to the project
- do not expend too much time or energy on securing ownership of individual guidelines
- let the enthusiastic staff locate the evidence and work on protocol development rather than trying to involve all of the doctors in the team
- do more work to understand the psychology of clinician behaviour. Work harder at implementing at least a limited check-list format which makes the protocol more robust
- consider ways in which the Internet could be used to gather and share evidence for protocols (and protocols themselves).

References

1 Sackett DL, Ellis J, Mulligan I and Rowe J (1995) Inpatient general medicine is evidence based. *Lancet.* **346**: 407–10.

2 Hurwitz B (1994) Clinical guidelines: proliferation and medico legal significance. *Quality in Healthcare.* **3**: 37–44.

3 Layton A and Morgan G (1994) *The Nuts and Bolts of Patient Focused Care. Clinical protocols.* Centre for Health Service Management, University of Nottingham, Nottingham.

4 McNicoll M (1992) Achieving quality improvement by structured patient management. *Quality in Healthcare.* **1** (Suppl.) S40–S1.

5 Layton A *et al.* (1998) Mapping out the patient's journey: experiences of devoloping pathways of care. *Quality in Healthcare.* **7** (Suppl.) S30–S6.

6 McNicoll M, Layton A and Morgan G (1993) Team working: key to implementing guidelines? *Quality in Healthcare.* **2**: 215–6.

7 Oxman AD, Sackett DL and Cook DJ (1993) For the evidence-based medicine working group. User's guide to the literature – how to get started. *JAMA.* **270**: 2093–5.

8 Guyatt GH, Sackett DL and Cook DJ (1993) For the evidence-based medicine working group. User's guide to the literature – 2. How to use an article about therapy or prevention. A. Are the results of the study valid? *JAMA.* **270**: 2598–601.

9 Guyatt GH, Sackett DL and Cook DJ (1994) For the evidence-based medicine working group 2. How to use an article about therapy or prevention. B. What were the results and will they help me in caring for my patients? *JAMA.* **71**: 59–66.

10 Jaeschke R, Guyatt GH and Sackett DL (1994) User's guide to the medical literature – 3. How to use an article about diagnostic test. A. Are the results of the study valid? *JAMA.* **271**: 389–91.

11 Evidence-based Medicine Working Group (1992) Evidence-based medicine: a new approach to teaching the practice of medicine. *JAMA.* **268**: 2420–5.

12 Baker R and Fraser RC (1997) Is ownership more important than scientific credibility of audit protocols? A survey of medical audit advisory groups. *Family Practice.* **14(2)**: 107–11.

13 Clemmer TP and Sphuler VJ (1998) Developing and gaining acceptance for patient care protocols. *New Horizons.* **6(1)**: 12–19.

14 Duff LA, Kitson AL, Seers K and Humpries D (1996) Clinical guidelines: an introduction to their development and implementation. *Journal of Advanced Nursing.* **23(5)**: 887–95.

15   Grimshaw JM and Russell IT (1993) Effect of clinical guidelines on medical practice: a systematic review of rigorous evaluations. *Lancet.* **342**: 1317–22.

16   NHS Centre for Reviews and Dissemination (1994) Implementing clinical practice guidelines. *Effective Health Care.* **8**: Dec.

17   Stiell IG, Greenberg GH, McKnight RD *et al.* (1992) A study to develop clinical decision rules for the use of radiography in acute ankle injuries. *Annals of Emergency Medicine.* **21(4)**: 384–90.

A&E protocols at
Central Middlesex

When asked if people could go back to working the way they had done, one survey participant enthusiastically replied:

> 'We can't stop now. We have a culture of evidence-based medicine in the department now. It's very dynamic. We couldn't go back to the way we were before.'

Another one was just as emphatic:

> 'No, no, no. They will definitely be sustained. For lots of reasons, they [the protocols] are totally embedded in the organisation.'

In teasing out those reasons, survey respondents mentioned several factors. One was the keen support of the A&E consultant, who is also the Project Manager. Another is the commitment from very senior staff such as the Chief Executive. A third is the use of protocols throughout the hospital. All of these have helped to create a climate that is right for clinical effectiveness.

Creating the right climate is one task; sustaining it is another. This project has been very adept in doing both. Key to its success has been the nurses.

When we first met this project team in June 1997, they mentioned that nurse adherence to protocols was 100%, while doctors' usage was much lower. Because nurse usage was so comprehensive, doctors had to think about why they were not using protocols. What's more, as nurses became more and more enthusiastic, they became 'product champions', using their considerable skills in working with resistant doctors to get them on board.

Nurse enthusiasm has grown, largely because protocols are very good for professional development. One said:

> 'With more protocols, we are updating our skills. Once we become happy with a case, we think "what next"?'

Another spoke of how the protocols were a part of ongoing education:

> 'This [a mistake] is usually identified from an audit meeting we have once a month. It's a constructive discussion. The consultant says, "This is great.

This is how I would like it to be done." … In group learning, we swap protocols. This is very beneficial. The professional learning is great.'

The same nurse commented that contrary to arguments put forward by those critical of evidence-based medicine, she found that since protocols don't cover everything, she needed her own knowledge and expertise. Protocols helped make her think. They did not take away her capacity for clinical judgement – they sharpened it.

The non-hierarchical team approach at the A&E department is also very important. One of the most enthusiastic survey participants was a manager, who definitely felt involved and excited about the changes within the department. Another practitioner, who had been on an awayday to an A&E department in another trust commented:

'I found it very hard because there was nothing innovative. In this department, it is nurse-initiated. At Hospital X, I had to hold back. Here, doctors just see the patients; everything else is done by the nurses. We wouldn't have got this far if doctors hadn't put their trust in us. It's a team.'

The long-term sustainability of this project looks very good. The A&E Department is one of the pilot sites for the trust's clinical governance policy. What's more, the project has been so successful that Central Middlesex A&E has now taken over administrative responsibility for urgent treatment services at Edgware Hospital and has introduced protocols. Said one survey participant:

'We will use our original protocols for Edgware. We are starting off there with box protocols; we are starting them off nicely… We [staff at Central Middlesex] have now moved on to more complex protocols. These ones develop your knowledge more.'

As one of the projects which has had the most success in becoming firmly embedded within the organisation, we believe this project has a great deal in its favour in repeating this success elsewhere.

4

Introducing open-access echocardiography in Brent & Harrow

Mark Dancy

Introduction/background

Central Middlesex Hospital is located in West London. Like many urban district general hospitals, it has an inherently high rate of referrals to out-patient departments from its GPs. The ethnic mix and level of deprivation of the local population contribute to the high incidence of cardiac disease, and, predictably, there is a considerable waiting time for clinic appointments. Long waits add to the (already) high levels of anxiety in patients and inevitably results occasionally in adverse cardiac events being suffered by patients who are waiting to be seen at the clinic.

Staff in the Cardiology Department have been aware for some time that a proportion of patients were being sent by their GPs for a *test* rather than a consultation (e.g. a 24-hour Holter* electrocardiogram (ECG) for a patient with palpitations). This has added to the wait experienced by people who really *do* need consultations, and was *not* based on sound clinical reasons. Rather, it was the consequence of an inflexible referral system which did not differentiate between patients simply requiring a test and those needing a full consultation, and compelled *all* to attend at outpatients.

The potential for changing these arrangements, in line with emerging research evidence of the clinical effectiveness of open access,[1,2] became apparent at roughly the same time as the offer of regional funding for Health

---

*This is a diagnostic test over a 24-hour period where a patient is fitted with a portable tape recorder which records the occurrence of irregular heartbeats.

Authority-led Implementation Projects. Members of the Central Middlesex Hospital Cardiology Department discussed these issues with Brent & Harrow Health Authority's Public Health Department, and the idea of establishing a local service as an Implementation Project began to coalesce. This would enable GPs to request tests directly from the department and, with a suitable report, act on the result without the need for consultations with the hospital doctors.

At a national level, open-access services have been a contentious issue, as is evidenced by recent debate, claim and counterclaim in the medical journals. On the whole, opinions seem to be divided between those who have set up a service, who generally find that it is well received and effective in changing the management of the relevant conditions,[2,3] and others who have raised fears that GPs may not have the expertise to act appropriately on the results of such tests, and that consequently patients having them should routinely be advised by a specialist.[4] Concern has also been raised that an open-access service might easily become overwhelmed, and this has led to suggestions that access should be restricted to patients whose condition satisfies certain criteria, such as equivocal evidence of heart failure[5,6] or abnormal ECG.[7,8]

In our own case, all the stakeholders were keen to document the efficacy of open access, and the appropriateness of the referrals. However, we were not uncomfortable with the thought that demand might be great because we took the view that if the quality, targeting of care and clinical outcomes were all demonstrably good, then the case for resourcing any additional volume of work could be well made.

There were a number of objectives for the service.

- To reduce the length of time patients would need to wait before being tested and receiving appropriate advice and treatment.
- By reducing the number of referrals to our overstretched outpatient service, reduce the waiting times for patients who had real need for a consultation and not just a test (i.e. by eliminating the need for patients requiring straightforward tests to join the waiting list for a consultation).
- To empower GPs to be more involved with the diagnosis and management of their patients with cardiac conditions. (When the choice of tests for a patient is left to the local cardiologist, there is little incentive for GPs to learn about the strengths and limitations of these tests. It seemed logical that if GPs were encouraged to become more familiar with the tests through having open access to them, they would be motivated to learn more about their use, and would be more comfortable about making management decisions for their patients.)
- To encourage the appropriate use of beneficial treatments, and to avoid inappropriate use of drugs. This is particularly relevant in the context

of heart failure where ACE inhibitors have been shown to prolong life in appropriate patients.[9] Locally, we were not only very keen to ensure that heart failure was considered and investigated, but also to reduce the number of patients being misdiagnosed with this condition.* It seemed reasonable to assume that an open-access service would encourage and enable GPs to use appropriate tests (echocardiograms) to make accurate diagnoses in their care for such patients.

Objectives, resources and the design of the service

In collaboration with the health authority a case was made for funding of an open-access service as part of the Health Authority-led Implementation Project. Initially targeted solely at an open-access echocardiography service, the main case rested on effective detection and diagnosis of heart failure.

The stated objectives were:

- to improve the management of heart failure by providing open-access echocardiography for GPs
- to increase the appropriate prescribing of ACE inhibitors
- to ensure the appropriate prescribing of diurectics
- to audit the use of the service by GPs and assess the impact on outpatient waiting times in the hospital Cardiology Department. The use of ACE inhibitors and diuretics would also be measured.

The main element of cost in the proposal was for staff. An estimate of the likely volume of additional work generated by an open-access service indicated that while there may be sufficient spare capacity within the existing equipment (i.e. the echocardiograph), additional technical staff time would be required.

Shortly after starting the service it became apparent that GPs were keen to gain access to more than just echocardiography, and that demand existed for a comprehensive open-access service offering a range of other tests (such as 24-hour ECG, 24-hour blood pressure (BP), 12-lead ECG and exercise ECG). We considered that expansion of the service in this way would not only meet this demand but would also be highly cost-effective, given that the main barriers to initiating any open-access service had been logistical and common

---

*A number of misdiagnosed cases of heart failure had come to light during recruitment for a clinical trial. It was thought that the observation of 'breathlessness' in patients had been taken by GPs as grounds for reaching the conclusion that a patient was suffering from heart failure, whereas in many cases subsequent echocardiography (during the trial recruitment) had confirmed that heart failure had not been the problem.

to *all* the different tests. Thus it was possible to offer a comprehensive service with relatively little additional investment.

Project funding enabled us to upgrade a vacant technician's post and recruit an echo-trained doctor whose responsibility has been to set up and run both the open-access service and the hospital echo service. We attribute the success of this arrangement to the involvement of this individual in the design, operation and audit of the service from an early stage.

In order to ensure that the open-access service would be used in a clinically appropriate way we identified a number of conditions which would have to be met.

- GPs needed to know which test would be appropriate in which circumstance, and to have a straightforward way of accessing investigations.
- The Cardiology Department needed to assure itself that GPs would provide information of the right type and of sufficient quality. This would be necessary to ensure that tests could be carried out safely, and in ways which would yield results of the sort which GPs could use as the basis of diagnosis and treatment.
- The Cardiology Department would need to provide a report which could be easily understood and applied by GPs. If successful, this would enable the majority of tests to be followed up by treatment by the GP in primary care rather than necessitating referrals to outpatient clinics. To achieve this, it would be important that both the Cardiology Department and GPs had confidence in their own ability to understand the reports. This would be dependent upon GPs having a reasonable level of knowledge about the uses, strengths and weakness of the various tests.

Preliminary, informal discussions with local GPs revealed great enthusiasm for the project, which encouraged us to undertake more detailed planning within the Cardiology Department, and a number of considerations emerged.

- It would be unreasonable to expect the GPs to have pre-existing detailed understanding of the various non-invasive tests used in cardiology departments (i.e. exercise ECGs, echocardiograms, 24-hour Holter ECGs, 24-hour BP recordings and 12-lead ECGs). It would therefore not be sensible to expect them to make appropriate referrals to an open-access service without some training. This implied that either we would need to provide the training or accept that a potentially high proportion of GP referrals would be inappropriate.
- In order to ensure that enough information was provided to the member of staff carrying out the tests we would need to design pro forma request forms for each of the tests.

- We would somehow need to take into account the varying levels of training and experience among GPs, particularly when writing reports and arranging follow-up of patients.
- In order to have some means of assessing the contribution of the service there would be a need to build in audit.

We planned to design the service within the department, and then to share the proposals with GPs, giving them the opportunity to criticise or improve on our ideas. We used a planning session for this purpose, and the GPs provided some very helpful feedback.

Box 4.1a–e gives an example of a referral pro forma. Design of the pro formas required some care. It was important to avoid unnecessary questions because in our experience long forms are often completed badly. Nevertheless there was clearly a basic minimum level of information required by Cardiology Department staff. Other questions on the pro forma were included for the following reasons:

- for the purpose of auditing the effect of the service on referrals to outpatients ('would you have referred this patient to the outpatient clinic if this open-access service was not available ?')
- for the purpose of auditing the appropriateness of the referral
- to enable the Cardiology Department to make management suggestions (e.g. patients with left ventricular impairment who were not taking an ACE inhibitor)
- for safety. Although there is no known risk to patients in undergoing the majority of non-invasive cardiac tests, there are potential hazards in exercise testing. It is generally held that one should not exercise patients with significant aortic stenosis because of the risks of syncope or sudden death. We therefore needed assurance that a GP requesting an exercise test not only knew about the potential risk in patients with aortic stenosis but was satisfied that his/her patient was not affected by this condition. To gain this assurance we included the following questions into the referral pro forma:
  - Have you examined the patient within the last ten weeks?
  - Is there any evidence of aortic stenosis?

The pro formas were initially written by the hospital staff, but subsequently modified by the GPs at the planning session. We believe that the consensual, joint approach was important, and was largely responsible for the fact that the forms have generally been completed appropriately.

Box 4.1a

Central Middlesex Hospital Open Access:
Exercise ECG Test Request

Episode no. ....   GP ....

Name ....   Address ....

DOB .... Gender ....

Address ....

....   Telephone ....

Telephone ....

Does this patient have:	**Treated**	**Untreated**
❒ Typical anginal pain	❒	❒
❒ Atypical pain – ? angina	❒	❒
❒ Possible anginal equivalent, e.g. breathlessness on exertion	❒	❒
❒ Hypertension	❒	❒
❒ History of myocardial infarction		

Is the patient taking:
❒ Nitrate   ❒ Beta blocker   ❒ ACE inhibitor
❒ Digoxin   ❒ Calcium blocker   ❒ Other

Does the resting ECG show:
❒ Normal ECG
❒ Previous myocardial infarction
❒ Possible ischaemia

Have you examined the patient within 10 weeks?   ❒ Yes   ❒ No

Is there any evidence of aortic stenosis?   ❒ Yes   ❒ No

Would you refer the patient to cardiology OPD if there was no open-access service?

❒ Yes   ❒ No

If the study is for the purpose of diagnosing angina, the patient should stop beta blocker and nitrate on the date of the test and resume them immediately after. Have you given instruction to this patient?

❒ Yes   ❒ No (please given reason:)

Signature ....   Date ....

Box 4.1b

Central Middlesex Hospital Open Access:
ECG Request Form

Episode no. ....

Name ....

DOB .... Gender ....

Address ....

....

Telephone ....

GP ....

Address ....

....

....

Telephone ....

Clinical diagnosis:

Medications:

❐ Digoxin   ❐ Beta blocker

Would you refer the patient to cardiology OPD if there was no open-access service?

❐ Yes   ❐ No

Signature .... Date ....

Box 4.1c

Central Middlesex Hospital Open Access:
24-Hour Blood Pressure Monitoring Request

Episode no. ....

Name ....

DOB .... Gender ....

Address ....

....

Telephone ....

GP ....

Address ....

....

....

Telephone ....

Is the diagnosis of hypertension:
❒ Borderline   ❒ New   ❒ Established

Is the patient taking:
❒ Diuretics   ❒ Beta blocker   ❒ ACE inhibitor
❒ Calcium channel blocker   ❒ Other ....

What is the reason for this investigation:
❒ Diagnosis   ❒ Monitoring therapeutic effects

Would you refer the patient to cardiology OPD if there was no open-access service?
❒ Yes   ❒ No

Signature .... Date ....

Box 4.1d

Central Middlesex Hospital Open Access:
24-Hour ECG Monitoring Request Form

Episode no. ....

Name ....

DOB .... Gender ....

Address ....

....

Telephone ....

GP ....

Address ....

....

....

Telephone ....

Is the clinical history:
❐ Palpitations
❐ Syncope
❐ Dizziness
❐ Other [please state]

Does the patient have:
❐ Ischaemic heart disease
❐ Valvular heart disease
❐ Thyroid disease

Would you refer the patient to cardiology OPD if there was no open-access service?
❐ Yes
❐ No

Why have you referred the patient?
❐ Diagnosis
❐ Management
❐ Confirmation of clinical diagnosis
❐ Reassurance for patient
❐ Other [please state]

Signature .... Date ....

Box 4.1e

Central Middlesex Hospital Open Access:
Echocardiography Request Form

Episode no. ....

Name ....

DOB .... Gender ....

Address ....

....

Telephone ....

GP ....

Address ....

....

....

Telephone ....

Does the patient have evidence of?

❐ Left ventricular failure
   [breathlessness, pulmonary oedema]

❐ Biventricular failure

❐ Right ventricular failure
   [ankle oedema, ascites]

❐ Previous alcohol abuse

Is there a history of heart disease?

❐ Ischaemic heart disease

❐ Valvular

❐ Thromboembolism

❐ Hypertension

Does the chest X-ray show evidence of heart disease?

❐ Cardiomegaly

❐ Pulmonary oedema

❐ Raised pulmonary venous pressure

❐ Left atrial enlargement

Does the ECG show any abnormalities?

❐ Old myocardial infarction

❐ Bundle branch block

❐ Left ventricular hypertrophy

❐ Ischaemia

❐ Arrhythmia, type ....

Clinical diagnosis: ....

If heart failure, where was the diagnosis made?

❐ General practice

❐ Hospital

If atrial fibrillation, choose type:

❐ New   ❐ Paroxysmal   ❐ Established

What treatment is the patient taking?

❐ Diuretic

❐ ACE inhibitor

❐ Nitrate

❐ Warfarin

Would you refer the patient to cardiology OPD if there was no open-access service?

❐ Yes

❐ No

Signature ....   Date ....

Planning, training, costs and concerns

We held an initial meeting with GPs to discuss their objectives for the service and to present our ideas as to how the service might be run. Invitations for this meeting were sent out by the local medical committee (LMC) and approximately 40 GPs attended. Important discussion points were:

- the nature of the service and the roles of the participants
- the organisational aspects of the service (contact numbers, introduction to key hospital staff, referral pro formas, audit forms, etc.)
- the appropriate use of the various tests, and the strengths and weaknesses of the different investigations
- the cost of the tests.

We were particularly keen to ensure that this first meeting with GPs engendered in them a sense that they had a stake in the design and development of the service, and that setting up open access was a joint effort. We think we succeeded in this aim, as modifications were made to our plans as a direct result of contributions from the GPs. Specifically, in discussing the roles of the different parties we had stated that we considered the role of the Cardiology Department in the open-access service would be purely technical. We stressed that we would not be able to take histories or examine patients (which in any case would have defeated the object of the scheme). We also envisaged that the majority of the patients referred for a test would be seen by a technician rather than a doctor. Not having detailed knowledge of the patients, we planned to write reports in the abstract, confining the conclusions purely to the test results. The GPs thought that this approach, if rigidly applied, would fail to make the best use of the service. They pointed out that the pro formas would contain a certain amount of clinical detail which the Cardiology Department could use to provide management guidance following the test results section in the report. A compromise was reached whereby the Cardiology Department would provide management advice provided that sufficient detail on the clinical background had been included, and subject to the caveat that the patient had not been examined in the department, and that ultimate responsibility for acting on any advice would remain with the GP.

We also had an interesting debate with the GPs about costs. In the prevailing contracting environment (at the time about half of the local GPs were fundholders) we were able to charge fundholders for tests, but unable to charge non-fundholders. We felt that it would be important to identify a way of paying for tests and supporting the service beyond the period of the funded Implementation Project, and the fundholders recognised this. They also appreciated that although on the one hand they were to be charged for tests, if they used the service appropriately this would be offset by the savings they would make through reducing their referrals to outpatient clinics. They did, however, raise a difficult question about charges which we were unable to resolve. They asked if it would be possible to be refunded for the cost of tests if a patient who had been referred for open-access tests subsequently required referral to an outpatient clinic (which attracted a fixed charge inclusive of tests). They argued (with justification) that in this situation they would in effect be charged twice for the tests. However, we were unwilling to agree to refunds, partly because of the administrative complexity, and partly because we felt that refunding the charges for tests would have encouraged fund-holders to refer to the cardiology clinics and would have been a disincentive to managing patients in primary care. We did stress, however, that we believed that all GPs would save money by using the service, and that we would attempt to provide evidence of this as the service was audited (*see* the later section on cost-effectiveness).

Exercise ECGs were a particular concern. To make the tests as safe as possible we wanted GPs to exclude patients with any condition which might cause an unwarranted risk (e.g. aortic stenosis). Many GPs felt they were not sufficiently familiar with cardiology to take this decision safely, and they worried that if they got it wrong (i.e. concluded incorrectly that a patient had no evidence of aortic stenosis) and there was a fatality, they would be blamed. After much discussion we reached the compromise that if a GP was unable to decide whether or not a patient had aortic stenosis we would carry out a rapid echocardiogram prior to the exercise to look specifically at the aortic valve so as to exclude aortic stenosis (which would entail an additional charge). Most GPs have taken responsibility for ruling out aortic stenosis, and in the few cases where we have carried out echocardiograms for this purpose we have not, at the time of writing, found a single case.

Training meetings

After the initial meeting, a series of further meetings was arranged to inform and educate GPs wanting to use the service about the tests that they would be requesting. They needed to know the indications for the different tests in order to avoid inappropriate referrals, and to understand the strengths and limitations of each test in order to be able to interpret and act on test reports. We took them through the tests one by one, covering technology, physiology, protocols, diagnostic criteria, risks and limitations. We also asked the GPs to estimate their frequency of use of the various tests. These meetings were arranged by a GP tutor and involved about 15 GPs in each group. In all, about 70 GPs came to the training meetings.

At the outset it had been our intention to make attendance at a training session mandatory for all GPs who wished to use the open-access service, primarily to prevent inappropriate referrals. However, we subsequently relaxed this stipulation because it would have been administratively cumbersome, and in fact there turned out to be a relatively low level of inappropriate referral. We would certainly not have turned away patients from GPs who had not attended a training session, nor has our experience indicated that these GPs are using the service any less appropriately than those who did. We concede that this may call into question the value of the training sessions as a means of ensuring appropriate use of the service.

The open-access service in use

The open-access service began in September 1996 and proved to be very popular with GPs. Copies of the referral forms were provided to all practices expressing interest, with a description of the service and how to access it, and details of how to get more forms. GPs were able to refer patients only with the appropriate forms, which could be mailed or faxed to the Cardiology Department. Patients were then contacted with appointment details. After the test had been carried out results were reported by the staff grade doctor and sent to the GP with the audit form to be completed and returned to the Cardiology Department.

The use of the service has been steadily growing since it started (*see* Figure 4.1). Initial estimates by GPs of the number of cases they would be likely to refer proved to be exaggerated, and the actual referral rate turned out to be about 25% of their initial estimate. (Fortunately this actual demand was much closer to our own estimates in the Cardiology Department, upon which the resource requirements for the service had been based.) From an original 30 GPs referring patients, the number has grown to 106 at the time of writing. However, about 25% of the GPs using the service have used it only once. To date 695 tests have been carried out (*see* Table 4.1 for a breakdown). Of the various tests, the least used is 24-hour BP monitoring, which we attribute to some GPs having alternative access to the necessary equipment.

Table 4.1   Referrals to the open-access service

	Total referrals	*Average wait for test* (days)*
Echocardiography	243	16
24-hour ECG Holter	162	20
Exercise testing	193	19
24-hour BP monitoring	97	21

*Number of days between receipt of the request and the date of the test.

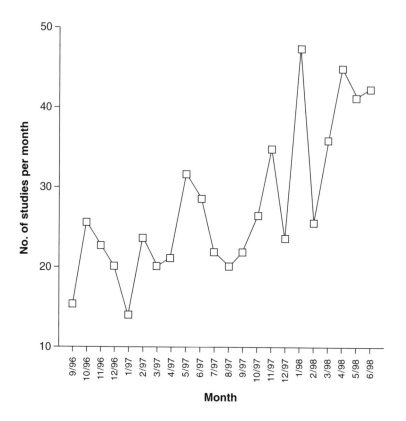

Figure 4.1 Open-access service activity.

Case mix and the efficiency of the service

The indications for echocardiography recorded on the referral forms were as follows:

Heart failure	76	(25 confirmed by echo)
Systolic murmur	45	
Atrial fibrillation	21	
Valvular disease	18	(10 confirmed by echo)
Increased CTR on Cxr	16	
LVH on ECG	16	
Palpitations	3	
Others	43	

Other reasons given included hypertension, transient ischaemic attack, family history of cardiomyopathy, congenital heart disease, ECG showing left bundle branch block (LBBB) and non-specific chest pain. Clearly some of these indications were inappropriate (e.g. palpitations), however, the level of inappropriate referrals from GPs has been no different from that which we expect from hospital doctors.

Table 4.1 (*see* p 79) gives the time taken to carry out the tests. This was measured as the time that had elapsed between the Cardiology Department receiving a request and the test being carried out. The average waiting time for an open-access test was about 19 days. This compares with an average waiting time for routine referrals to the Cardiology Outpatient Department of 119 days. We recognise that there is considerable scope for reducing the time between referral and open-access test results, given additional resources to reinforce the staffing of the scheme and reduce the pressure on equipment. However, bearing in mind that in our project the process has been managed by one individual (without cover for leave or absence) and that no new equipment has been purchased, we consider that the benefits already achieved are very worthwhile. In simple terms, for the majority of patients, not having to wait for an outpatient appointment saved an average of 100 anxious days. In the few cases who were at risk of cardiovascular events, the increased speed of accurate diagnosis (and the subsequent introduction of appropriate treatment) was of inestimable benefit.

Audit results

An audit form was sent back to GPs with each set of test results (*see* Box 4.2). We encouraged the GPs to complete the form and return it by stressing that the continuation of the service would be dependent on demonstrating its value. There was a reasonable degree of compliance (the response rate was 64.3%), but with hindsight we realise that the message exhorting GPs to complete and return the forms may well have influenced the answers they gave (i.e. they might have exaggerated the value of the service in order to ensure its continuation). The audit form repeated a question from original referral pro forma (phrased in a slightly different way) asking GPs if they intended to refer the patient to the outpatient clinic. Comparing the proportion who *would have* referred their patients to the cardiology outpatient clinic (had there been no open access to tests), with the proportion who *subsequently* intended to refer patients for consultations gave us a feel for the impact of the service. These questions and the collated responses are shown in Table 4.2. The first question was posed on the referral pro forma and the remainder were from the audit form.

If we assume that the audit forms returned were reasonably representative of the total population of patients referred to the service, the results suggest that the provision of the open-access service has enabled GPs to manage

Box 4.2

Central Middlesex Hospital Open Access: Audit Form

Please complete and send to:
Dr H B Xiao
Cardiology Department
Central Middlesex Hospital
Acton Lane
Park Royal
London
NW10 7NS

Episode no. ....   GP ....
Name ....   Address ....
DOB .... Gender ....
Address ....
....   Telephone ....
Telephone ....

1 Does this report provide you with helpful information?

Yes   No   Not certain

2 On the basis of this report would you alter your management?

   a To prescribe   Diuretics   Beta blocker   ACE inhibitor
       treatment?   Digoxin   Nitrate   Warfarin   Others

   b To discontinue   Diuretics   Beta blocker   ACE inhibitor
       treatment?   Digoxin   Nitrate   Warfarin   Others

3 Are you going to refer the patient to cardiology OPD?

Yes   No

Further comments

Signature .... Date ....

Table 4.2   Responses to audit form

Question from the referral pro forma	Yes/No
Would you be referring the patient to OPD if there was no open-access service?	615/75*
Questions from the audit form	**Yes/No**
Are you going to refer the patient to cardiology OPD?	69**/378
Does this report provide you with useful information?	436/11
On the basis of this report are you going to prescribe new treatment ?	101/346
On the basis of this report are you going to discontinue any treatment ?	32/415

*Five patients had two tests, therefore while 695 tests were performed, 690 patients were tested.
**Twenty-eight (40%) of the 69 were recommended for referral in the report from the hospital.

about 85% of the patients in primary care (378/447). This contrasts with the 88.5% who would have been referred to the Cardiology Department had the open-access service not been available (from the original referral forms, 615/695). It was also reassuring to learn that the vast majority of GPs who responded had found the reports useful (97.6%).

In writing reports we tried to strike a balance between including all potentially useful information and detailing every minor abnormality. To a certain extent this was a skill we learned as the service developed, and GPs' feedback from our early reports led us to make alterations to the style. For example an early echocardiogram report included the comment 'trivial tricuspid regurgitation', and the patient's GP telephoned the department to ask the significance of this observation. When told that it was clinically unimportant, the GP suggested that in the circumstances it had been unhelpful to include this reference, and we took this point, modifying our subsequent reports to included only clinically or potentially clinically important pathology.

Cost-effectiveness and evidence of changes in care

A crude estimate of the financial implications of the open-access service can be made by using notional costs. If we were to assume that all users of the service had paid the tariffs for tests which applied to the GP fundholders, the total cost of the 695 tests would have been about £83 000. Despite the availability of the open-access service, 104 patients were still referred by their GPs to the Cardiology Outpatients Department for tests at a cost of approximately £24 000. Putting these two figures together derives a notional cost of approximately £107 000 for non-invasive cardiology tests over the period (approximately 18 months). Had the open-access service not existed (and consequently all patients been referred to outpatients), the cost would have been over £141 000 (£230 per patient). The notional saving from having the service was therefore in the region of £34 000.

However, focusing in this way on charges from one part of the NHS to another may not reflect the real value added by the service. It fails to take account of the improvement in waiting times and quality of the outpatient service resulting from the reduction in referrals to outpatients (i.e. for tests), and does not recognise the value of reducing the anxiety in patients. Unfortunately, concurrent changes in staffing configuration in the Cardiology Department made it impossible to demonstrate a direct effect on outpatient waiting times, and we acknowledge the weakness of our cost calculations. Nevertheless, we were pleased that it was at least possible to make a case for the open-access service being economically effective as well as clinically desirable.

About one third of patients had a change in their management as a direct result of the report received from the hospital. With regard to heart failure, of the 239 echocardiograms performed (for all indications), 151 audit forms were returned, and these indicated that 18 patients had been prescribed ACE inhibitors for the first time following the tests, and that in four cases this prescription had been stopped. Although we cannot be sure that all changes in clinical management were appropriate, the audit data suggest that reports were sufficiently informative and authoritative to enable GPs to take decisions which would have been impossible without the service. Without the open-access service many of these decisions would have been made, typically 100 days later, by hospital doctors in the outpatient clinics.

Conclusion

The service is highly valued by those GPs who use it and we believe that the audit shows that it is having an impact on the management of patients with heart conditions. Nevertheless, if the numbers of patients who have been started on ACE inhibitors as a result of the service are compared with the estimated incidence of heart failure in the community, we are reminded of the modesty of our progress, as it seems that as yet we are addressing only a small proportion of unmet need.[6] There are undoubtedly opportunities for wider use of the open-access service, particularly in the context of heart failure. Our view is that increased uptake will be dependent on two key factors: first GPs' recognition of the importance of considering and investigating heart failure in breathless patients (an educational issue); and second, making GPs more aware of the service and how to access it (better advertising). Notwithstanding the limitations, and bearing in mind the admittedly crude measures of impact and cost, we have been encouraged by the introduction of the open-access service, and feel confident that it will prove beneficial in terms of both clinical effectiveness and cost-effectiveness.

Lessons learned

- GPs needed to be involved and to have an opportunity to shape the service.
- Training sessions were valuable, but more for the purpose of announcing the service and building consensus than for avoiding unnecessary referrals.
- Initial fears about the department being overwhelmed by open-access work proved to be unfounded.
- GPs have similar thresholds for referral for non-invasive tests to hospital doctors.
- Providing the service has helped to foster a new, patient-focused philosophy to the department.
- GPs preferred reports to be written in a firm, focused style.

Things we would do differently if we were starting tomorrow

- hold fewer training sessions (unless specifically requested by GPs)
- not make any stipulation about the need for GPs to attend training in order to be able to use the open-access service
- put more effort into advertising the service
- look at ways of integrating referral pro formas into GP information systems to reduce the proliferation of different forms.

References

1   Thomas E, Cotzias C and Handler CE (1995) General Practitioners' requirements from a hospital cardiology department. *International Journal of Cardiology.* **48(3)**: 295–301.

2   Murphy JJ, Frain JP, Ramesh P, Siddiqui RN and Bossingham CM (1996) Open-access echocardiography to general practitioners for suspected heart failure. *British Journal of General Practice.* **46(409)**: 475–6.

3   Francis CM, Caruana L, Kearney P, Love M, Sutherland GR, Starkey IR, Shaw IR, Shaw TR and McMurray JJ (1995) Open-access echocardiography in management of heart failure in the community. *BMJ.* **301**: 634–6.

4   O'Toole L, Oates A and Channer KS (1995) Open-access echocardiography. Open access to specialist opinion is preferable. *BMJ.* **311**: 326.

5   Davie AP, Francis CM, Caruana L, Sutherland GR and McMurray JJ (1997) Assessing diagnosis in heart failure: which features are any use? *QJM.* **90(5)**: 335–9.

6   Slovick DI (1995) Open-access echocardiography. Service should be reserved for equivocal cases. *BMJ.* **311**: 327.

7   Houghton AR, Sparrow NJ, Toms E and Cowley AJ (1997) Should general practitioners use the electrocardiogram to select patients with suspected heart failure for echocardiography? *International Journal of Cardiology.* **62(1)**: 31–6.

8   Houghton AR and Cowley AJ (1997) Managing heart failure in a specialist clinic. *Journal of the Royal College of Physicians of London.* **31(3)**: 276–9.

9   The SOLVD investigators (1991) Effect of enalapril on survival in patients with reduced left ventricular ejection fractions and congestive heart failure. *N Engl J Med.* **325**: 293–302.

Non-invasive cardiac assessment

As external evaluators, it is difficult to say anything with confidence about this project. The project leaders were reluctant to take part in the evaluation as they felt the grant by North Thames was too small to warrant full participation. Apart from attendence at one workshop in January 1998 and a survey with three local professionals in March 1998, we have very little information.

But the little information we do have is positive. This was the smallest of all of the North Thames projects in terms of money (£11 500), but it delivered great value. As one survey respondent said:

'[We've learnt that] ... without putting lots of money into it, you can improve the service and roll it out to other areas.'

What's more, all three survey participants mentioned how the service not only speeded up access to test results, but also educated GPs about cardiovascular disease. The Project Manager said:

'We are beginning to see that if we give GPs the power to give tests, then we help make them better doctors. There is a de-skilling effect if they over-refer.'

Education, latched on to setting up a much-valued service, has worked well in generating GP enthusiasm, as shown by the excellent turnout of 40 GPs to the objectives meeting and 70 GPs to training meetings. These training meetings may not have helped much in the reduction of inappropriate referrals, as intended, but they do offer a valuable opportunity for GPs and consultants to meet and discuss cardiovascular disease.

The key question for evaluating open-access services is: Do they help keep patients in the community or do they still use hospital outpatient services? If patients are still using other hospital services, other than those indicated by the open-access test results, then the service becomes an add-on rather than an 'instead of'.

Unfortunately asking GPs if they *intend* to manage patients in the community is not enough (audit question 'Would you refer the patient to cardiology OPD if there was no open-access service?'). As we have seen from other projects (hypertension in elderly people, Kensington, Chelsea & Westminster cardiac), what clinicians say they do and what they actually do can be very different.

In looking at how well this service has done at keeping patients in the community, it looks like roughly 13% (104/794) of the patients who were referred to the Central Middlesex for cardiac tests went to outpatients. It would be good to know why these 104 patients were still referred to outpatients despite the existence of the open-access service. Did they originally have open-access tests and then further tests in outpatients were indicated? Did the GP not know about the open-access service? Did s/he know and was not happy with it? The service seems to be doing well at keeping patients in the community. With a proper audit of the 104 who went the outpatient route, we would know how to improve it still further.

What is clear is that with very little development money, this project team has developed a service that is valued and popular with many GPs. As one survey participant put it:

'It works!'

5

Helicobacter pylori eradication in Camden & Islington

Julie Ferguson

Introduction

Peptic ulcer disease is a common disorder of a chronic, relapsing nature. The disease has relatively low mortality but results in substantial human suffering and high economic costs.[1] According to the Prescription Pricing Authority, in 1996/97 over £399m was spent on ulcer-healing drugs nationally, and in Camden and Islington alone more than £2.2m was spent on this group of drugs. This accounted for 8.8% of the total primary care prescribing budget for the health authority.

The treatment of peptic ulcer disease has changed dramatically over the years, especially in the last decade. Historically, peptic ulcers were treated with antacids, which act by neutralising the acid in the stomach. In the 1970s, a new type of drug called an H_2 antagonist was introduced. This reduces the amount of acid secreted and the treatment proved much more effective in promoting ulcer healing than antacids.[2] Another type of drug was developed in the 1980s, the proton pump inhibitor, which provided another improved treatment for peptic ulcers. Despite the increased effectiveness of these drugs, a large proportion of patients suffer a recurrence after healing, and a cyclical pattern of ulcer & pain → treatment → freedom from ulcer → ulcer & pain → treatment has been common. This has been managed either by repeating treatment doses of drugs when ulcer pain is experienced, by continuous (and potentially life-long) prescribing of low doses (so-called maintenance), or by a combination of these methods. The discovery of *Helicobacter pylori* and its association with peptic ulcers in the mid-1980s is the most radical development of all in this area of medicine. It has led to a transformation in the way ulcers are viewed and treated, enabling the cycle of treatment and suffering to be broken by curing ulcers and eradicating the bacteria which are now known to be instrumental in causing the disease.[3]

H. pylori is probably the most common chronic bacterial infection found in humans, and is present in about 50% of the world's population.[4] In Western countries, its prevalence rises with age and the percentage of any age group infected approximately equates to the age of the group.[5] Prevalence is higher in developing countries and in lower socio-economic groups.[5,6] Not everyone infected with *H. pylori* will develop peptic ulcers (current evidence suggests that less than 20% of infected individuals will suffer any clinical consequences from their infection),[7] however, there is now widespread agreement that eradication of *H. pylori* is recommended in all infected patients with confirmed peptic ulcer.[1,5,8,9] This includes patients with a past or present diagnosis, including those in remission or receiving anti-secretory maintenance treatment. This is based on the evidence that 95% of patients with duodenal ulcer and about 75% of patients with gastric ulcer are infected with *H. pylori*.[5] The association is so strong with duodenal ulcer that it is considered unnecessary to check for infection in the absence of another precipitating factor such as non-steroidal anti-inflammatory drug (NSAID) use.[5,10]

Eradication of the organism has been shown to reduce the relapse rate of duodenal ulcer from over 80% per year to less than 10%.[5] In one recent study with a one-year follow-up, the relapse rate in patients with benign gastric ulcer in whom the organism was eradicated was 7%, compared with 48% in patients who remained infected.[11]

Objectives

The objective of the project was to promote the implementation of the strong research evidence for the benefits of *H. pylori* eradication in patients with peptic ulcer disease in Camden & Islington. This entailed increasing the appropriate uptake of eradication therapy locally, with the expectation of ensuring better value for money for expenditure on ulcer-healing drugs and reducing the numbers of patients receiving long-term acid suppression (maintenance).

Method

Literature search

Many papers and articles have been published on this subject in recent years as new evidence about the nature of the disease and developments in treatment has emerged. It was a precondition for funding that the project should be based on firm research evidence and therefore in the early stages of the project, time was committed by the audit facilitator (who was also the project manager) to studying the evidence on *H. pylori* eradication in patients with peptic ulcers.[1-13] This was important in establishing clarity on important issues such as who to treat, which diagnostic tests to use and how best to prescribe.

Networking

Time was spent networking with others who had been involved in similar work. This included participation in the workshops for the North Thames projects facilitated by the King's Fund. The purpose of these was to facilitate discussion around managing change in practice. They were not specific to *H. pylori* but provided a helpful forum for exchanging general ideas and experiences in the context of changing clinician behaviour based on research evidence. In addition, contact was made with the leaders of several of the PACE (Promoting Action for Clinical Effectiveness)* projects which were also concerned with *H. pylori*. This proved to be useful by offering a chance to share subject-specific concerns and benefit from others' experience in tackling issues directly related to the topic, such as guidelines. Individuals and bodies who had an interest in the project, such as gastroenterologists from the local NHS trusts, members of the local medical committee, local pharmaceutical committee and the community health councils were also informed about the project. In addition, the local Medical Audit Advisory Group (MAAG) offered help with the design of audit data collection which would be important in establishing the impact of the project (*see* Table 5.1).

Steering group

A steering group, with representation from primary and secondary care, was set up to oversee the project. The members included a consultant gastro-enterologist, a university professor of clinical pharmacology and therapeutics, a consultant microbiologist, a GP and the health authority prescribing adviser. A relatively small group was convened in preference to one representative of all involved parties in the interest of effective management.

---

*PACE is a national clinical effectiveness programme, which provided resources and network-ing opportunities to 16 projects across England.[15]

Table 5.1 Data collection form

Surgery Name.................................

Patient name	NHS no./ DOB	Current ulcer-healing medication	Diagnosis and how made – where known	Meet criteria for eradication? Y/N	If yes, patient called for an appointment? Y/N	Patient attends the appointment? Y/N	Has patient had a history of complicated ulcer disease? Y/N	To have H. pylori test? Y/N	Diagnostic test used NPS/HS/ UBT/RUT*

Table 5.1 *continued*

Patient name	H. pylori status? +/–/?	Eradication therapy prescribed? Y/N	Regimen prescribed	Symptoms relieved at one month? Y/N	Comments	Symptoms relieved at six months? Y/N	Comments

* NPS – near-patient serology; HS – hospital serology; UBT – urea breath test; RUT – rapid urease test (at endoscopy)

Audit pack

Different approaches have been tried in Camden & Islington in recent years, with the aim of influencing clinician behaviour in various contexts. In this case it was felt that audit would be the most suitable method to use to promote *H. pylori* eradication because it would ensure appropriate identification of patients and enable follow-up of outcomes. It was also seen as a practical intervention which would lend itself to the time frame and cash-limited nature of the project. An audit pack was produced for GPs by the audit facilitator with input from the steering group. This pack contained:

- background information on *H. pylori*
- suggested practice standards
- dyspepsia management guidelines
- a comparison of eradication regimens
- audit data collection forms
- a suggested letter to the patient.

In addition, it was suggested that summary guidelines would be helpful and user friendly for the busy GPs, and a flow diagram with summary notes and a *step-by-step* guide to the audit was produced.

Support pack for pharmacists and patient information

Successful eradication of *H. pylori* is dependent on the patient taking the medication correctly. Community pharmacists play a key role in advising patients how to take their medicines and addressing any concerns they may have. To support this role, an information pack was prepared which contained background information on *H. pylori*, counselling points for patients and information on the different eradication regimens. The audit facilitator also presented a session on the issues surrounding *H. pylori* infection and treatment, as part of a community pharmacy study day. It was also anticipated that patients may have queries about their treatment. To pre-empt these, a patient-oriented fact sheet was produced, explaining in basic terms the rationale for eradication therapy (*see* Box 5.1).

The pilot – targeting GPs

It was decided that the impact of the project would be maximised if efforts were concentrated on those practices which had most to gain from analysing their prescribing behaviour with regard to the treatment of peptic ulcers. It

Box 5.1 Patient fact sheet

PATIENT FACT SHEET

'Got a stomach bug?
... Let's eradicate it'

It has recently been discovered that a bacterium (bug) is involved in the development of stomach ulcers.

Treatment of ulcers usually involves taking medicine to reduce the acid in the stomach. This will work for a while, but often ulcers will come back.

A new treatment is available which destroys the bug. The treatment typically consists of an ulcer-healing medicine, with two different antibiotics. The treatment involves taking several tablets a day, but has been made as simple as possible. **Treatment is typically for just one week!**

This leads to a cure of the ulcer in most patients. It also reduces the risk of the ulcer coming back.

This is good news, as it means that many patients will be able to stop taking their usual ulcer-healing medication.

Some patients may need to stay on a medicine that reduces acid if they continue to have problems with heartburn. **Your doctor will advise you if you can stop your usual ulcer-healing medication.**

If the tablets are taken as directed by the doctor and pharmacist, there is a high chance that your ulcer will be cured.

The course of tablets should be finished, EVEN IF YOU START TO FEEL BETTER.

As with all medicines, you may experience some side effects. Your pharmacist will advise you about these when you collect your prescription. Any side effects will usually be mild, and you should continue to take your medication. **If you develop any side effects that you are worried about, speak to your doctor or pharmacist.**

Produced by Camden & Islington Health Authority, May 1997.

was thought that in the first instance working with ten practices would be a manageable task, so a means of identifying the 'ten practices with most to gain' was sought. Because of the maintenance prescribing and the cycle of ulcers recurring it seemed logical that one indication that a practice may not be using eradication therapy to best advantage would be the size of its drug bill in respect of ulcer treatments, i.e. the *more* being spent, the *less* likely that *H. pylori* eradication therapy had been used widely. A weighted measure of prescribing costs, STAR Prescribing Units,* was used to identify the ten practices within Camden & Islington with the highest prescribing cost per (weighted) patient for ulcer-healing drugs. (There was an approximately six fold difference between the most and least costly practices in this regard across the health authority.) Letters were sent to the top 25 practices in terms of highest cost/STAR-PU. Practices that agreed to participate were offered the incentive of assistance from the audit facilitator in setting up the audit. Of these 25, 12 did not wish to take part and four failed to respond despite the invitation being followed up by telephone calls. The remaining nine practices were visited by the audit facilitator to discuss the audit and prescribing for peptic ulcers. Four of these practices agreed to participate in the audit, however, one subsequently pulled out and another decided to postpone the work owing to other priorities. One declined to participate following the visit, and the remaining four said that they were interested, but felt unable to take on the work at that time.

As this initial approach had failed to recruit ten practices (only two of the 25 approached being willing and able to take on the audit), invitations were sent to the next nine practices on the list, based on ranking by cost/STAR-PU. Responses followed a similar pattern to the first group, and, after visits from the audit facilitator, three practices agreed to take part in the pilot, of which one subsequently dropped out. At this point it was decided for practical reasons that the pilot should proceed with the four recruited practices rather than ten as had been planned.

---

*In an attempt to make comparisons of prescribing costs valid, a weighting factor, called the prescribing unit (PU), was introduced in England in 1983 to take account of the greater need of elderly patients for medication. In 1993, a more sophisticated weighting system using ASTRO-PUs was adopted, which took account of sex and temporary resident status, as well as a greater number of age bands. There are differences in the age and sex of patients for whom drugs in specific therapeutic groups are usually prescribed. To make such comparisons STAR-PUs have been developed (Specific Therapeutic group Age-sex Related Prescribing Units). [From *Prescribing Measures and their Application: an explanation*, Prescribing Support Unit, Brunswick Court, Bridge Street, Leeds LS2 7RJ]

Roll-out

Camden & Islington's approach to developing evidence-based practice in pre-scribing has been to organise prescribers' forums where groups of GPs meet to discuss prescribing topics and agree on quality markers which attract prescrib-ing incentives. The audit was offered as a quality marker in the Camden & Islington Prescribing Incentive Scheme following discussion at a prescribers' forum held in December 1997 (i.e. nine months into the project). Thirty-two practices selected *H. pylori* eradication as a quality marker for the 1997/98 Prescribing Incentive Scheme (this includes the practices that were piloting the audit). Additionally, one fundholder (who was ineligible for the Pre-scribing Incentive Scheme) was involved in the pilot, which gave a total of 33 practices expressing an interest in carrying out the audit. This represented a third of all practices in Camden & Islington. The audit facilitator visited or telephoned the majority of these practices to offer support and guidance. In three cases, practices requested more 'hands-on' help from the facilitator, which involved trawling notes and making patient-specific recommendations. (Dis-appointingly two of these practices failed to act on the recommendations. This is discussed in greater detail in the section on observations on audit on p 103.)

Notwithstanding the fairly narrow focus of the project, the nature of the subject and the lack of convenient boundaries in the real world of primary care led to the extension of the involvement by the audit facilitator. For example, recommendations were made not only about *H. pylori* eradication, but also about the drug treatment of other upper gastrointestinal disease, such as reflux oesophagitis. This is unsurprising as patients are prescribed acid-suppressing drugs for a number of conditions affecting the upper gastro-intestinal tract. Inevitably, an audit of patients on acid suppressants designed to identify those for whom *H. pylori* eradication would be beneficial, will, by default, also identify those for whom this treatment would *not* be recommended. Nevertheless these patients may well be candidates for therapeutic review, and it was noted that while setting well-defined parameters to a project may be relatively straightforward in the planning stage, in the context of imple-mentation a balance has to be struck which is sensitive to both project object-ives and the pragmatic opportunities that may occur during the work.

Distance learning and use of the Delphi technique

At the time of writing, the *H. pylori* quality marker is in the process of being tested with all Camden & Islington GPs through a distance-learning pack, and application of the Delphi technique.[12] All GPs have been sent a copy of the quality marker with references to the literature. The GPs are asked to agree or disagree and to comment, and responses are chased up by a researcher to maximise participation. The results are analysed and fed back to all GPs, showing the level of consensus and frequency of alterations, disagreement or recurring comments. GPs are again asked to agree, disagree or comment to test whether their opinion has been changed by the feedback of information. A total of three cycles are performed. The technique has been successfully applied in Camden & Islington in other therapeutic areas, such as the prescribing of diuretics.

Experience

Practices were requested to give details of their progress with the audit in July/August 1998. A standard form was provided to practices setting out the required details, ensuring that information would be provided in a uniform format. To encourage return, pre-paid envelopes were used, and after follow-up in August, 26 of the practices had made a start on the audit. This represented 79% of those practices who had 'signed up' to the audit and 25% of all practices in Camden & Islington. (However, this does include some practices (eight) whose small degree of progress, though symbolic, was not materially significant, as is discussed later.)

Of the seven practices that had not started work on the audit, it was noticeable that six were single-handed (this is considered in the section on observations on audit on p 103).

Aggregate results from the audit were as follows:

- no. of patients identified by the searches = **2646**
- no. who met the criteria for eradication = **509 (19%)**
- no. reviewed to date = **413 (81% of 509)**
- no. subsequently prescribed eradication therapy = **317 (62% of 509)**
- no. with improvement in symptoms noted in medical records after eradication therapy = **247 (78% of 317)**.

(Note: different search terms were used in different practices to identify relevant patients from the practice records. This is explained in the section on modifications on p 102.)

There was considerable variation between practices in the proportions improving after eradication, but this may have reflected differences in recording of symptoms.

PACT analysis

Prescribing (PACT) data for the practices have been examined. The time periods examined were April–June 1997 (before implementation of guidelines

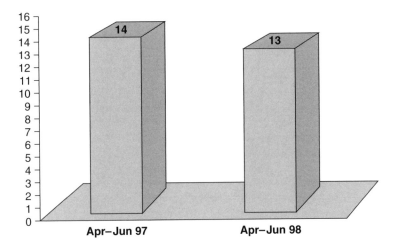

Figure 5.1   Cost/STAR(97)-PU for GI drugs for C&I (pence).

and audit) and April–June 1998 (after the implementation of guidelines and audit), and the British National Formulary section examined was section 1.3 – *Ulcer-healing drugs*.

PACT data analysis is a useful tool when examining prescribing. However, it is important to recognise its limitations, such as the fact that it does not link the use of a drug to a specific clinical condition in the patient. In the context of this project, where the drugs of interest are also used for the management of other (non-ulcer) forms of gastric disorder, this means that PACT data alone cannot show the extent of prescribing attributable to peptic ulcer 'maintenance'.

Figure 5.1 shows the change in cost/STAR(97)-PU for gastrointestinal prescribing for Camden & Islington between April–June 1997 and April–June 1998 **(–8.95%)**.

Figure 5.2 shows the change in cost/STAR(97)-PU for gastrointestinal prescribing for the audit practices, between April–June 1997 and April–June 1998 **(–7.89%)**.

For most practices there were reductions in costs, some more pronounced than others. For a minority there was an increase in costs.

Conclusions

During the course of the project many useful lessons have been learned about different aspects of trying to implement research evidence into clinical practice. In addition to these specific lessons, it was noted that awareness of one key fact could impact on all of the dimensions of implementation in this

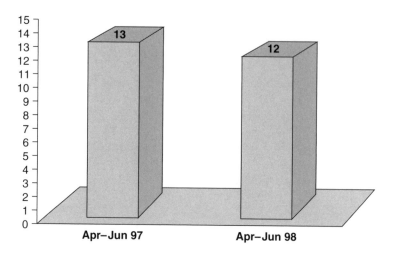

Figure 5.2   Cost/STAR(97)-PU for GI drugs for audit practices (pence).

context (i.e. general practice). This was the recognition that GPs are individuals with different interests, working styles and motivations. Accordingly, the single most important lesson from the project was the need to have sufficient flexibility in approach and in the levels of information and support offered, to meet GPs' differing levels of need and to appeal to their different motivations. Flexibility really is the key.

Guidelines

With an area of medicine where there is relatively new evidence and controversy over patient management, having guidelines seems intuitively to be helpful. In the Camden & Islington project, the time invested in researching and producing the guidelines and audit template (which involved working with representatives from primary and secondary care) was considered to be well spent. Not only did the process unearth high-quality research evidence on which the guidelines were based, it also contributed to the sense of local ownership in the project, and helped to avoid the feeling that the project and guidelines were 'external' and simply another facet of the health authority seeking to impose its will on practitioners.

Nevertheless, there is a balance to be struck between investing in guideline development and the other aspects of implementation. There is always the danger that the interesting but academic tasks of literature searching, critical appraisal and guideline development can erode so far into the time and resources available for an implementation project that the other, essentially manual aspects of the project can be squeezed out, threatening the viability of the project as a whole. It also goes without saying that it is vital to ensure that any guidelines developed are based on the best available research evidence, and that 'local ownership' does not compromise the credibility of an implementation project's claim to be evidence-based.

Because GPs receive such a large volume of paper through the post daily, it was considered important that guidelines and supporting material should be designed with an eye-catching format, which would not only get attention, but be user-friendly. This led to the decision to employ a graphic designer in pursuit of these objectives. The resulting documents have, on the whole, been well received. Nevertheless, it noted that appreciation of the style was not universal, and despite the effort put into presentation it is hard to avoid the conclusion that it is impossible to please everyone. As with other aspects of guideline development, the issue of style and presentation may be best settled by setting aside a sensible proportion of effort and resource, but the temptation to seek the unattainable (i.e. universal approval) to the detriment of the whole project should be resisted.

Recruiting for the pilot

As described in the earlier paragraph on targeting GPs, the process of recruiting practices to the pilot proved to be more difficult than had been envisaged. Likely reasons for this were as follows.

- The time of year – recruiting was attempted over the summer months, i.e. holiday period. Decisions about such a piece of work are preferably made with all partners in attendance. This is difficult at the best of times, but over the holiday period this is inevitably harder.
- Practices were involved in other audits, had limited resources (most importantly *time*) and were therefore reluctant to take on any additional work.
- Practices did not see the pilot as a priority in terms of day-to-day work.
- Practices had participated in a similar pharmaceutical company-sponsored audit a short time previously.
- Targeting practices with the highest ulcer treatment prescribing costs may have made recruitment more difficult than if the same number of practices selected at random had been invited to participate.

Incentives

Following initial visits to the practices, when the resource implications of diverting practice staff time into audit was raised on several occasions, it was suggested that a monetary incentive (other than that from the prescribing incentive scheme) might provide a helpful stimulus to getting the project started. This was possible within the budget, and it was therefore decided that practices would be offered a modest and limited additional amount of money to cover the costs of staff involved in the audit (£250). In fact, only four practices subsequently applied for this money, of which three were successful. Despite patchy uptake, it was felt that the signal given by offering additional resources may have been influential in getting the project off the ground. This was a further instance where awareness of barriers and motivations, and the capacity to offer a flexible and appropriate response were critical in keeping up the momentum of the project.

In addition to the offer of a financial incentive, all 33 practices were also offered hands-on support from the audit facilitator. Three practices requested this support, and in these cases the audit facilitator reviewed notes and identified appropriate patients for *H. pylori* eradication therapy. Notwithstanding this flexibility in financing audit time and the offer of direct input by the audit facilitator, 15 of the 33 practices had either failed to make any progress or had done very little by August 1998, and this underlines the limitations of incentives and offers of support in an implementation project of this nature. In the final analysis, it may be concluded that while practices may be encouraged by the knowledge that financial and physical support is there, other factors, such as time pressure, conflicting priorities and in this case GPs' individual perceptions about audit, may ultimately be more important in determining whether a practice will participate in an implementation project.

Modifications

As a result of piloting the audit, modifications were made to the design of the data collection forms to make them more user-friendly (one practice preferred the original form and continued to use it). It was also decided that for pragmatic reasons there should be flexibility with respect to the search criteria. For example, for some practices, reviewing notes for all patients who had received acid suppressants within a two-year period represented an unmanageable level of extra work. In such cases, a more realistic approach was to consider those patients who had received acid suppressants on repeat prescription within the past six months. Another alternative approach, even less demanding, was to limit the review to just those patients who were being prescribed specific types of ulcer-healing drugs. Typically, a single-handed and/or non-computerised practice would find a comprehensive search too daunting a prospect to contemplate, but would be prepared to undertake a quicker, limited search. Allowing this flexibility encouraged practices to attempt the audit. Our philosophy was that we would rather practices start small and attempt a piece of audit than not participate at all. It seems plausible that having made a start, such practices will be more likely to progress towards a more thorough audit in the future, with its scope widening as interest, time, confidence and resources permit.

These adjustments, which were made in the light of the pilot phase, although not dramatic, were undoubtedly important in enabling the next phase to proceed smoothly, and the importance of testing the audit through piloting is stressed.

Observations on audit revealed by the project

Assessment of performance in a particular clinical area, and comparing actual performance against agreed standards, with a commitment to changing practice in the direction of the standards, is the basis of audit. The work involved is largely paper-based, in that it requires the detailed scrutiny, maintenance and analysis of records. This contrasts with the central component of a GP's work, which relies more on interpersonal and manual skills than on clerical activity. GPs, whose main function is primary care, quite rightly rank the day-to-day care of their patients as a higher priority than audit, which is often perceived as bureaucratic and of lesser merit. The GPs who were invited to participate in this project were not untypical, in that their workload was daunting and the pressure on their time was great. In this context it was not surprising that despite widespread acceptance that involvement in this audit would be worthwhile, the majority of the GPs invited to participate were unwilling to commit themselves to it. This clearly touches on a deeply rooted problem and is likely to prove to be a barrier to any implementation project that is reliant on GPs' involvement in audit.

In the cases of the practices that *did* participate, the project revealed wide variation in the levels of interest and skills required to perform audit effectively. While some practices needed no assistance at all, others found support essential.

As stated earlier, of the seven practices who had not started work on the audit, six are single-handed practices and one is a two-partner practice. This may reflect the time and support that is required for audit, which it seems may not be addressed simply by the offer of external support, as only one of these practices has expressed interest in help offered by the audit facilitator.

In the cases of the three practices with whom the audit facilitator did work closely to identify the patients who may fit the criteria for *H. pylori* eradication, disappointingly two have failed to act on the work done in identifying patients likely to benefit from *H. pylori* eradication therapy. Again workload and the priority given to audit may offer an explanation as to why this is the case. When questioned as to why they had failed to take the work forward, GPs from each practice stated that they simply had not had the time to action any of the audit facilitator's recommendations. A rough calculation comparing the number of patients per full-time GP (a crude indicator of the time pressure on each partner) shows that the two practices which failed to implement the audit have an *above* average number of patients per GP, while the practice which has taken the audit forward has a *below* average number of patients per GP. Obviously this is by no means conclusive evidence, but it does support the hypothesis that time pressure (as well as other factors, such as GP interest in the subject and the level of computerisation of records) is a barrier to both *undertaking* and *acting on* the results of audit in general practice.

GPs offered the following comments on problems/practical difficulties that had been faced:

'It was time-consuming. It took one week (instead of surgeries) for two doctors to go through the notes and send out letters, blood test forms and prescriptions. We will need to pull most of these notes again to find out outcome.'

'We haven't started the audit due to workload.'

'The main problem is the time needed to go through all the notes and to obtain all the necessary information.'

'Very time-consuming exercise...'

'The gathering of data (i.e. finding out which patients met the criteria for eradication therapy) has been straightforward but time-consuming.'

'It is all a lot of work and the clinical decisions are not as easy as it appears on paper!'

'Used system of "when next seen" rather than calling patients up and GP prompts – but not all GPs are as good at responding to opportunistic approach!'

'Only recently computerised.'

'Not all patients attend for review.'

The audit facilitator herself made two observations about the process of undertaking the audit which arose from the work she did in the three practices where her support was requested:

'The process of reviewing notes that are poorly summarised really is a time-consuming business!'

'A diagnosis is often absent or unconfirmed in this field of medicine. Patients may have "dyspepsia" or "acid" documented in their notes. This makes it difficult to apply guidelines based on more tightly defined diagnoses, and consequently identify all appropriate patients.'

Results

Of the patients identified to meet the criteria for eradication therapy, 81% had been reviewed at the time of writing. There is wide variability in progress between practices. It was commonly reported that many patients failed to attend for review or for *H. pylori* testing. Patients' symptoms are often well-controlled on acid suppressant therapy and there is therefore not always a clear incentive to try a new treatment. The Patient Fact Sheet (*see* Figure 5.1) was produced as an attempt to overcome this issue by informing patients of the potential long-term benefits of *H. pylori* eradication therapy. From the aggregate data, 35% of patients were tested prior to receiving eradication therapy. There was, however, wide variability between the practices, with one practice not testing at all and several testing each patient. This was surprising, as the guidelines clearly stated which patients should be tested, and suggests that at least some GPs were not following the guidelines, perhaps because they remained unconvinced by the evidence on which they were based.

The results have been used to derive a simple success rate (the percentage of patients prescribed with eradication therapy whose symptoms had improved) of 78%. Improvement was ascertained by GPs, either by questioning patients about their symptoms or through monitoring their requests for repeat medication. Although clearly this method of follow-up lacks rigour, the direction of travel was most encouraging, and the magnitude of the effect is not incompatible with trial evidence for the effectiveness of *H. pylori* eradication in patients with peptic ulcers.[13] Once again, however, there were wide variations between practices, which may be attributable to a range of factors such as inappropriate targeting or patients' lack of commitment to stick to the eradication regimen. Certainly the discipline required from patients in adhering to a typical eradication regimen (which usually involves taking three different medicines, two or three times a day for a week) may make concordance difficult and emphasises the need to win over patients as well as GPs. It is, of course, also possible that the range of success rates reflects the lack of precision of the criterion used, and with hindsight it may have been advantageous to have applied a more tightly defined measure of impact.

PACT analysis

There had been an 8.95% decrease in cost/STAR(97)-PU for gastrointestinal prescribing for (all) Camden & Islington between April–June 1997 and April–June 1998 (*see* Figure 5.1). For the audit practices there had been a corresponding decrease of just 7.89% (*see* Figure 5.2). The fact that the decrease was less for the audit practices came as a surprise. Several explanations can be offered. One possibility is that the results of those practices that *have* carried out the audit have been diluted by those that *have not*. When a sub-analysis is carried out, identifying those practices that have made progress with the audit (but excluding those with a query over whether the audit had been carried out) the decrease in cost/STAR-PU is 8.81%, which is similar to the figure for all Camden & Islington. Another possibility is that insufficient time has passed for changes in prescribing to become apparent in PACT data. This seems plausible, as a number of practices started the audit later than planned, and at the time of writing several had not yet completed the audit. Alternatively, the lack of differentiation between the prescribing costs for ulcer drugs of practices participating in the audit and those not participating, may be attributable to the fact that *all* GPs in Camden & Islington were sent the Audit Pack and guideline, which may have influenced prescribing in the non-audit practices as well as in those directly involved in the project. This possibility seems unlikely, however, in the light of the Cochrane Systematic Review on the effectiveness of distributing printed guidelines.[14]

Examination of the cost/STAR(97)-PU for gastrointestinal prescribing for the individual audit practices between April–June 1997 and April–June 1998 shows that for most practices there is a reduction in costs. The initial sixfold variation in costs means that clearly some practices had much more scope than others for achieving reductions in costs. It should also be noted that the cost of two of the major ulcer-healing drugs, omeprazole and ranitidine, decreased by 15% and 18% respectively during the year. This will obviously have had an impact on the decreases in cost/STAR(97)-PU observed. (The use of more sophisticated prescribing measures, such as Defined Daily Doses or Average Daily Quantities, would have permitted more accurate assessment of the impact of the project. However, this level of analysis is not currently available through the electronic PACT system.)

Feedback from patients

Although feedback from patients on their perceptions of their treatment was not formally sought, a number of unsolicited comments have been volunteered by patients, and these have been passed on by GPs:

> *'Several patients were delighted with triple therapy and said it had "almost changed their lives".'*

> *'I have received several letters of thanks.'*

> *'One miracle cure and a thank you letter.'*

Awareness of the evidence

Coverage of *H. pylori* and its relationship with peptic ulcer disease has been widespread in recent years, both in the medical/scientific press and in the popular media. Nevertheless, the project showed that there remains a large degree of variability in GPs' understanding of current evidence on the criteria for appropriate use of testing and eradication therapy, and in knowledge of the effectiveness of eradication. For example, it was clear that in some cases patients had been prescribed the wrong medication or had been tested for *H. pylori* inappropriately. Feedback from practices visited by the audit facilitator was positive in this respect, suggesting that in at least some cases visits had been successful in delivering key messages and raising awareness of the research evidence. One GP commented as follows:

> *'Awareness of* H. pylori *has definitely increased in the practice. More serology tests [for* H. pylori*] are now ordered by all partners, especially in newly presenting patients.'*

As discussed above, it was apparent from this project that some practices need more support than others in getting to grips with audit. It is not realistic for one person (such as the audit facilitator in this project) to provide the necessary level of support to a large number of practices, and for larger projects it would be wise to consider finding alternative means of support.

Lessons learned

- GPs are individuals whose interests, priorities, motivations and needs all differ. An attempt to engage them must recognise and adapt to these differences. *Flexibility in approach is key.*
- It is important that guidelines and supporting material are designed in a *user-friendly* and eye-catching format. However, different styles of presenting information appeal to different people. It is therefore difficult to please everyone.
- It is important to be responsive and adaptive in order to keep up the momentum of a project.
- Incentives may have a role; however, they have limitations. Factors such as time, priorities and perceptions about the proposed change may be more critical.
- Projects should be piloted to identify any unanticipated difficulties and enable the necessary changes to be made.
- The methods for measuring outcomes should be agreed and clearly defined.
- The clarity of the evidence, the perceived benefit from change and the difficulty of incorporating the change into practice are all important factors which will impact on a research implementation project. All need to be thoroughly considered before a project begins.

Things we would do differently if we were starting the project tomorrow

- put greater emphasis on searching for evidence that the implementation method adopted is likely to be effective in the context of the target environment and desired change. Our literature searching focused almost entirely on the evidence about the condition and the therapy. Conversely (and paradoxically) the decision to use audit as the vehicle for change appears with hindsight to be based on relatively scant evidence
- if audit is to be used, pilot it with practices with a keen interest in audit rather than a 'high-need group' (in our case those with the highest prescribing costs). Practices with experience of audit would be better placed to provide constructive criticism, and it would be better to encourage the high spenders to participate in the main phase of the project
- pilot a full audit cycle rather than just part of one (this would have exposed difficulties/weaknesses around measuring success/outcomes which we recognised when it was too late to rectify them)
- assign more time to physically helping practices to conduct audit
- invest more time in developing and standardising access to relevant diagnostic testing across the health authority. (A lot of hard work in educating and persuading people to change what they are doing can be undermined by practical limitations such as inequality of access to necessary services.)

References

1 NIH Consensus Development Panel (1994) *Helicobacter pylori* in peptic ulcer disease. *JAMA.* **272**: 65–9.

2 *British National Formulary* (1998) (36e). BMJ Books/Pharmaceutical Press, London.

3 Marshall BJ and Warren JR (1984) Unidentified curved bacilli in the stomach of patients with gastritis and peptic ulceration. *Lancet.* **1**: 1311–15.

4 The Eurogast Study Group (1993) An international association between *Helicobacter pylori* infection and gastric cancer. *Lancet.* **341**: 1359–62.

5 Scottish Intercollegiate Guidelines Network (SIGN) (1996) *Helicobacter pylori* eradication therapy in dyspeptic disease. *Pilot Edition.* **August**. http://www.show.scot.nhs.uk/sign/home.htm

6 Sanders D (1996) *Helicobacter pylori* eradication. *The Pharmaceutical Journal.* **257**: 720–2.

7 Blaser MJ (1997) Not all *Helicobacter pylori* strains are created equal: should all be eliminated? *Lancet.* **349**: 1020–2.

8 The Maastricht Consensus Report (1997) Current European concepts in the management of *Helicobacter pylori* infection. *Gut.* **41**: 8–13.

9   British Society of Gastroenterology (1996) *Dyspepsia Management Guidelines.* September. BSG, London.

10 Medical Resources Centre (1997) Dyspepsia, peptic ulcer and *Helicobacter pylori. MeReC Bulletin.* **8**(2).

11 Axon ATR *et al.* (1997) Randomised double blind controlled study of recurrence of gastric ulcer after treatment for eradication of *Helicobacter pylori* infection. *BMJ.* **314**: 565–8.

12 Jones J and Hunter D (1995) Consensus methods for medical and health services research. *BMJ.* **311**: 376–80.

13 Phull PS, Halliday D, Price AB and Jacyna MR (1995) Is absence of dyspeptic symptoms a useful test to access *H. pylori* eradication? *Gut.* **36** (Suppl. 1): A12.

14 Grimshaw J and Russell IT (1993) Effect of clinical guidelines on medical practice: a systematic review of rigorous evaluations. *Lancet.* **342**: 1317–22.

Camden & Islington commentary

Helicobacter pylori

In our survey of local participants, one summarised the rationale of this project as:

> 'There is enormous variation in how dyspepsia is managed. Lack of education provided to GPs is one of the commonest causes of patient referral by GPs. GPs are very keen to learn and want to be told.'

Although not all Camden & Islington GPs are interested in learning, some are. So it made sense that this project team used a pragmatic, educational approach. They involved all Camden & Islington GPs by sending out a distance self-learning pack using the Delphi technique. More specifically, they emphasised self-learning through audit for the pilot practices.

Those GPs who did participate in the audit found it worthwhile. They were especially positive about the user-friendly flowchart by a graphic designer. They were also pleased that the audit was in stages so practices could do as much or as little as they wanted. So, this project team designed an excellent resource.

But having an excellent resource is only the first step. The next is motivating practices to want to use it. Using an educational approach successfully, especially one that relies heavily on audit, requires certain pre-cursors – mainly that GPs and their practices make time to concentrate on learning. As one GP pointed out:

> 'It's an enormous audit – 220 patients in this practice alone ... One weakness is that just giving practices the paperwork is not enough. You need to help practices to do everything, from pulling notes on.'

One of their great strengths is that the team were very resourceful in trying to find ways round such obstacles. But even with offers of hands-on help from the audit facilitator and extra incentives such as money, many practices still did not feel they could participate, or participate fully. Models reliant on self-learning will have a limited impact unless participants have enough time, or can get themselves motivated enough to make time, to take on the extra workload.

By default, this team chose a historically difficult type of practice to focus on, since they selected practices on the basis of highest spending. Nearly 60% of the highest-spending practices invited to participate were single-handed. Many of the other North Thames project teams commented that they wanted to reach single-handed practices, but were unsure how to do it. Although the

Camden & Islington team found it disappointing that so few of the small practices wanted to take part, at least they made the effort in trying to get them on board, and in some cases succeeded.

As the second cycle of the *H. pylori* project draws to a close (1998–99), it is disheartening that even fewer practices have taken part. As it is a part of the prescribing incentive scheme, the project team hoped that as practices heard about the pack and its benefits through 'word of mouth', uptake would spread.

Unfortunately that hasn't happened, as only 17 practices signed up to the audit in its second cycle, as compared to 33 during the lifetime of the project. Since the project has finished and the audit facilitator has moved on to another post, no one is actively recruiting practices or able to offer an extra pair of hands. So, even fewer practices are interested or able to take an audit of this magnitude on board.

This project team ended up with a difficult group to work with. Despite a number of considerable hurdles, they did well in getting a number of practices interested enough to consider tackling the audit. Perhaps in time, the new pharmacists appointed to the PCGs can build on this team's work.

6

Establishing a computerised diabetes register in Ealing, Hammersmith & Hounslow

Raymond Jankowski, Suzanne Smith
and Sarah Davies

Diabetes: the broad context and effective treatment

The St Vincent Declaration[1] set the standards of care for people with diabetes worldwide, with its targets to reduce the long-term complications of the condition. Its goals strive to achieve reductions in blindness, renal failure and amputations. It also aims to reduce the mortality and morbidity due to stroke and coronary heart disease in people with diabetes and to normalise pregnancy outcomes for women with the condition. The British Diabetic Association[2] identifies collaboration and teamwork as pivotal in the care of people with diabetes in both primary and secondary care. They further recommend that implementation of district-wide diabetes guidelines can be enhanced by the development of district diabetes registers. The National Health Service Executive[3] sets out the role of health authorities in setting local standards of care and being responsible for the co-ordination of this across all agencies.

There is considerable evidence that morbidity can be substantially reduced by attention to preventative measures.[4,5] Specifically, this includes optimisation of blood glucose and blood lipid control, reduction in smoking, control of blood pressure, simple foot-care measures to prevent ulceration and amputation, surveillance for sight-threatening eye damage and prescribing aspirin for ischaemic heart disease. Until recently, the link between tight control of blood glucose has been more convincingly proven for Type I diabetes.* However, the recent UK Prospective Diabetes Study (PDS),[4,5] a nine-year follow-up of 1000 non-insulin-dependent diabetics aged 25–65 has demonstrated that this is also true for Type II diabetes. Approximately 25% of all diabetics have retinopathy of some degree, and in about 10% of cases this is severe enough to require laser therapy.[6] If these are detected early enough, usually before vision is affected, laser treatment will prevent 70% from going blind. Likewise with neuropathy, as many as 60% of diabetics have some evidence of this, and diabetics are at least 50 times more likely to have some form of foot ulceration, which in turn can result in amputations.

It is therefore essential that known diabetics are reviewed at least annually, either by their GP or hospital to ensure any complications are detected as early as possible. It is difficult to estimate the precise impact of good diabetes control on the number of diabetics who die prematurely each year. However, the recently published results of the PDS[4,5] indicate that tight control of blood pressure can reduce diabetic complication rates by as much as 24%, and death rates by up to 32%. Reductions for specific complications varied from 57% for heart failure and 44% for stroke to 37% for microvascular disease. This is partly due to the high prevalence of hypertension in the Type II diabetic population (estimated at between 40 and 60%). The magnitude of reductions by strict blood pressure control appears to be higher than those reported for intensive blood glucose control: 12% reduction in diabetic complications and 25% reduction in microvascular disease.

It is estimated that expenditure on diabetes, mainly the treatment of complications, is approximately 4–5% of the total NHS annual budget.[7]

Diabetes: the local picture in west London

Ealing, Hammersmith & Hounslow (EHH) has a population of approximately 650 000. The proportion of local residents aged over 65 is above the national average, and 26% of the EHH local population is from ethnic minorities, (the third highest such proportion in England and Wales).[8] Within the district there are 390 GPs, over one third of whom are single-handed.

The large scale of the diabetic population of west London was first documented in the Southall Study[9] which identified that 5% of the population in this part of EHH suffered from diabetes. The EHH population comprises 22%

---

*Type I diabetes is insulin-dependent diabetes, which is the less common form of the disease, but more prevalent in young people. Type II diabetes is non-insulin-dependent diabetes, which is a more common form of the disease, but rare in patients under the age of 35.

South Asian origin, and because people from this ethnic group are more commonly afflicted by diabetes, e.g. the prevalence of Type II diabetes in these groups is likely to be at least twice that of comparable European populations.[8] (The proportion of EHH residents with diabetes is 2.33% compared with the national average of 1.05–1.3%.[10]) Recent figures from general practice chronic disease management reports show that in different localities of EHH, diagnosed diabetics range from 1.4 to 4.4% of the local population. In terms of numbers, EHH Health Authority has responsibility for commissioning care for around 14 700 people with diabetes. Based on the age and ethnic structure of the population and using nationally published age- and ethnicity-specific prevalence rates, the true figure has been estimated to be nearer to 20 000, which implies that there is a serious degree of undiagnosed diabetics in the community.

The gathering of data at district level, as recommended in the St Vincent Declaration, can enable the evaluation of the effectiveness of diabetes services in improving the health of diabetic patients. In the NHS, health authorities (and now primary care groups) need detailed, high-quality information about the local population in order to plan, implement and evaluate care. We believed that a computerised diabetic register in EHH could offer an important intelligence resource for the NHS in our district.

Objectives

The Southall Study had identified diabetes as a local health issue in 1983. In the same year, the Diabetes Chronic Disease Management (CDM) Programme[9]* was launched and the British Diabetic Association (BDA) recommended that comprehensive local diabetes registers should be developed. Between that year and the early 1990s, clinicians from Ealing Hospital working in diabetic care developed close links with local GPs and set up pioneering, nurse-led clinics in practices. An early attempt was made at a hospital-based diabetes register (using a stand-alone system), however, at that point practice-level information technology was still relatively crude, and the information produced was limited to paper reports to GPs based on data from the hospital diabetic clinics. In 1992, Burnett et al.[11] suggested that an 'identification of all diabetic patients registered with a practice is an essential starting point for structured care'. Although the CDM Programme required individual practices

---

*The Chronic Disease Management Programme is an approval programme whereby practitioners forward activities relating to diabetes care within their surgery. Each eligible GP will be entitled to claim payments as defined in 30.1 of General Medical Services Regulations.

to submit information on their diabetic patients, this required only limited details, such as the numbers of insulin- and non-insulin-dependent diabetics, numbers having had an annual review and place of care (i.e. hospital, general practice or shared). No clinical information was recorded (e.g. levels of HbA1c and blood pressure control, how often patients have a fundoscopy,* etc.). Discussions at the health authority led to a decision that a diabetes register which provided a clinical management system, as well as the ability to collect demographic and epidemiology data, was required. The local diabetes advisory group developed a minimum data set (MDS) to support GPs in the collection of standardised clinical data, including annual reviews, etc., to feed into the diabetes register (*see* Box 6.1).

The project

In December 1995, a bid to develop a pilot diabetes register was submitted to the Regional R&D Implementation Programme (*see* Box 6.2 for its aims and objectives). Funding was agreed in October 1996, and a project manager was appointed for one year to lead the work. A project team was established comprising a GP, a health promotion adviser, the health authority commissioning director and a public health consultant. A tendering process led to the purchase of the Hicom Diamond system, a database running on Microsoft Access, which was at the time being used at about 20 other sites for trust-based diabetes systems.

The plan for the whole project up to this point had been to extract data from hospital clinical management systems and hold this centrally at the health authority. However, the practicality of this approach was soon challenged by the variation in the computer systems in use at the local trusts (Ealing, West Middlesex, Charing Cross and Hammersmith hospitals) and the lack of compatibility between the clinical systems and the Patient Administration System (PAS). It was therefore necessary to change the focus of the project, from a register based on records from secondary care to one based in primary care, so interest was sought from GPs. The project group ensured that each practice wishing to participate met certain criteria, i.e. that they used either EMIS or Meditel as their clinical system, that they cared for 100 or more diabetics and that they had been approved by the CDM Programme (*see* Box 6.3). We were aware from word of mouth that diabetes registers in other health authorities had failed, and that over-ambition in their early stages was

---

*A fundoscopy is a direct examination of the fundus of the eye, used for the detection of retinopathy and other diabetic complications.

Box 6.1 Ealing, Hammersmith & Hounslow Health Authority – minimum data set for diabetes

NHS number [ ][ ][ ][ ][ ][ ][ ][ ][ ][ ]   GP Code [ ]

Name   ....

Address   ....

            ....

Post Code   [ ]

Date of Birth [/   /   ]   Gender M [ ]   F [ ]

Ethnicity   White   [ ]
              Black Caribbean   [ ]
              Black African   [ ]
              Black other (non-mixed)   [ ]
              Black other (mixed)   [ ]
              Indian   [ ]
              Pakistani   [ ]
              Bangladeshi   [ ]
              Chinese   [ ]
              Other ethnic (non-mixed)   [ ]
              Other ethnic (mixed)   [ ]
              Not given   [ ]

Type of diabetes   IDDM [ ]   NIDDM [ ]

If NIDDM   Diet treated   [ ]
                   Tablet treated
                   Insulin treated

Year of diagnosis   [/   /   ]

Smoking   Cigarette smoker   [ ]   Date status recorded
            Cigar smoker   [ ]   [/   /   ]
            Pipe smoker   [ ]
            Current non-smoker [ ]

Body Mass Index (BMI) % [ ]   Date [/   /   ]

HbA1c   [ ]   Date [/   /   ]

Date Fundi Reviewed [/   /   ]   Date of Annual Review [/   /   ]

Lead Clinician   GP [ ]   Consultant [ ]   Shared [ ]
(who does annual review)

Latest Blood Pressure   Systolic [ ]   Diastolic [ ]
& Date [/   /   ]

Box 6.2   Aims and objectives of the project

- Initially the aim of this project is to provide a computerised system which supports clinicians in both the primary care and secondary care setting to provide and maintain good quality care for people with diabetes.
- The computerised diabetes register will ensure accurate documentation of annual review, and facilitate an efficient system for call/recall of patients.
- To record accurately the number of known diagnosed diabetics for which services have to be provided and funded in EHH.
- To check that these patients have a minimum of an annual review.
- Provide comparative data and information about service activity, thus ensuring service provision meets the needs of the local population.
- To enable practices to take part in more sophisticated clinical audit to help improve patient care.
- In the longer term to ensure that multidisciplinary input is provided to diabetics, especially at the time of annual review.
- To try to record diabetic complication rates and monitor the progress of their reduction (e.g. registered blindness, amputations, renal failure, etc.).
- To provide a reliable recall and review of all people with diabetes in EHH.
- To improve communication between all health professionals caring for people with diabetes.

---

blamed. We therefore decided that it would be sensible to limit the number of GPs involved in the pilot stage of the project (we had a maximum of 20 in mind). We reasoned that working with a small number of GPs would enable us to ensure that problems could be detected and sorted out at an early stage. We wanted to be able to give maximum time and support to the practices involved, and ensure that their systems could be adapted as necessary. We were keen to feed back the data collected as quickly as possible, and in each case it seemed that objectives would be more easily achieved with a small number of practices participating. A clinical information facilitator was recruited to support the practices taking part in the collection of data. This involved adaptation of systems as well as extracting the data using a software package called Miquest.*

We were sure that gaining the interest and engagement of GPs would be critical to the success of the project, and we were therefore keen to convince them of the value of the register. We set about this in two ways: first by ensuring that meaningful data was fed back to them and second by identifying

---

Miquest (Morbidity Information Query & Export Syntax) is a software package designed to extract anonymised health data from selected GP systems.

Box 6.3   Chronic disease management programme for diabetes mellitus

Standards of excellence
It is proposed that any practice recognised as achieving a 'standard of excellence' for provision of an organised programme for the care of patients with diabetes mellitus would include the following.

1 A register
To have and keep up to date an immediately available register of all patients with diabetes. The register should include a marker for identification of those patients in particular 'at risk' groups.

2 Call and recall
To ensure the systematic call and recall and response of patients on the register is taking place either in a hospital or general practice setting at a minimum of six-monthly intervals. Thus two visits should be recorded in a 14-month time period, allowing for delayed response, and the number of calls should be appropriate to the needs of the individual and at more frequent intervals for those in 'at risk' groups.

3 Education for newly diagnosed diabetics
To ensure that all newly diagnosed patients with diabetes (or their carers when appropriate) receive appropriate education and advice on management of and prevention of secondary complications of their diabetes.
    To provide for each patient a check list of aspects of education, to be discussed to ensure that all appropriate areas are covered.

4 Continuing education for diabetics
To ensure that all patients with diabetes (or their carers when appropriate) receive appropriate continuing education.
    (Need to define what continuing education is and what aspects should be covered.)

5 Individual management plan
To prepare with the patient an individual management plan.
    Each patient to be issued with a patient-held shared care card which includes the individual management plan. The latter should be discussed with the patient and attention given to ensure the latter understands his and the GP's responsibilities.

6 Clinical procedures
On initial diagnosis and annual review, a full review of the patient's health should be carried out, including measurement of BP, HBA1c, weight, fundoscopy, visual acuity.

Box 6.3 *continued*

The interim review should include checks for any potential areas of complication previously highlighted and a review of the patient's own monitoring records.

The GP with the responsibility for the diabetic programme should be on site while any such checks are conducted, and easily accessible by whoever is undertaking the check.

7 Our professional links
The GP and practice-based team should demonstrate a team approach to the care of diabetes, including links with other professionals, e.g. dieticians, chiropodists. Any health professional involved in the care of patients in the programme should have undergone approved training in the management of diabetes.

The GP advising on chronic disease management care for diabetes should also have undergone approved training and assessment for the care of diabetes. This may be in the form of portfolio and distance learning.

8 Referral policies
Patients should be referred promptly to other necessary services, and other relevant support agencies using the locally agreed referral guidelines.

9 Record keeping
The practice should demonstrate the maintenance of records of results of all the above procedures, incorporating information from other local providers involved in the care of patients.

10 Audit
The practice should carry out regular clinical audits of the care of patients with diabetes against the aforementioned criteria, and including reference to outcome.

---

a local GP *project champion*. The plan for a computerised diabetes register was taken to the local medical committee (LMC), and the health authority asked the members to discuss and agree the undertaking of a central register in their area. A number of issues were raised and, subject to certain conditions (including confirming the status of the register as a voluntary project and a commitment to seek patients' consent for records to be held), the register was accepted by the LMC. That the committee had focused on the issue of confidentiality was not surprising, given the pertinence of this issue to any system for keeping electronic patient records, and given concurrent debate in the specific context of diabetes registers in the medical press. We addressed the issue of confidentiality throughout the pilot in the following ways:

- the patient database was a stand-alone system at the health authority. It was password-protected and could be accessed only by the clinical information facilitator, the public health consultant and a member of the information technology team
- practices were encouraged to gain written consent from all diabetic patients to include their details on the register
- we gave practices the option of either running a call and recall system themselves or letting the health authority run it for them.

The project also received agreement and backing from the local diabetes advisory group.

From the criteria we had set, 43 practices were eligible, and 13 responded to an invitation to participate. The pilot began with these practices in December 1997, with a workshop to discuss the workings of the register. Presentations were made by the health authority project group, the supplier of the register (Hicom Diamond) and the Miquest Consultancy, to explain the process of the data flow and the potential benefits of the register. It had been agreed by the project team that Miquest would be used to write a set of 'queries' based on Read codes,* to be held on floppy disk, asking the GP clinical systems to extract the data requested on the minimum data set. Data would then be downloaded from the GP clinical system on to floppy disk. Hicom then had the task of writing an 'upload' programme to enable the register to store the data. As is often the case with information technology (IT), this process took considerably longer than had been anticipated.

Early queries were 'Would Diamond and Miquest be compatible?' and 'Would it be possible to import into Diamond the data extracted from the GP clinical system using Miquest?' In fact, less sophisticated questions needed to be tackled first. An initial set of queries was written and data extraction was undertaken at one practice to provide Hicom with an example of the format in which data would be presented for uploading on to the register. It was at this point that we started to realise that despite keeping the project to a manageable scale and working with only practices satisfying sensible criteria, acquiring the data and putting it into the register was going to be much more of a challenge than we had envisaged. First, although the project team had realised from the outset that large chunks of information may not be present on practice computer systems, we had not anticipated that practices would not be using their clinical systems for data entry *at all*. This, however was what we found in several cases. Even though practices had EMIS or Meditel

---

*Read codes are a comprehensive structure created to facilitate the recording of health information.

clinical systems installed, these systems were in some cases being used only for prescriptions. The amount of information recorded depended on the level of education and skill in using the system within individual practices. Second, when the MDS was written it had been assumed that if practices used their computer, they would be recording the relevant information automatically using the Read codes identified within the MDS. However, it became apparent that each practice was recording information in a completely different way, and although Read codes had been identified, there were many other ways practices were recording this information. For example, three types of codes were being used by practices:

- Read codes – two versions were being used
- codes specifically devised and provided by the EMIS clinical system suppliers
- customised practice codes – for those items not covered by the above two coding structures.

It was the task of the clinical information facilitator to enable the MDS to be set up on to each of the participating practices' clinical systems' templates or protocols using the standardised Read codes. When information was being recorded on to the computer but using a different code, the facilitator liaised with the clinical system suppliers to transfer information from the existing code to the standard code. It was agreed that future data entry would be made using the standard Read codes.

A further difficulty remained in two practices which were recording similar information with different words and Read codes. The MDS stated that ethnicity should be recorded for all diabetics to enable the health authority to identify numbers of diabetics within each ethnic group. The problem arose with practices where *country of origin* was being recorded rather than *ethnicity*. This was not simply a case of code conversion because, for example, patients born in Australia of Indian parents could be regarded as Australian under the term country of origin, but would be regarded as Indian under the term ethnic group. This would affect the quality of the data and could result in serious skewing of potentially valuable information on ethnicity in diabetes. It was therefore decided that these practices' records could not be included as they stood, but that accurate ethnicity data should be sought from patients and included in records at consultation. This is the main reason for the gaps which remain in records of ethnicity in the data analysis.

Another difficulty of Read codes which affected the data collection came in the recording of the diabetic blood test results. The Read code structure allows practices to enter HbA1 and HbA1c* on one Read code only. Practices have

---

*The blood tests HbA1 and HbA1c are measurements of blood glucose control over a six-week period. Different hospital laboratories measure in different ways to produce either HbaA1 or HbA1c.

historically either entered the two readings under one code, or created an individual practice code for one or other type of test. For these reasons, it has been impossible to undertake comprehensive, accurate analysis of the levels of the blood tests as the combination of the two sets of results would cause distortion.

Although the criteria stipulated participating practices required the use of EMIS or Meditel clinical systems, three practices using other systems were particularly keen to participate. Two of these used the Microsolutions clinical system which was not accredited for use with Miquest, while the other was non-computerised. These practices completed forms for each diabetic, and data collected in this way were entered on to the Diamond system manually at the health authority.

By March 1998, 13 practices had forwarded their diabetic data to the register (ten using Miquest and three using manual records). Anonymised versions of different formats of report were produced and discussed at a workshop for project participants and a wider group of EMIS and Meditel system users, diabetes nurse specialists, diabetologists, chiropodists and dieticians. Practices were asked to present their anonymised reports for discussion between participants and non-participants with a view to improving diabetic services. The potential value of information collected and the appropriateness of its presentation were key areas of debate. One particular topic discussed was the high proportion of unknown or unrecorded information. This problem persists to some extent. However, Table 6.1, which compares data from March 1998 with that available in November 1998, shows that some progress has been made in capturing more complete data (e.g. smoking status). Discussions with participating practices have focused on missing patient data and ways of improving the quality of data recording. The clinical information facilitator has contributed suggestions as to ways in which specific problems can be solved. All GPs expressed interest in producing reports detailing patients with no record of an annual review in the last year, and those with no record at all. This report lists all diabetic patients alongside all their latest information and these are currently being provided to each participating practice. All practices are now using this list as a reminder during consultations to improve the record keeping and care of their diabetic patients.

Since the initial pilot phase the project has expanded, and at the time of writing 42 practices, comprising EMIS and Meditel users, are now participating. To enable data to be forwarded by the practice and analysed at the health authority on a quarterly basis, a system guide has been written. Training has also been made available for all participating practices on an individual practice basis to ensure that at least one person at each practice is competent to undertake the data extraction.

Table 6.1 Diabetes register project analysis comparison – March–November 1998 – 13 GP practices

The analysis undertaken below for the diabetes register centres around the 13 GP practices beginning the register at the initial stage of the pilot study (March 1998). Although the register to date has 43 practices participating and also has recent agreement from the Hounslow PCG to take the register forward on a PCG level, the analysis below concentrates on comparing data from the 13 practices between two periods in time.

The health authority has received quarterly extracts from all but two of the participating practices. (Both practices have sent written forms on not such a frequent basis as quarterly extracts from GP clinical systems.) This may average out the effort put in by the more enthusiastic practices.

Smoking status	Mar 98		Nov 98	
Smoking status	N	%	N	%
Non-smoker	1091	77	1060	70
Smoker	195	14	459	30
Unknown	130	9	0	0
Total	**1416**	**100**	**1519**	**100**

HbA1c	Mar 98		Nov 98	
HbA1c (9 practices)	N	%	N	%
HbA1c <6 mmol/ls	86	8	177	17
HbA1c 6–7 mmol/ls	130	13	196	18
HbA1c 7.1–8.9 mmol/ls	197	20	304	28
HbA1c >9 mmol/ls	192	19	196	18
Unknown	396	40	199	19
Total	**1001**	**100**	**1072**	**100**

HbA1	Mar 98		Nov 98	
HbA1 (4 practices)	N	%	N	%
HbA1 <7.5 mmol/ls	49	12	55	12
HbA1 7.5–8.7 mmol/ls	58	14	66	15
HbA1 >8.8 mmol/ls	196	47	226	51
Unknown	112	27	100	22
Total	**415**	**100**	**447**	**100**

Table 6.1 *continued*

Annual review	Mar 98		Nov 98	
Annual review	N	%	N	%
Record in last year	615	43	850	56
Record more than 1 yr ago	565	40	354	23
Unknown	236	17	315	21
Total	**1416**	**100**	**1519**	**100**

Place of care	Mar 98		Nov 98	
Place of care	N	%	N	%
Practice-based	346	24	497	33
Hospital	874	62	413	27
Shared	0	0	143	9
Unknown	196	14	466	31
Total	**1416**	**100**	**1519**	**100**

Fundoscopy	Mar 98		Nov 98	
Fundoscopy	N	%	N	%
Record in last year	240	17	104	7
Record more than 1 yr ago	239	17	401	26
Unknown	937	66	1014	67
Total	**1416**	**100**	**1519**	**100**

Ethnicity	Mar 98		Nov 98	
Ethnicity	N	%	N	%
White	270	19	297	20
Black Caribbean	20	1	23	2
Black African	13	1	15	1
Black other	0	0	0	0
Indian	157	11	168	11
Pakistani	22	2	25	2
Other	16	1	16	1
Unknown	918	65	975	64
Total	**1416**	**100**	**1519**	**100**

Benefits for patients, practices and primary care clinicians

Organisational aspects of diabetes care

The diabetes register has brought about distinct benefits to the practices' organisation of diabetic care. The register has replaced the need for manual feedback for the CDM Programme. Many practices, particularly those which are single-handed, did not keep a register of their diabetic patients. Instead, every year at the time of requesting the CDM information, written notes of their diabetic patients were hand-searched to identify whether they were insulin- or non-insulin-dependent, whether they had had their annual review and if so, where. This system was very much prone to errors, often the consequence of someone without adequate knowledge undertaking the search and being unable to check the notes thoroughly and to pull out the right information. This method could also easily miss patients and lead to the submission of incomplete and inaccurate figures. It was also very time-consuming.

The health authority understood that, in the short term, additional time would have to be invested by participating practices to set up the register, design the template, etc. This was recognised by a small reimbursement of £100 to each participating practice and considerable support offered by the clinical information facilitator. This role provided the advice and training to participating practices and enabled them to get the most from their practice systems.

Clinical aspects of care

In terms of clinical advantages, use of the template or protocol in each consultation has led to clinicians concentrating on the most important aspects of diabetic care, in a systematic way agreed by the diabetes specialists within the diabetes advisory group. From this standard approach to data entry, each member of the primary healthcare team within the practice was able to identify whether a patient had received his/her annual review or fundoscopy. This enables quick and precise clinical audit within each practice. A call/recall service is provided for practices' diabetic annual reviews where requested.

Peer support and the PCG effect

Each participating practice knows which practices are undertaking the register within their own PCG and surrounding PCGs. This provides a project network of practices to gain peer support in terms of diabetes care which indirectly benefits the patients. Regular workshops are organised by the health authority to provide support for this network and to encourage discussion on improving care and services for diabetics. Practices also receive standardised comparative data, both at practice level and now also at PCG level. This is both a basis and a stimulus to practices in discussing among themselves ways of improving performance relative to diabetic care.

Discussion

The success of the pilot project depended on the key stakeholders, both in the health authority and within primary care, in developing skills around project management, often requiring a change in management approach, i.e. persuading and influencing, articulating and solving information technology problems as they arose. The differing levels of IT skills in primary care made it essential to invest time and effort in ensuring that all participating practices had the minimum necessary competencies.

The sustainability of the project depends not only on continuing funding, but also the motivation of clinicians in primary care, which we think will be assured if the benefits to patients of maintaining a diabetic register are clearly demonstrated. While there remain issues about the quality of data being collected in terms of completeness, accuracy and timeliness of feedback to practices, these have all improved since the pilot began. We think that this improvement is attributable to timely feedback to the practices during and between register workshops.

Throughout the lifetime of our project, diabetes has been a high priority for the health authority. It is now one of two local priorities for the Health Improvement Programme. The link between diabetes and coronary heart disease (CHD) has been apparent for some years. The UK PDS has reinforced this link. As a result EHH Health Authority has decided to combine the diabetes register with its Coronary Heart Disease Risk Reduction Programme. This programme uses data from primary care to calculate a 'score' for at-risk patients. Reports are generated for practices categorising patients by risk order, enabling the practice to identify and focus on those at most risk. The programme helps practices to prescribe appropriately, and cost pressures on PCGs will ensure that this information continues to be valued. It is planned that the future development of the diabetic register system should link into the CHD programme so that detail on cardiovascular conditions in diabetic patients is captured. Currently negotiations are taking place with the clinical governance and IT leads of the local PCGs, which we hope will secure the future development of a combined register.

Lessons learned

- The most important lesson learned in the course of the project was the importance of setting up good channels of communication.
- We found it important to be able to emphasise to practices that participation would not create additional work for them, but would provide support for them in their care of diabetic patients.
- We came to appreciate the importance of piloting the diabetes register with a small number of participating practices because it enabled us to iron out the problems which came to light (such as coding transfers) before rolling out to a large number of practices.
- We found it important to enlist the support of key people, and in the case of directors this was achieved by the project group emphasising the value of the project as a commissioning tool for the health authority/PCGs, and as an information service to primary care.
- We found it helpful to engage a GP project champion whose enthusiasm and commitment to the project was influential in 'marketing' it to colleagues in primary and secondary care.

Things we would do differently if we were starting tomorrow

- include only practices with appropriate computer systems. Those practices returning data through the use of paper forms are not using the register to its full potential. The register is unable to pick up all diabetics from these practices (as data are gathered from patients attending clinics), therefore in these instances it is not achieving its aim of identifying patients who have not had an annual review
- advertise the register to all relevant bodies at each GP clinical system supplier used by EHH practices (so as to encourage them to make their systems compatible with the register). Ensure that the importance of the register to practices (and now PCGs) is noted to assist in commissioning services, together with the increasing importance of Miquest at practice level, thus increasing the likelihood of bringing the use of Miquest further to the top of other GP clinical system suppliers' agendas

continued opposite

- liaise further with companies supplying general practice computer systems to ensure that MDS and standard Read codes are suitable for data recording and that they combine with current systems for data recording
- merge with data being received and analysed from the CDM Programme still being collected from non-register practices
- increase effort at practices in areas where there are considerably higher numbers of diabetics, e.g. Southall and Hounslow, to maximise benefit to practices.

References

1   Department of Health (1992) *St Vincent Task Force for Diabetes*. Department of Health and British Diabetic Association, London.

2   British Diabetic Association (1994) *Response to the Report of the Clinical Standards Advisory Group*. BDA, London.

3   NHS Executive (1997) *Key Features of a Good Diabetes Service*. HSG (97) 45. Chronic Disease Management Registers. HMSO, London.

4   UK Prospective Diabetes Study Group (1998) Tight blood pressure control and risk of macrovascular and microvascular complications in Type III diabetes: UK PDS 38. *BMJ*. **317**: 703–13.

5   UK Prospective Diabetes Study Group (1998) Intensive blood glucose control with sulphonylureas or insulin compared with conventional treatment and risk of complications in patient with Type II diabetes (UK PDS 33) *BMJ*. **352**: 837–53.

6   Mather H (1995) *Ealing Hammersmith & Hounslow Practical Guide to Diabetes Care*. EH&H HA, London.

7   Williams R (1994) Diabetes mellitus. In: A Stevens and J Raftery (eds) *Health Care Needs Assessment, Vol 1*. Radcliffe Medical Press, Oxford.

8   Ealing, Hammersmith & Hounslow Health Authority (1998–2001). *Better Health for West London*. (Annual Public Health Report.)

9   Mather HM and Keen H (1985) The Southall Diabetes Survey: prevalence of known diabetes in Asians and Europeans. *BMJ*. **291**: 1081–4.

10 Ealing, Hammersmith & Hounslow Health Authority (1997) *Chronic Disease Management Data for Diabetes*. EH&H HA, London.

11 Burnett SD, Woolf CM and Yudkin JS (1992) Developing a district diabetes register. *BMJ*. **305**: 627–30.

Ealing, Hammersmith & Hounslow commentary

Diabetes register

Early on, this team had to 'sell' the project in two directions – to the Executive Board and to primary care teams. They have managed very well in getting initially reluctant senior managers on board. As one health authority employee new to the project mentioned:

> 'It has a high priority within the HA. People already think it's a good idea, so you don't need to convince them. They're already convinced.'

This had not always been the case.

The team has also been well led and managed. The three key members worked well together, made their meetings sancrosanct from other work and ensured that they met on a systematic rather than ad hoc basis to review progress. The project worker, in particular, was particularly well regarded by primary care staff, one of whom went so far as to say that her visits were the 'highlight'.

The first step of this project has been to establish a computerised register of all diabetics in the district. Because setting up a data collection process is so challenging, the project team has had to be careful not to lose sight of their focus. The emphasis can easily slip from improving clinical practice to setting up an accurate, reliable, user-friendly data collection process. As one survey respondent put it:

> 'What are you going to do with the data? And are there resources to back up data findings ... It's all right having registers but it's more important to see patients than just to know that they are there. Everyone knows that we have a lot of diabetics here.'

As a consequence of the register, everyone now knows that there are a lot more diabetics than they first thought. Seventeen percent more diabetics were identified on the diabetes register than on the chronic disease register within the 13 pilot practices. One GP we spoke with mentioned that he had found over 150 diabetics within his practice alone that were not on the consultant's list. So, the project team have been successful in achieving their first objective of identifying unknown diabetics.

The team now hopes that as the numbers of hidden diabetics rises, commissioning bodies will put more money into diabetic care. This looks like it's beginning to happen, as recently, the diabetes advisory group at the health authority agreed funding for extra diabetes nurse specialists at the local trusts.

But there is a lot more work needed, especially from primary care groups. As one practitioner said:

'The information obtained must inform service development. That loop is not completed. As a PCG, we're keen to look at how to respond.'

In the meantime, survey respondents indicated that the register is having a limited impact on improving clinical practice. The project team hoped that by feeding back better-quality information, practices would look at their care and improve weak areas. This does not seem to be happening. Practices need more than better information; they need help in developing the skills necessary to improve their practice.

The strength of this project is that they have laid the foundation to work intensively with practices to develop those skills, if they choose to. Over 70 practices are now willing to share their data with the health authority, so this team has gone a long way in gaining the practices' trust. Even more importantly, some practitioners want to invite the team in still further – they want closer contact on a one-to-one basis. One respondent commented:

'There are not enough people to help us. Facilitators are too thin on the ground ... I would like the register reviewed with me at a six-monthly meeting in which my practice could be compared with other practices ... I want to know – how can you make good excellent?'

This team has been operating under the premise that 'better information leads to more informed decisions which then lead to better clinical practice'. What the project has shown is that better information leads to a modest improvement in information and service provision, but there is still some way to go before we can say it results in better care.

7

Leg ulcer care in East London

Sally Gooch, Alison Hopkins and Francesca Scott

Introduction

Context

The East London Leg Ulcer Project ran between 1996 and 1998 as one element of a larger action research project in Tower Hamlets Healthcare NHS Trust (THHT), the Best Clinical Practice Project*. The larger project, which began in 1994, was concerned with developing, implementing and auditing multiprofessional care programmes for use across primary and secondary care settings.[2–4]** The Leg Ulcer Project followed this pattern, but was focused solely on care for this condition. It was funded mainly by the regional office as a Health Authority-led R&D Implementation Project, through the support of the local health authority (East London & The City).[6,7] Small, additional, amounts of funding for specific features of the project were provided by the trust and from commercial sponsorship.

---

*Action research is concerned with everyday situations in which individual and group reflection within the development groups creates 'the capacity and reality of change'.[1]
**Care Programmes are tools for clinical practice developed by clinicians at Tower Hamlets Healthcare Trust which incorporate clinical guidelines for assessment, treatment and care, aids to clinical decision making and measurable patient outcomes.[4] The project which generated this definition and the Care Programmes is known as the Best Clinical Practice Project or the Care Programme approach. The approach uses care pathways[5] to specify key events, tests and assessments to help achieve the best possible outcomes, given the available resources.

Locality

Tower Hamlets is an economically deprived part of east London approximately 21.6 km^2. It has a diverse (estimated) population of 200 000. It is served by a large acute NHS trust and a community and mental health trust that also incorporates an integrated elders* service.

The need for the project

Leg ulcers affect 1% of the population.[8] The majority are venous in origin and can be healed relatively easily when a correct and timely diagnosis is made and effective management provided.[9] Approximately 85% of people with leg ulcers have their care managed within primary care.[10] There is now a large body of research evidence that has established good practice for the prevention and management of venous ulcers,[10,11] yet until the project, Tower Hamlets did not have a consistent approach to this care, and there were no trust-wide guidelines for leg ulcers. The use of assessment tools (e.g. Doppler ultrasound) was inconsistent, and the use of effective compression bandaging variable, despite a well-established educational programme. Documentation was ad hoc and it was clearly common for delays in diagnosis to occur (evident from the condition of patients referred to the clinical nurse specialist). In terms of clinical pathways, there was no clear route for patients to receive optimum domiciliary and clinic-based management, with ready access to experts when appropriate (for example to treat non-healing wounds). We considered that the lack of consistency in the (then) current organisation of care, combined with the powerful research evidence for the effectiveness of timely diagnosis and appropriate treatment, and the high prevalence of the condition in the local population made this a very suitable candidate for a research implementation project.

Organisational background and methodology

It is important to view the project in its historical and organisational context. As stated, the project was part of a bigger initiative (the Best Clinical Practice Project) which was itself one component of a wider development agenda in the trust. We consider that the design of any research implementation/ clinical practice development project needs to be congruent with the other objectives and underlying values of the organisation because collaboration

---

Integrated Elders is the local inpatient elderly care unit.

between managers and clinicians in developing services is critical.[11] In this respect we were, from the outset, keen to emphasise that although the Leg Ulcer Project was receiving dedicated external funding (from the Regional R&D Implementation Programme), its function and motivation was common with, and part of, the wider development of the trust.

The Leg Ulcer Care Programme[12] can be regarded not only as part of a broad range of developments in the trust but also as the culmination of local development work on this particular topic over several years.[13] This included setting up a leg ulcer clinic, the training of district nurses in care of patients with leg ulcers, the provision of assessment forms, appropriate use of Doppler ultrasound to detect arterial insufficiency and the use of compression bandaging. In addition, the Well Leg Project,[14] which was an initiative of the Stepney Nursing Development Unit,[15] had focused on user groups and included a local campaign to raise awareness about good leg ulcer care. Many features of the programme can be traced back to the learning contributed by these related activities which pre-dated the project.

As an *action research* project, the East London Leg Ulcer Project (in common with all other action research) had two central concerns: improvements in practice, and increased knowledge and understanding.[16] The methodology requires a flexible approach which means that objectives and methods cannot be rigidly or precisely determined in advance.[17] In an implementation project, we regard this ability to adapt to circumstances as an important advantage. We are aware that this flexibility and the absence of tight, pre-determined objectives may be construed as a lack of a robust approach. We believe this to be a misconception and that the opposite is true, however, we have recognised the presence of a critical perspective throughout the project and hope that we have demonstrated that an action research is a viable approach for a research implementation project.

The project

Aim

The aim of the project was to improve the service and management of leg ulcers for patients of THHT, through the provision of the Leg Ulcer Care Programme and community leg ulcer clinics.[18]

Objectives

- to educate, train and facilitate health professionals within THHT in the Care Programme approach to leg ulcer management

- to set up nurse-led leg ulcer clinics with the support of general practitioners and district nurses
- to meet the needs of service users with support and education
- to reduce variability in care across the trust
- to develop the programme within a clinical audit and quality assurance framework
- to reduce inappropriate referrals to the Complex Wound Clinic
- to continue links with East London and the City Health Authority to ensure that commissioning would reflect good practice.

With hindsight it is clear that the original objectives (which were less specific than those set out above) were over-ambitious, not least because the Care Programme on which the project was based was not published at the time that funding was secured and the project due to commence. The objectives were revised during the course of the project, on the one hand making them more realistic and achievable, and on the other, making them firmer and more detailed. Our project was not unique among the North Thames Implementation Projects in having to adjust its objectives; the issue of 'moving targets' being a point noted by the external evaluators.[5]

Appointing a project worker

Funding was secured in 1997 for a short-term post (nine months) for a part-time project worker (30 hours per week) who was a clinical nurse specialist in tissue viability ('G' grade). Her role was to assist the clinical nurse specialist ('H' grade) in setting up locality-based leg ulcer clinics within Tower Hamlets and to educate practitioners on the subject (based on the Care Programme). Attempts to recruit by internal secondment failed; however, the post was filled in November 1997 by a registered nurse with a first-class honours degree in podiatry. Our project worker was astute, competent and enthusiastic, and the significance of the individual's personal qualities in driving the project along cannot be overstated. Her practical approach to leadership was critical, particularly in the early stages of the project.

Changing the whole service

It was important to look at the whole service provided to patients with leg ulcers, and to refashion it, implementing changes which would provide the best chance that patients would receive optimal care at any stage of their treatment. This awareness of the whole picture and willingness to consider changes to how it fitted together was at least as important as implementing more focused changes, such as training district nurses in bandaging techniques or improving the supply of bandages and access to equipment.

The service provides continuity of care for patients living at home; ease of access to primary care-based leg ulcer clinics staffed by highly skilled nurses working closely with GPs and a clinical nurse specialist; and ease of referral to the Complex Wound Clinic.* Guidelines ensure that clients are seen within the correct setting without delay.

In order to shift the focus from 'hospital' care to a service centred on the needs of patients, with the provision of care based on clinical effectiveness and patients' best interests, it was important to rethink the role of the clinical nurse specialists. In practical terms this meant changing their job descriptions (in July 1997) to reflect their key function as *consultants* on leg ulcer care. In addition to setting out their specific responsibilities for clinical practice and service development, education and training, and research and development,[19] the clinical nurse specialists were given a trust-wide remit which enabled them to work much more effectively across the primary/secondary care interface, and their perspective shifted from *hospital* to primary care orientation.

The Leg Ulcer Care Programme

The Care Programme was developed over three years by a multiprofessional group with the aim of facilitating improved management through evidence-based practice and careful documentation of leg ulcers. Our belief that management of this could be improved was supported by a large body of evidence which shows that healing rates have improved following implementation of guidelines, and the introduction of effective training and resources.[20,21]

Auditing

While some auditing of leg ulcer care had been performed in the trust, a complete baseline audit (as described by Tinkler *et al.*, 1999[22]) was not undertaken. With hindsight we recognise this as a weakness in our approach, however, at the time a range of factors led to our decision not to attempt to measure the baseline. We justified this decision on the following grounds.

---

*The Complex Wound Clinic (also known as the East London Wound Healing Centre) comprises a multiprofessional team with a consultant physician, consultant dermatologist, podiatrist, clinical nurse specialist, medical photographer and other nursing staff. It includes an outpatient clinic and inpatient beds and the system is bound together by the clinical nurse specialist, who has contact with patients in each area of care.

First, we had difficulty with determining an appropriate point at which a 'baseline' should be measured. The gradual take-off of the project and the ongoing nature of training and the development of the Care Programme meant that assessment procedures and referral pathways were clarified over a period of time. Because work was already underway before the project was funded, and progress was incremental and continuous, no specific point in time could be regarded as the baseline.

Second, we were aware that it would have taken months to devise a way of obtaining the audit data required as none of the requisite systems were in place. We took the view that our priority was to make progress rather than to establish the status quo (which we felt that we understood in general terms, and wanted most of all to improve upon).

Finally, we were aware of detailed audits from other centres which had found that the type of care provided by district nurses was variable, ad hoc and ineffective.[21,23] We had no reason to think that healing rates and clinician competence would be any higher in our trust than in these other centres which were also providing a service without consistent standards or effective clinical guidelines.[21]

With hindsight we think that we should have undertaken a simple baseline audit, which would have provided basic information on the number of patients being treated for leg ulcers and length of time they had been suffering from them. This would have provided an important comparison with the audit conducted in October 1998.[24] Nevertheless, we think that the most important measurement is that which compares current treatment with best practice. This shows the distance from optimal healing rates, and focuses on the gains yet to be realised rather than any progress already achieved. Reflecting on a percentage improvement in healing rates (which would have been possible if a full audit/re-audit cycle had been performed) might have diverted attention from the fact that *despite* significant progress, care remains suboptimal.

Guidelines

Producing guidelines required someone to produce drafts, co-ordinate the contributions of colleagues and ensure that the task was completed.[4] The development phase took over two years, which was not an unsurprising length of time given the empirical nature of the task and the fact that other priorities were competing for attention (including the parallel development of a Pressure Sore Care Programme).[25] Draft national guidelines were not available during the life of the project but were finally published in September 1998.[26] Notwithstanding these difficulties, we were keen to produce good, evidence-based local guidelines, because we were not content with the applicability of the few evidence-based guidelines which it would have been possible to 'import'. (For example, our view was that the work undertaken at Charing Cross[20] was biased towards the exclusive use of four-layer bandaging at that time.) Lessons had been learned from the implementation and audit of the Tower Hamlets Pressure Sore Care Programme and these were incorporated into the format of the assessment tool (*see* Appendix 2). This has resulted in the routine capture of information about the factors affecting the healing of particular ulcers as well as their actual healing *rates*. The final draft of the Care Programme was sent out to wide consultation in March 1998 to district nurses, hospital consultants, hospital nurses and GPs. A number of helpful comments were received and incorporated into the Care Programme. A common message from those consulted was that familiarity with the Care Programme approach within the trust and their understanding and acceptance that clinicians would be expected to *use* the documents had reinforced their motivation for appraising the Leg Ulcer Care Programme.

Obstacles to implementation

Printing

Working with commercial printers (in producing the Care Programme documentation) was a learning experience for the project team, and a number of problems resulted in the failure of the contractor to meet the deadlines (and the delay of the launch from July to September 1998). With hindsight it would have been advantageous if, rather than organising this ourselves, we had drawn on the expertise of others in the trust.

Sponsorship

The trust had been successful in securing sponsorship from drug/dressings companies to assist in the print costs for previous Care Programmes. Despite great efforts, only one company involved in leg ulcer management made a contribution to the publication of the Care Programme (although a second company did contribute to the cost of the launch). This meant that the trust had to bear most of the total cost (over £4000 for 500 ring-binder file copies). We think that the difficulty in attracting sponsors in this case can be attributed to the fact that dressing products were named only generically in the Care Programme. This meant that companies that were potential sponsors felt that their products would not necessarily be promoted, and that consequently sponsorship was not commercially attractive.

Launch

The Leg Ulcer Care Programme was launched in September 1998 at a lunch-time gathering, sponsored by two companies. The event was attended by members of the Trust Board, consultants, nurses and many other colleagues who had been involved in developing the programme. Representatives from carers' groups and leg ulcer patients themselves attended (which encouraged the project team). More patients may have come had we been able to offer them transport.

Dissemination

Copies of the Care Programme were sent to all ward, district and practice nursing teams, to each GP, and to consultants and managers in the trust. Additional copies were made available to other local clinicians who had expressed interest. In working to secure the implementation of the Care Programme, a variety of strategies, including continuing professional education, mailings, audit and targeted feedback delivered by the clinical nurse specialists, were used.[27] Conference presentations and listings in relevant network directories are increasingly used as means of sharing ideas and products from projects, and we have been keen to promote our Care Programme in this way. To date copies of this Care Programme have been sold to other providers in the UK, Europe, Hong Kong and Australia.*

Education

Briefing sessions were arranged for practitioners to show them how to use the new programme and how to obtain the clinical documentation which was necessary to follow it. Workshop sessions allowed practitioners to familiarise themselves with the Care Programme approach and the assessment tools, relating the guidelines to real patients. An existing two-day, in-service course on leg ulcer management for registered nurses was re-structured around the Leg Ulcer Care Programme.

Audit

Audit time had been secured for 1997/98 and due to the delay in the implementation of the Care Programme we were in danger of 'losing' this. It was therefore decided in January 1998 that we would launch the Assessment Tool

---

*Readers wishing to purchase a copy of the Leg Ulcer Care Programme should contact Alison Hopkins at Tower Hamlets Healthcare NHS Trust, Primary Care Building, Mile End Hospital, Bancroft Road, London E1 4DG. At the time of writing the cost is £25.

and Treatment Plan in advance of the full Care Programme (in addition to supporting information, *Doppler Guidelines* and *Use of the Assessment Tool*), so that the audit time identified could be used productively. A documentation audit of the effectiveness of the initial implementation of the Care Programme was conducted in March 1998 with the assistance of the trust's Clinical Audit Department.[28]

It showed that two months into implementation of the Assessment Tool and Treatment Plan there was variable compliance with the Care Programme's specifications for the documentation of information (the range was 62.5% to 86% compliance across the 26 patient records audited). Confirmation of agreement to the Treatment Plan with the patients' GPs was rare (evidenced from a tick-box on the Treatment Plan document). However, when compared with an audit six months previously (of pressure sores, where wound care would be similar), the use of the wound assessment and evaluation forms suggested that there was likely to have been substantial improvement in wound bed evaluation. Recommendations following the audit have focused on the content of the training provided, management action to ensure that all nurses assessing receive training, and the continued involvement of the clinical nurse specialists in increasing the competence of colleagues. A leg ulcer healing and documentation audit was carried out after completion of the project in September 1999. Healing data is still being collated – however, preliminary results show that 91% of clients are now assessed using the Care Programme, with 38% of clients being seen in community clinics. It was noteworthy that 33% of clients remained on the Prevention Care Plan and were not simply discharged when their ulcers had healed.*

The leg ulcer clinics

Community leg ulcer clinics are usually staffed by district nurses, who treat patients from the local area with support from a clinical nurse specialist. Patients who cannot travel to the clinic continue to be treated in their own homes and others are treated by practice nurses within general practice. The advantages of clinics are that treatment can be standardised across the geographical patch covered by a trust, practitioner expertise is built up and staff travelling time is reduced.[21] It is also easier to compare and focus attention on improving the healing rates for each patient. The project team adapted a model of development that had been applied successfully in a neighbouring trust (Newham Community Health Services NHS Trust)[21] to meet the needs of the local teams and their patients. It comprised locality-based clinics managed by the district nursing teams.

---

*To obtain results from the re-audit readers should also contact Alison Hopkins.

Securing commitment from clinicians

The project team was fully aware of the evidence that leg ulcer clinics would facilitate improved management and healing rates,[20,29] and assumed that colleagues in primary care would share this understanding and react positively towards setting up leg ulcer clinics. In fact, in the majority of cases, this assumption was incorrect. It had been based on the team's contact with a small number of enthusiastic and vocal clinicians, who were not typical of their peers. This led to a significant underestimation of the amount of work required in getting the clinics established.

The clinical nurse specialists set out to generate interest among district nurses and GPs in hosting clinics through meetings, training sessions and by letter. It seemed important to set out the vision for the clinics and their place within the local Tissue Viability Service. Presenting the 'bigger picture' was found to engender enthusiasm and commitment. The role of the clinical nurse specialist and the support that would be offered to practitioners and patients was made explicit.

Some district nurses appeared to be interested until they realised the degree to which they would personally have to be involved. They worried about the time commitment, particularly as the clinics were to be founded on the principle that they would treat patients who were not solely part of their 'own caseload' and who may require time-consuming care. A key issue was whether nurses should be involved if they had only a few patients who could attend the clinic. The incentive offered by clinics to district nurses, that it would reduce home visits, was in this case not relevant. However, the educational aspects for staff and students were appreciated and this became the focus of involvement for teams which had only small numbers of patients able to attend a clinic.

We were aware that the district nurses had always perceived the role of the clinical nurse specialist to be one of 'helper', a colleague from whom they could expect support and assistance. If district nurses were sceptical about the project there was a risk that their relationships with the clinical nurse specialists (who were driving the project) could be adversely affected. We considered it essential to try to understand the perspective of the unenthusiastic clinicians and to find some common ground. The clinical nurse specialists also found it effective to focus attention on the most enthusiastic member of each team, looking for (and often achieving) a 'knock-on' effect to their colleagues. We found that the persuasive influence of enthusiastic practitioners was very important, both in terms of fostering commitment to the Care Programme approach within the team and in promoting the project to other teams.

Some of the more reluctant practitioners questioned whether they needed any additional clinical nurse specialist input at all, as they believed that they already had good healing rates (however, they did not have data to support this view). A telephone survey as part of the project's evaluation revealed that staff felt that (previously) they had not 'been providing the quality of care that they should have been'.[6] We believe that since their introduction the clinics have become generally accepted as high-quality learning environments for pre-registration nurses, new team members and experienced practitioners alike, and that the reluctance of some practitioners to get involved has diminished as this acceptance has taken root. Several practitioners have stated that despite teething problems, an increased workload and less than ideal premises (such as carpeted rooms with only one sink), they are committed to the success of the project because they can see that the benefits outweigh any inconveniences.

The location of clinics

The decision as to number and site of these clinics was based on the following criteria:

- the needs of the population
- the commitment of enthusiastic key practitioners
- the availability of premises
- knowledge of the teams' development track record.

Two clinics have been established during the period of the project and a third clinic opened later during the summer of 1999.

Staffing

The first clinic, Newby Place, was staffed by the same practitioners each week, whereas the second clinic, Steels Lane, was staffed by several different nursing teams from the locality. The model of staffing used at Newby Place required less input from the clinical nurse specialists as the district nurses' own expertise increased quickly through their growing familiarity with the work. The Steels Lane clinic involves seven district nursing teams, treating patients from four group practices. A three-monthly rota has been used to share the work fairly across all teams and assure cover. The clinic has been staffed for a two-hour period by a 'G' grade district nurse, and two associate nurses ('D' or 'E' grade), and they generally see around eight patients per clinic. The clinical nurse specialists' input has been greater due to the reduced opportunity for staff to become experienced at leg ulcer management. In both clinics, student nurses placed with the registered nurses have been encouraged to participate.

Non-pay costs

The cost of setting up the clinics was initially low (in the region of a few hundred pounds for buckets for soaking patients' legs, stationery and minor items of equipment for each clinic), however, more funding was required for double sinks (essential for good practice) and this was secured from the trust. (These cost in the region of £400 each.) Staff costs were already covered as were the costs of dressings and bandages which were either obtained on prescription by the patient or provided by the district nurses from stock.

Premises

Establishing all clinics within trust premises proved expedient. We thought that the second clinic would be easy to establish, because a twice-weekly leg ulcer clinic (exclusively for one practice's *own* patients) had been running there since 1989. In fact, it proved difficult, because the clinic was located in a part of the health centre used by GPs, who foresaw problems if patients from other practices were treated there. As the district nurses were keen to establish the clinic without the need for protracted negotiations it was relocated to alternative (though less appropriate) trust premises. Subsequently a successful bid for capital to refurbish another room for the purpose has led to the clinic being moved again.

Problem solving

A number of problem-solving strategies were developed which helped the leg ulcer clinics to be established and to work well. We were able to present once-weekly clinics as not only a more convenient alternative to traditional, twice-weekly attendances, but also to reassure nurses that compression bandages are effective over this interval.[30] It was emphasised that appropriate weekly care at a clinic would be more effective than less well-structured care, even if the latter involved more frequent dressing of wounds.

One team had wanted the clinic to be implemented but felt it did not have the time to set it up. The project worker facilitated progress by preparing packs containing standard GP letters and patient information, and giving tips based on how to make leg ulcer clinics work. These included the type of equipment and stationery that each clinic would need to hold, and addressed issues of infection control and manual handling. Furthermore, the following protocols were developed to cover the use of buckets which are used for soaking patients' legs:

- the use of 'clean' and 'dirty' sinks
- lifting buckets
- distances to the disposal area
- the provision of couches
- correct bending techniques for bandaging.

Future provision

The third clinic, close to a borough boundary, was proposed by an experienced district nurse working within a supportive and innovative GP practice based at Bromley-by-Bow Health Centre. The nursing team was keen to set up a leg ulcer clinic at these premises and despite difficulties with the lease of the building and delays surrounding the provision of a sluice this clinic was opened in summer 1999.

A fourth target area was identified, however, it was not assumed that all GPs here would be keen for leg ulcer clinics to be set up. In planning this clinic, each GP in the area was sent an individual letter explaining the project and inviting comments on the proposal to establish a fourth clinic within their locality. Four responses were received from 70 letters sent, and two of these were negative. The low response may be attributable to GP workloads or possibly a general lack of interest in leg ulcer care. If a fourth clinic is to be set up, there is clearly a need for a considerable amount of preparatory work which is, of course, way beyond the lifetime of the project. However, there is keen interest from nursing staff, and a fourth clinic remains a distinct possibility.

Experience

The Leg Ulcer Care Programme

The Leg Ulcer Care Programme is an evidence-based, patient-centred tool, which users have reported as being easy to use. It is in operation in Tower Hamlets and there has been interest from other centres, either in adopting the tool as it is or in adapting to other local circumstances. We believe that the Care Programmes enable 'generalist' practitioners to assess and manage clinically more of the patients' needs to a higher standard than they would otherwise be capable of doing. If our view is correct it follows that the improved quality of care provided within primary care will contribute to the avoidance of a proportion of referrals to secondary care.

Guidelines

Even the best guidelines will not necessarily change practice, and short-term impact is most unlikely to result from their dissemination. We have found that continuous effort is required to embed the use of guidelines into everyday practice, and we would suggest that this is a process which is best considered in a time frame of years rather than months. A corresponding commitment to auditing patient outcomes and an economic analysis of the changes in practice achieved is also desirable. Our view is that a long-term, comprehensive approach to the implementation of guidelines will be necessary if the potential for guidelines to contribute to clinical governance is to be fulfilled.[3]

Education for evidence-based practice

As part of the Care Programme, clinicians in Tower Hamlets have had access to high-quality clinical documentation for assessment and care planning, and ongoing, evidence-based, practical training in leg ulcer management. The clinical nurse specialists have been readily available to provide telephone advice and joint assessments which we have found enabled practitioners to make progress in changing their practice to reflect the research evidence.

Reducing variability in patient outcomes and costs

The Leg Ulcer Care Programme was designed first and foremost to reduce variability in the standard of care by standardising treatment across the trust. Cost benefits have been achieved through prompt and appropriate management, and through reduced referrals from primary care to the Complex Wound Clinic and earlier discharge from the Complex Wound Clinic. The Care Programme approach facilitates audit, both of its use and healing rates.

A sample audit comparing the first 20 new referrals to the Complex Wound Clinic in 1997 with the first 20 new referrals in 1999 indicates the change in referral pattern (i.e. in 1999 there were fewer inappropriate referrals from the local area, and more appropriate referrals, including some from further afield). However, small numbers limit the robustness of the findings.

Meeting the needs of service users

Service users' need for information has been addressed within the Care Programme with guidance for staff providing verbal and written information about leg ulcers. In addition, a leaflet about the Care Programme has been produced to inform the public (*see* Appendix 3). The clinical nurse specialists have been well received when they addressed local carers' groups. The structure of care offered to patients with leg ulcers is now explicit, ensuring that there is clarity about referral pathways, particularly for persistently non-healing wounds. Our experience has been that this is highly valued by patients because it alleviates their anxiety.

Working across professions and organisations

The Care Programme benefited from the input of a number of clinical professions in its development phase, although its implementation has been driven by nurses. (It has also most affected the practice of nurses.) This may not be surprising, given the nature of the clinical condition, however our much lower rate of success in engaging doctors (especially GPs) with the Care Programme has been somewhat disheartening. We think that this difficulty may be the consequence of their view of wound care as the 'nurse's domain' and GPs' belief that the Care Programme is not something which they would personally use regularly.

Our view is that it is essential for local GPs to be more involved and committed to best practice in leg ulcer care if more clinics are to be set up. Experience in the project taught us that involvement of GPs is particularly advantageous when doctors are well informed about the current evidence-base for management, because nurses feel supported in their decision making and more comfortable in asking for medical advice. As a consequence, further steps will be taken to canvas GPs before any attempt is made to set up further clinics.

The involvement in the project of colleagues from neighbouring acute and community trusts, and an individual GP, was significant, and given the complexity of the relationships between provider organisations during the lifetime of the project, quite surprising. It relied heavily on personal professional relationships built up between individuals, and our view is that the cultivation of cross-organisational alliances such as this will almost always be an essential pre-requisite for the success of an implementation project. In our case the clinical nurse specialists were key to the project's success. The work fitted neatly with their core functions[19] and undoubtedly extended the range and level of their skills, and changed the nature of their clinical work and relationships with colleagues and patients. They were empowered by their participation in the project, and led parts of the work autonomously. Nevertheless the view of the project manager is that they could not have functioned effectively without the contributions and support of the expert medical colleagues in the team.

Conclusions

Our project was not just 'trial and error'[31]; we regard it as being systematic, rigorous and methodical.[17] It was based on knowledge and experience of the development processes that are likely to be effective.[4] It worked on a clinical topic where closing the gap between theory and practice was feasible. Initiatives were carefully selected and planned, and there was a high level of awareness of the risks of failure, which included potential damage to the clinical effectiveness drive in the trust.

Ensuring the sustainability of the project

It is doubtful whether at the beginning of the project many trust staff recognised that the work on leg ulcers was a distinct project with dedicated funding. It proved difficult at times to ensure that organisational support for the project was in place, despite the fact that the work itself was very clinically focused. It took a long time for the potential of Care Programmes to become apparent to all senior managers in the trust. Over time, however, the project has become more visible, and we think that this has helped to underscore the primary care emphasis of tissue viability. The desire to bring about improvements in leg ulcer care is now shared by many practitioners, and the impetus for change no longer lies solely with the clinical nurse specialists. We are optimistic that momentum will be sustained and we regard the success of bids for funding to improve clinic facilities as a good sign. Overall, reflecting on the project has enabled the team to visualise new opportunities for development and growth.

Plan for the future

Priorities for the first year after the close of the project include:

- further discussions to clarify the role of the clinical nurse specialist to reassure general practice that there is no intention to de-skill community nurses
- opening further clinics as opportunities arise

- managing clinical risk (principally infection control and manual handling issues), i.e. ensuring that new clinics have the proper equipment and the understanding of how to use it
- further development of educational work with patients and carers
- further work on the training packages for use with a variety of professionals in conjunction with the East London Wound Healing Centre
- continuing audit
- seeking funding for an additional clinical nurse specialist post to replace the project worker.

Acknowledgements

The authors acknowledge the funding and support provided by the Implementation Group of the North Thames R&D; the role of the external evaluators; and the contribution of many clinicians, managers, audit and other support staff in the trust. The consistent support of Dr Richard Bull (Consultant Dermatologist) and Dr Gerry Bennett (Consultant Physician) was particularly important due to their clinical expertise and a vision for a co-ordinated service.

Lessons learned

- **Overambition.** The project team overestimated what could be achieved with relatively small resources in a short timescale. In our view the project was saved by having the flexibility to amend the timetable and refocus objectives once we appreciated the impracticality of aspects of the original plans.
- **The value of dedicated project staff.** The appointment of a dedicated project worker was essential, as was the consistent involvement of the clinical nurse specialist (project manager) whose vision was critical to the project, and who has continued the work beyond the lifetime of the project.
- **Measuring change.** Although we believe we had good reasons for not doing a baseline audit at the time, with hindsight a simple audit of leg ulcer care within the trust would have been valuable in measuring progress. Although we can now obtain healing rates, the lack of 'before' information means that we cannot compare these objectively with care before the project began.
- **Being political.** It was important to try to ensure that individuals with the power to influence the progress of a project were supportive (or at the very least not threatened nor offended). Corporate support mattered.
- **Being committed to a multiprofessional approach.** We found that it was important to constantly revisit this important dimension of a

continued overleaf

Multiprofessional approach to the project to avoid losing it. We found that the multiprofessional consensus was threatened by delays, organisational change and the risk of enthusiasts running too far ahead of the broader, multiprofessional constituency of practitioners, whose commitment was vital to sustaining the changes achieved.

- **The importance of maximising support.** The sympathetic support of the funding body and the evaluators was very important to the morale of the project staff, which undoubtedly affected their performance. Action research involves working with a level of uncertainty that can be uncomfortable for a bureaucratic organisation,[4] and with hindsight we think that the pace of progress in the project could have been increased if:
  - the nature of action research had been better understood by the project team at the start, and that understanding had been more widely shared
  - project management techniques had been adopted earlier
  - the host organisation had been signed up to contributing necessary supplementary resources at an earlier stage.

- **Working with printers and sponsors.** Experience is required if pitfalls of working with external organisations are to be avoided. Lessons we learned included:
  - maximising economies of scale when getting material commercially printed (e.g. ordering more copies than the minimum required – 1000 instead of 500)
  - ensuring that prices quoted are inclusive of VAT and 'finishing' (e.g. hole punching)
  - being assertive and specifying in writing details such as the colour and format of printed materials at the outset
  - including financial penalties in contracts with external suppliers (if they fail to meet deadlines)
  - sponsors need to be nurtured and kept in regular contact. Staff changes within a sponsoring organisation can lead to disappointment unless a commitment is formalised and both parties keep in touch.

- **Investing in people with influence on the ground.** The project workers found that spending time influencing people, sharing the vision and promoting the ideas behind the project was a worthwhile investment. Keeping in regular contact with all parties and ensuring that none felt left out of the decision-making process was important. We think that it also helped to 'second-guess' the likely views of some staff in advance, so that potential problems could be worked through and avoided. We were also aware that on occasion verbalised views may not have reflected individuals' true feelings, and it was important to recognise these instances.

- **Incremental small changes.** Our view, based on the experience of the project, is that change must continue if further improvements in leg ulcer care are to be achieved. We believe that making this small project a component part of a wider agenda of changes in clinical practice and service development was critical to both the credibility and sustainability of the work.

> **Things we would do differently if we were to start tomorrow**
> - **Project planning.** We underestimated the importance of thorough project planning at the outset. With the benefit of hindsight we can see that it would be helpful to:
>   - be realistic in project planning and test rigorously whether the project plans are deliverable before the project plan is submitted
>   - be careful not to base a project on untested assumptions about colleagues' acceptance of the evidence for changing practice
>   - not assume that managers will sign up to a project; their support may require investment, but their commitment is vital
>   - work hard to keep focused on the multiprofessional dimensions of the project.
> - **Baseline audit.** We would invest a proportion of the project's resources in a baseline audit because demonstrating improvement in healing rates provides the ultimate proof that an initiative to upgrade the care of patients with leg ulcers is working.

References

1   Bellman LM (1996) Challenging nursing practice through reflection on the Roper, Logan and Tierney model: the enhancement approach to action research. *Journal of Advanced Nursing.* **24**: 129–38.

2   Hopkins A, Gooch S and Danks F (1998) A programme for pressure sore prevention and management. *Journal of Wound Care.* **7(1)**: 37–40.

3   Chadburn S, Haggar V and Gooch S (1998) Developing a continence care programme. *Professional Nurse.* **14**: 1.

4   Gooch S (1998) An evaluation of an action research project: Care Programme development, implementation and audit in a NHS Trust. South Bank University, London. Unpublished MSc thesis.

5   Wilson J (1994) The multidisciplinary pathway to improved quality, cost and outcomes. *Clinician in Management.* **3(6)**: 2–5.

6   Smith L and McClenahan J (1997) *Putting practitioners through the paces: initial findings in our evaluation of putting evidence into practice.* King's Fund, London.

7   Smith L and McClenahan J (1998) *Snakes and Ladders: initial findings in our evaluation of putting evidence into practice.* King's Fund, London.

8   Cullum N and Roe B (eds) (1995) *Leg Ulcers: nursing management. A research-based guide.* Scutari Press, London.

9   Blair S and Riddle E (1988) Sustained compression and healing of chronic venous ulcers. *BMJ.* **297**: 1159–61.

10 Callam MJ, Ruckley CV, Harper DR and Dale JJ (1985) Chronic ulceration of the leg: extent of the problem and provision of care. *BMJ.* **290**: 1855–6.

11 Fridsma DB, Gennari JH and Musen MA (1996) Making generic guidelines site-specific. *Proc AMIA Annual Fall Symposium:* 597–601.

12 THHT (1998) *Leg Ulcer Care Programme.* Tower Hamlets Healthcare NHS Trust, London.

13 Hopkins A (1991) *Proposals for the effective treatment of leg ulcers in the Community and Priority Services Unit of The Royal London Trust* (internal paper).

14 Hopkins A and Forsyth J (1995) Giving patients power. *Community Nurse.* **October**.

15 Gooch S (1993) Nursing development units. Health options. *Nursing Times.* **89(8)**: 41–3.

16 Malterud K (1995) Action research – a strategy for evaluation of medical intervention. *Family Practice.* **12(4)**: 476–81.

17 Room G (1986) *Cross-national Innovation in Social Policy.* Macmillan, London.

18 Thorne E (1998) Community leg ulcer clinics and the effectiveness of care. *Journal of Wound Care.* **7**: 94–9.

19 Hamric AB (1989) History and overview of the CNS role. In: AB Hamric and J Spross (eds) *The Clinical Nurse Specialist in Theory and Practice.* Grune and Stratton, New York.

20 Moffatt C *et al.* (1992) Community clinics for leg ulcers and impact on healing. *BMJ.* **305**: 1389–92.

21 Dowsett C (1997) Improving leg ulcer care in the community. *Professional Nurse.* **12(12)**: 861–3.

22 Tinkler A, Nelson EA and Edwards L (1999) Implementing evidence-based leg ulcer management. *Evidence-Based Nursing.* **2(1)**.

23 Cornwall JV, Dore CJ and Lewis JD (1986) Leg ulcers: epidemiology and aetiology. *British Journal of Surgery.* **73**: 693–6.

24 City and Hackney Community Services NHS Trust, Newham Community Services NHS Trust, Tower Hamlets Healthcare NHS Trust (1998) *East London Wide Leg Ulcer Audit March.* Unpublished report.

25 THHT (1997) *Pressure Sore Care Programme.* Tower Hamlets Healthcare NHS Trust.

26 Royal College of Nursing (1998) *Clinical Practice Guidelines: the management of patients with venous leg ulcers.* RCN, London.

27 Madhok R and Green S (1994) Orthopaedic outpatient referral guidelines: experience in an English health district. *International Journal of Quality Health Care.* **6(1)**: 73–6.

28 THHT (1998) *An Audit of the Leg Ulcer Care Programme: the assessment and treatment plans.* Tower Hamlets Healthcare Trust, London.

29 Lambourne LA, Moffat CJ, Jones AC, Dorman MC and Franks PJ (1996) Clinical audit and effective change in leg ulcer services. *Journal of Wound Care.* **5(8)**: 348–51.

30 Nelson EA (1996) Compression bandaging in the treatment of venous leg ulcers. *Journal of Wound Care.* **5(9)**: 415–8.

31 Rolfe G (1996) Going to extremes: action research, grounded practice and the theory–practice gap in nursing. *Journal of Advanced Nursing.* **24**: 1315–20.

Appendix 1 Leg ulcer treatment plan

Leg Ulcer Care Programme

Leg Ulcer Treatment Plan

ON CARE PLAN ☐   Has the treatment been agreed with the client's GP?   Yes ☐   No ☐

Patient's name _____   Date _____

Record No. _____   Ward/ clinic _____

		Right Leg	Left Leg	Notes
Cleansing/ Soaking	*Emollient*			
	or Irrigate			
	or Antiseptic			
Skin Care	*Emollient*			
	Steroid			
	Antibacterial			
	Other			
Dressing	*1*			
	2			
	3			
Bandaging	*1*			
	2			
	3			
	4			
Information	*Dressing Frequency*			
	Hosiery			
	Pain Control			
	Review Comments			

Please ensure all preparations used in treatment are detailed above.
Please sign and date below each time the above treatment plan is used.

Date										
Signature										

Page 11

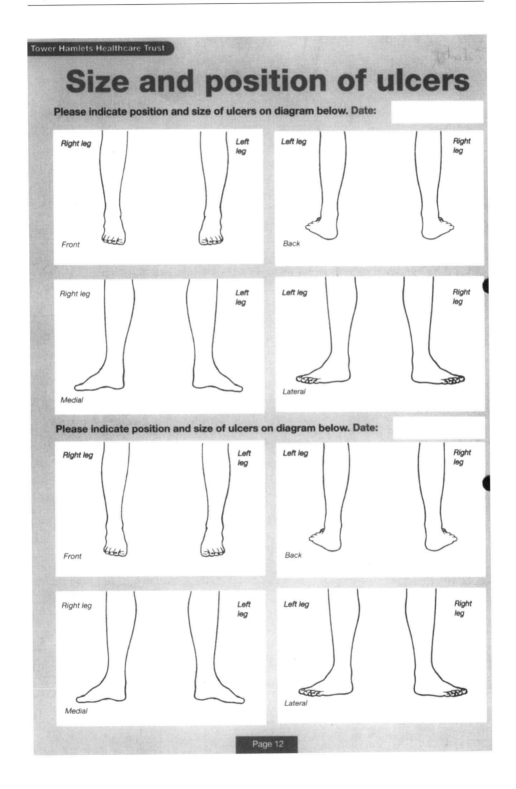

Tower Hamlets Healthcare Trust

Size and position of ulcers

Please indicate position and size of ulcers on diagram below. Date:

Right leg — Left leg
Front

Left leg — Right leg
Back

Right leg — Left leg
Medial

Left leg — Right leg
Lateral

Please indicate position and size of ulcers on diagram below. Date:

Right leg — Left leg
Front

Left leg — Right leg
Back

Right leg — Left leg
Medial

Left leg — Right leg
Lateral

Page 12

Leg Ulcer Care Programme

Quality of Life Assessment

Dear patient,

We would be grateful if you would take five minutes to complete the following questionnaire by circling the most appropriate number on the scales. After three months we will ask you to complete the same form again so that we can see whether the treatment of your leg ulcer has made a difference to you. Please ask your nurse if you need help filling in the form. Thank you for your time.

At the present time, do you experience pain from your ulcer?

0	1	2	3	4	5	6	7

Not at all   *very much so*

Do you currently have trouble sleeping?

0	1	2	3	4	5	6	7

Not at all   *very much so*

Do you currently find it difficult to get about because of your ulcer?

0	1	2	3	4	5	6	7

Not at all   *very much so*

Is your appetite currently:

Better than it was/ Yes/No   **Worse than it was/ Yes/No**

Does your ulcer currently prevent you from working?

0	1	2	3	4	5	6	7

Not at all   *very much so*

Does your ulcer currently prevent you from carrying out household duties?

0	1	2	3	4	5	6	7

Not at all   *very much so*

Does your ulcer currently prevent you from enjoying leisure or social activities?

0	1	2	3	4	5	6	7

Not at all   *very much so*

Does your ulcer currently affect your personal relationships?

0	1	2	3	4	5	6	7

Not at all   *very much so*

Does your ulcer currently make you feel low in mood?

0	1	2	3	4	5	6	7

Not at all   *very much so*

Have you felt more anxious since having a leg ulcer?

0	1	2	3	4	5	6	7

Not at all   *very much so*

Do you feel that your ulcer limits your life or makes you feel isolated?

0	1	2	3	4	5	6	7

Not at all   *very much so*

Tower Hamlets Healthcare Trust

Care Plan 1 PREVENTION OF VENOUS LEG ULCERS

- Cients whose clinical condition puts them at risk of venous leg ulcers
- Clients whose venous leg ulcer has healed

OUTCOMES

All patients with venous ulceration will be fitted with compression hosiery after 4 weeks of healing

90% of patients identified as at risk of venous ulceration will be fitted with compression hosiery

70% of patients will remain healed at 18 months

60% of patients will remain healed after 3 years

ASSESSMENT

Comments, date & signature

- Document Leg Ulcer assessment.

- Refer to appendix for characteristics of venous disease and hosiery.

- Ankle Brachial Pressure Index should be greater than 0.8. Refer to appendix 1.

- If ABPI < 0.7, hosiery may still be applicable: refer to CNS.

MANAGEMENT

Comments, date & signature

- Life time compression hosiery therapy is essential, ideally with Class 2 . See hosiery appendix 3.

- Leg measurement (to determine stock or made-to-measure). Document measurements on diagrams on back of treatment plan.

- Assess need for aids for application of hosiery.

- If unable to tolerate hosiery, please document the reasons for this and refer on to CNS.

- Rehydrate any dry skin with Aqueous or Diprobase cream.

Page 14

CLIENT INFORMATION

- The aims and expectations should be discussed and supported by written client information of treatment e.g. *'A Patient's Guide to Graduated Compression Hosiery'* (3M).

- Report any traumatic leg wounds to the district nurse to ensure prompt treatment.

- Discuss self-help strategies e.g.

  - Basic exercises for walking and when at rest

  - Discuss with client how to avoid trauma to leg e.g. wearing thick socks and extra caution in high risk places e.g. in supermarkets (trolley trauma)

  - Discourage smoking

  - Ensure correct fitting shoes and socks

Comments, date & signature

REVIEW

- Review at least every six months for repeat ABPI and check leg measurements.

If client is wearing FP10 hosiery, they will need a review after 3 months for new hosiery but continental class hosiery only needs renewing every 6 months.

If previously unable to tolerate hosiery, review the factors causing this and assess for possible hosiery at 6 month intervals.

Comments, date & signature

Tower Hamlets Healthcare Trust

Care Plan 2 — VENOUS LEG ULCERS

- For clients assessed as having a venous ulcer
- For clients with non-healing traumatic leg wounds

OUTCOMES

Healing rates: 60% of patients will be healed twelve weeks after assessment.

Healing rates: 70% of patients will be healed six months after assessment

Healing rates: 85% of patients will be healed one year after assessment

All patients will have an improvement in their pain after assessment

All patients will have a quality of life assessment on enrolment to care plan and 3 months later.

All patients will be referred on for specialist advice if there is no improvement in healing after three weeks of treatment.

ASSESSMENT

Comments, date & signature

- Document Leg Ulcer assessment.

- Refer to appendix for characteristics of venous disease.

- Ankle Brachial Pressure Index should be greater than 0.8. Refer to appendix 1.

- Document nutritional assessment.

MANAGEMENT

Comments, date & signature

- Ideally, soak leg in warm water with emollient such as Hydromol. If soaking is not possible, apply aqueous cream to the legs and wash or shower off. Bathing is not contra-indicated.

- Pat dry and moisturise the leg (Aqueous cream or 50% white soft paraffin/ liquid paraffin mix) using downward strokes. Remember to check expiry date of creams and ointments.

- Apply simple low adherence dressing. This is adequate for most ulcers but practitioner discretion or client preference may dictate otherwise.

- Apply bandaging system (see over)

Page 16

- Choose the compression system, in liaison with the clients' GP/Consultant, that is judged to be the most appropriate based upon the ankle circumference and client preference. A gentle introduction to compression such as Velband, crepe and Elset only for the first session may increase patient tolerance to compression.

N.B. All bandages are applied spirally unless otherwise indicated.

Comments, date & signature

1.   MULTI-LAYER SYSTEM

Ankle Circumference	Bandage Combinations	Ankle Circumference	Bandage Combinations
Less than 18cm	2 or more Velband 1 Crepe 1 Elset (Fig. 8) 1 Coban	18cm-25cm	1 Velband 1 Crepe 1 Elset (Fig. 8) 1 Coban *(4 Layer Bandage System)*
25cm - 30cm	1 Velband 1 Tensopress/ Setopress/Surepress 1 Coban	Greater than 30cm	1 Velband 1 Elset (Fig. 8) 1 Tensopress/Setopress Surepress 1 Coban

If reduced compression is required, (e.g. discomfort, borderline ABPI)omit the final layer until full compression is tolerated.

Comments, date & signature

2. SHORT-STRETCH
For patients who are fully mobile or who have non-ischaemic pain at night Comprilan or Rosidal K may be appropriate.

Comments, date & signature

3. LONG-STRETCH
e.g. Tensopress, Surepress or Setopress over a Velband type layer.

- Use caution when applying compression to clients who have any inflammatory disease or evidence of heart failure as they may not tolerate it.

Comments, date & signature

CLIENT AND CARER INFORMATION AND EDUCATION

Comments, date & signature

- The aims and expectations should be discussed and supported by written client information about venous disease treatment eg. *'A Patients' Guide to Venous Leg Ulcers'* (3M)

- Discuss self-help strategies e.g.basic exercises that will improve venous circulation

  - Moving feet up and down at the ankle

  - Elevating the leg to level of thighs when resting *NB A low foot stool is not adequate*

  - Discourage smoking

  - Encourage correct fitting shoes and socks

REFERRAL

Comments, date & signature

- To GP. if required

- To Nurse Specialist, Tissue Viability if no improvement or reduction in size after 3 weeks of enrolment on to the programme

REVIEW

Comments, date & signature

- Reassess bandages prior to removal, noting slippage or *'strike through'* ie. oozing through the bandage. If slippage occurs despite good application then a different bandage system should be tried otherwise treatment time is being wasted.

- Formally observe, re-assess and document condition weekly, recording any changes on the Treatment Proforma

- Once healed, measure for hosiery, remaining in full compression for 1 month

- Enrol on to the Prevention of Venous Ulcers Care Plan (Care Plan 1)

Care Plan 3   ARTERIAL ULCERS

● **For clients assessed as having an arterial ulcer**

● **For clients with an ABPI of less than 0.8**

NB: If signs of venous disease or gross oedema refer to Clinical Nurse Specialist Tissue Viability

OUTCOMES

All patients will have an improvement in their pain level after assessment.

All patients will receive education to prevent further or recurrence of ulceration.

All patients will have a quality of life assessment at enrolment onto the care plan and 3 months later.

All patients will be reviewed every 3 months to prevent deterioration and reinforce education.

ASSESSMENT

	Comments, date & signature
● Document Leg Ulcer assessment including size ● Refer to appendix 5 for characteristics of arterial disease ● Complete doppler assessment to confirm degree of arterial insufficiency (ie. <0.8) ● Nutritional Assessment	

MANAGEMENT

	Comments, date & signature
● Irrigate using warmed water or saline and apply appropriate primary dressing, securing with a conforming bandage ie. a bandage that gives no compression and only holds the dressing in place and protects the leg. Avoid applying tape directly to the skin. ● Liaise with GP for pain control and further referral if ABPI dictates .	

CLIENT AND CARER INFORMATION AND EDUCATION

	Comments, date & signature
● The aims and expectations of treatment should be discussed and supported by written client information of treatment e.g. 'A Patients' Guide to Arterial Leg Ulcers' (3M) ● Discuss self-help strategies e.g. ■ Basic exercises for walking and when at rest, depending on level of claudication present	

Tower Hamlets Healthcare Trust

CLIENT AND CARER INFORMATION/EDUCATION contd.

Comments, date & signature

- Keep feet warm

- Discourage smoking

- Encourage/ensure correct fitting shoes & socks

REFERRAL

Comments, date & signature

- If ABPI is less than 0.6 and rest pain and claudication are present, the G.P. must be informed

- If ABPI is less than 0.5 and the ankle systolic pressure less than 70mmHg, the G.P. should be asked to refer patient to vascular consultant

- To footwear clinic in Podiatry Dept. if required

- To Clinical Nurse Specialist Tissue Viability if no improvement or decrease in size after 3 weeks

- To smoking cessation clinic/Specialist, if appropriate

REVIEW

Comments, date & signature

- Re-assess and document condition weekly for 2-3 weeks or as appropriate after healing. Once healed, in addition to self-help strategies discuss with the client how to avoid trauma to leg e.g. wearing thick socks and extra caution in high risk places e.g. in supermarkets (trolley trauma).

- The patient may then be discharged with a contact number in case of future difficulties.

Page 20

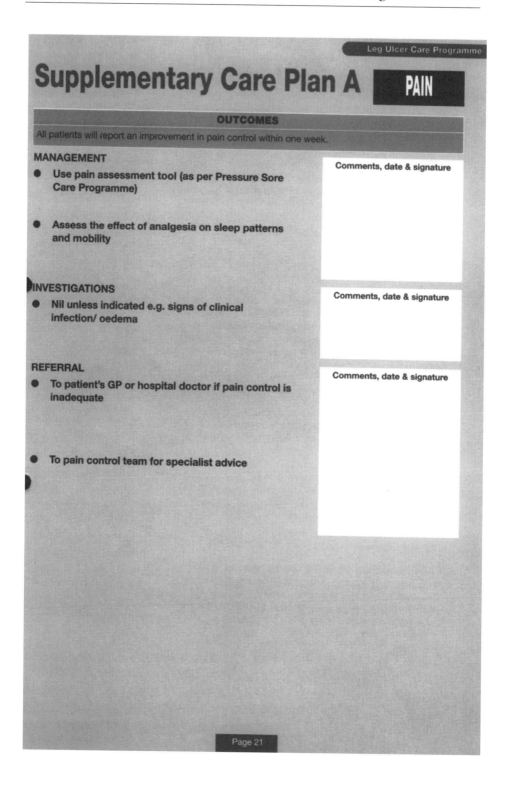

Leg Ulcer Care Programme

Supplementary Care Plan A   **PAIN**

OUTCOMES

All patients will report an improvement in pain control within one week.

MANAGEMENT

- Use pain assessment tool (as per Pressure Sore Care Programme)

- Assess the effect of analgesia on sleep patterns and mobility

Comments, date & signature

INVESTIGATIONS

- Nil unless indicated e.g. signs of clinical infection/ oedema

Comments, date & signature

REFERRAL

- To patient's GP or hospital doctor if pain control is inadequate

Comments, date & signature

- To pain control team for specialist advice

Page 21

Tower Hamlets Healthcare Trust

Supplementary Care Plan B

OUTCOMES

Clinical signs of infection will be absent in 100% of patients within one week.

ASSESSMENT

Comments, date & signature

● Note signs of clinical infection e.g. cellulitis, pain, malodour, delayed healing, friable bright red granulation tissue, increased exudate or increasing erythema around the wound.

● Take swab for microscopy, culture and sensitivity (M, C & S) after thorough cleansing of the wound either by soaking or irrigation with 0.9% Sodium Chloride and after as much slough as possible has been removed, which is a harbour for bacteria.

● *NB. All wounds are colonised by bacteria to some extent and healing is not necessarily affected. However, signs and symptoms of clinical infection, accompanied by positive microbiological results, may indicate the need for systemic antibiotic treatment.*

TREATMENT

Comments, date & signature

● Dress as required, seeking advice from the Clinical Nurse Specialist Tissue Viability.

● Daily dressings may be indicated initially so that the wound can be carefully observed. This will also help to eradicate pseudomonal infection as increased moisture and exudate facilitate its growth. Therefore, if exudate looks green , consider daily dressing changes until exudate is no longer green.

● If the exudate on the dressing remains green after one week of daily dressing changes and regular soaking/ irrigation of the ulcer, then Silver Sulphadiazine (Flamazine) can be applied to the wound for 2 weeks. This is effective against pseudomonas infection and soothing for the patient but avoid application to surrounding skin to prevent maceration.

● Do not use topical antibiotics in creams or dressings.

Page 22

REFERRAL

- To GP or hospital doctor if signs of clinical infection are present. Encourage liason with Medical Microbiology prior to treatment with antimicrobials.

Comments, date & signature

- To the Clinical Nurse Specialist Infection Control or Tissue Viability if persistent infection present or culture reveals resistant organisms.

REVIEW

- Re-assess and document condition weekly, noting when infection no longer present.

Comments, date & signature

- It is recommended that the same practitioner should assess and undertake these reviews to improve continuity and effectiveness of care.

Supplementary Care Plan C   DIABETES

● **For clients who have leg ulcers but are also diabetic**

NB. This Treatment Plan is not for use with diabetic foot ulcers.
Clients with diabetes may have microvascular disease, which would not be revealed by use of the Doppler Ultrasound. The ABPI may then have a false 'normal' reading or elevated due to calcification of the arteries.
In addition, peripheral neuropathy may also be present, reducing sensation to the foot. The client will thus be unaware of bandage constriction.

OUTCOMES

Any complications of diabetes that render compression a hazard will be identifed

All diabetic patients with leg ulcers will aim to maintain their blood sugars within the optimal range for wound healing.

MANAGEMENT

Comments, date & signature

● Monitor blood glucose levels each review. The optimum for wound healing is <8 mmols/L.

● Monitor that medication is being taken correctly.

● Encourage the client to comply with dietary regime.

● Check feet daily to detect problems at an early stage.

Appendix 2 Assessment tool from the care programme

Tower Hamlets Healthcare Trust

Date

Leg Ulcer Assessment

Patient's Surname

Forename

Address

Date of Birth

Hospital No. if known

Tel. No,

Sex: Female ☐ Male ☐

Health Centre ☐ **Ward** ☐ **GP Surgery** ☐   Source of referral

GP
Address

Has assessor attended THHT Leg Ulcer
study days?   Yes ☐ No ☐

Tel. No.

Was the Doppler carried out by the above
person?   Yes ☐ No ☐

Do not complete this section if details are already held in other records.

Name of next of kin

Name of carer
(if applicable)

Address

Address

Tel. No.

Tel. No.

SUMMARY

Care Plan (please tick✓) 1 ☐   2 ☐   3 ☐   **Both Legs**   **YES** ☐   **No** ☐
Supplementary Care Plans   A ☐   B ☐   C ☐   D ☐   E ☐

Date					
API *(Please note right and left)*					
Compression Bandaging					
Hoisery Size, class & make					

AUDIT INFORMATION

Date ulcer(s) treatment started

Past & Present Referrals

Speciality	Date	Comment/Outcome

Date limb is ulcer-free: Left   Right

Ulcer size (cm²)   Time ulcer present

Any previous ulceration?   Yes ☐ No ☐

Fixed or stiff ankle?   Yes ☐ No ☐

Seen in Leg Ulcer clinic?   Yes ☐ No ☐

If Yes, where?

Page 8

1. Assessment of Leg

ULCER HISTORY	SWELLING

Date of onset?

Is swelling present? Yes ☐ No ☐ sometimes ☐

Cause of onset? *(Spontaneous/Trauma)*

If Yes, for how long?

Treatment so far *(left and right)*

Does the swelling reduce overnight?
Yes ☐ No ☐ sometimes ☐

Previous ulceration: *location, treatment & response*

Is there a family history of swollen legs?
e.g. lymphoedema

Location and size (cm²)? Please state site. See back of Treatment Plan

PAIN Yes ☐ No ☐ If Yes, see Supplementary Care Plan for assessment.

Client's understanding of and response to ulceration: What do they think will heal the ulcer?

Please tick (✓)	Right	Left	ANKLE BRACHIAL PRESSURE INDEX		
			Please tick (✓)	Right	Left
Varicosities	☐	☐			
Oedema	☐	☐	Brachial	☐	☐
Lymphoedema	☐	☐	Ankle: dorsalis pedis	☐	☐
Induration	☐	☐			
Staining	☐	☐	Ankle: posterior tibial	☐	☐
Atrophe blanche	☐	☐	ABPI	☐	☐
Ankle flare	☐	☐			
Eczema: W=wet D=dry	☐	☐	SOUNDS:		
Palpable Pulses	☐	☐	Biphasic	☐	☐
Dry skin or scaly	☐	☐	Monophasic	☐	☐
Colour/warmth	☐	☐			
Ankle circumference	☐	☐			

For assessment of ulcer & leg: see *Wound Assessment and Evaluation form*

Tower Hamlets Healthcare Trust

2. Supporting Information

PATIENT PROFILE	BP	Pulse	Urine or BM result *(if not a known diabetic)*

MEDICAL HISTORY

Please tick (✓)	Yes	No
Stroke	☐	☐
M.I.	☐	☐
Diabetes	☐	☐
Diabetes stable?	☐	☐
HbA1		
Hypertension	☐	☐
Heart failure/angina	☐	☐
Overweight	☐	☐

Please tick (✓)	Yes	No
Recurrent cellulitis	☐	☐
Osteoarthritis	☐	☐
Site of arthritis:		
Rheumatoid arthritis	☐	☐
Malignancies *(eg skin, bowel)*	☐	☐
Anaemia/ polycythaemia	☐	☐
No. of pregnancies		
Family history of leg ulcers	☐	☐
Smoker	☐	☐
Used to smoke?	☐	☐

Previous surgery

Relevant occupation

Previous leg fractures: Yes ☐ No ☐   **Site**

Claudication *(please note walking distance and rest pain)*   Yes ☐ No ☐

MEDICATION *(State dose here if applicable)*

Antibiotics

Diuretics

Antihypertensives

Steroids (including creams)

Ascorbic acid/zinc supplements

VENOUS HISTORY

	Right		Left		Not known
DVT	Yes ☐	No ☐	Yes ☐	No ☐	☐
Phlebitis	Yes ☐	No ☐	Yes ☐	No ☐	☐
Venous surgery	Yes ☐	No ☐	Yes ☐	No ☐	☐

MOBILITY Immobile/chairbound ☐ Limited ☐ Fully mobile ☐ Fixed (stiff) ankle Y/N

SLEEPING ARRANGEMENTS Chair? ☐ Bed? ☐

SOCIAL Visitors: Yes ☐ No ☐ Gets out of the house Yes ☐ No ☐

PETS Yes ☐ No ☐ **HEATING:** Does the client feel it is adequate? Yes ☐ No ☐

ASSESSMENT SUMMARY

Appendix 3 Leaflet for users

A Tower Hamlets Healthcare NHS Trust
response to

LEG ULCERS

This may be of use to you or someone
you care for.

WHAT IS A LEG ULCER

♦ A leg ulcer is an area of broken skin, on the leg, which has been evident for a period of longer than 6 weeks.
♦ Leg ulcers may initially be caused by injury, such as a knock, or by scratching the leg in response to skin irritation. They may also occur as a result of a specific medical condition.

WHO IS AT RISK

Those who,
♦ have varicose veins
♦ have high blood pressure
♦ have a high fat/cholesterol diet
♦ are overweight
♦ smoke
♦ are immobile
♦ have done a lot of sitting/standing
♦ have a particular medical condition eg diabetes, rheumatoid arthritis
♦ have had surgery on their legs
♦ have had injured or broken legs
♦ have had inflammation of leg veins
♦ have had multiple pregnancies

WHAT AFFECTS HEALING

How quickly your ulcer heals depends on a variety of reasons. Among them:

◆ how at risk you are (see previous section).

◆ the circulation in your legs. You may have a problem either with your veins, arteries or both, that you are unaware of.

◆ the condition of the surrounding skin eg any swelling or irritation.

◆ any underlying medical condition, (eg diabetes) which is not at present controlled.

◆ any underlying medical condition which has not been previously diagnosed.

WHAT YOU CAN DO

If you have a non-healing wound on your leg seek medical advice. Ulcers can quickly develop and the longer you have them the more difficult they can be to heal. They can also reoccur.

WHAT YOU CAN EXPECT FROM TOWER HAMLETS NHS TRUST

In September 1998 the Trust launched the *Leg Ulcer Care Programme.* This has been introduced in order to offer expertise in the management of leg ulcers and advice in leg ulcer prevention.

It is important that you and your leg ulcer are correctly assessed. Any factors contributing to or delaying healing must be identified including the underlying condition of your circulation. All of this can only be done effectively by seeking professional guidance. A correct course of management can then be discussed with you.

WHAT YOU NEED TO DO

If you suspect that you have a leg ulcer you can contact your GP or district nurses. Your GP will be able to give you your nurses phone number. Alternatively you can contact the tissue viability nurses on
0171 377 7000 extn 4331

East London & The City
commentary

Leg ulcers

This project did not have an auspicious start. Early on, the community trust where the project team was based underwent a massive reorganisation, resulting in the loss of many staff. During and following this upheaval there was (understandably) a culture of resistance to change and low morale.

It also took the team over 18 months before a project worker came into post. Their original plan to second internally was not feasible and external candidates were not attracted to the short-term (nine months), part-time nature of the post.

Despite these difficulties, this project team has made excellent progress. A key factor in their success has been enthusiastic leadership of the project manager. She persisted with the project despite organisational turbulence and the lack of staff to take it forward. Several survey participants commented that this enthusiasm, coupled with her well-respected skills in tissue viability were vital in getting the leg ulcer clinics off the ground.

Keeping them going has been possible because staff have noticed improvements very quickly in two areas. One is continual professional development. Because district nurses see the clinical nurse specialist (who is also the project manager) about once a month, their skills are constantly being updated. One district nurse who was contacted opportunistically said:

'Having (the clinical nurse specialist) there to discuss different things makes a difference. When you are seeing seven leg ulcers in a row, it leads to better practice. We are using the leg ulcer care programme lots... The professional development is the best part of it.'

The other key to the early and continued success of the clinics is that nurses see how much happier patients are. Several survey participants remarked that patients were pleased with the new arrangements, some even seeing the weekly clinic as a social occasion. What's more, their leg ulcers are healing faster. One district nurse said:

'Even in the short time I've been here (two months), I've seen wounds heal.'

Getting to this point has not been easy. They have been fortunate in that the evidence on leg ulcers is very robust and simple to understand. But although the evidence is convincing, they have had a number of practical, operational difficulties in finding appropriate premises and getting them up to an acceptable standard.

One of the biggest lessons the team has learned is to be wary of over-reliance on 'opinion leaders'. Although a number of studies mention that getting opinion leaders on board is essential, the issue is much more complicated than it first suggests. Primary care practices operate as separate organisations and a person who has a great deal of influence within his or her own practice may have very little impact on outside colleagues. Even if a project team can identify the more innovative GPs within a community, they may not represent the views of others. What's more, it may be too much to expect one or two innovative 'opinion leaders' to have sufficient influence needed to change someone else's beliefs and behaviour. Getting key people on board is essential, but relying on them to convince others may not work.

The money for this project was small (£18 700), but they have used it wisely to establish a new service that now runs on its own. As one survey participant explained:

'Rather than just use extra money to parachute in, try to use the money to build capacity for the training and development of staff. Once you have a clinic in there, if you've reorganised the systems then when the money goes away, the system's still in place.'

As this approach has worked so well with leg ulcer care, the trust is now replicating it for other conditions, such as diabetes and incontinence. The same survey participant spoke of the new energy within the organisation, commenting:

'We're evolving a whole new approach around facilitating and enabling clinical nurse specialists to learn from each other. It's really exciting. You get them together and one says, "Oh, do you do that? We could try that too."'

Perhaps this is the team's greatest achievement. They have contributed to replacing a severely fragmented, demoralised organisation with one where staff are enthusiastic and open to learning. Nurses no longer work in isolation and they have a much better sense of how to locate their practice. Even more importantly, this is one of the few North Thames projects where patients clearly have benefited.

8

Self-directed learning groups in primary care: a sustainable initiative? A local research implementation project in Enfield & Haringey

Peter Sheridan

Background, aims and methods

The theory of self-directed learning requires an individual to reflect on their own situation, diagnose their learning needs and decide on the competencies needed in order to develop. With the support of peers, the necessary resources can be identified and a learning strategy planned. Group work offers mutual support and motivation, and self-directed learners are encouraged to evaluate their learning so that an individual can appreciate what is the most effective stimulus for their own learning.[1]

An earlier project in part of Enfield & Haringey under the London Implementation Zone Educational Initiative (LIZEI)* had demonstrated that local GPs appreciated the opportunity of learning in self-directed learning groups, which they considered to be an effective method of learning.[2] Taking this approach to the part of the health authority outside the LIZ area (where

---

*The London Implementation Zone (LIZ) was established following The Tomlinson Report's[3] (1992) recommendation of investing in inner-London primary care. The Educational Initiative (LIZEI) funded a range of projects aimed at developing primary healthcare teams within inner London.

practitioners had not been able to benefit from the LIZEI initiative) and testing its impact on clinical practice was selected as the subject for Enfield & Haringey Health Authority's R&D Implementation Project. The aim of this project was to observe the group processes involved in negotiating changes in clinical behaviour, and to see if participation in a group would help practitioners to consider and implement changes in their own clinical behaviour. Attention would be focused on the negotiation of changes in practice in the light of evidence of clinical effectiveness. The project had the support of the Medical Audit Advisory Group (MAAG) and general practice tutors, and was seen as building on existing local work and being rooted in local general practice.

GPs were recruited at a MAAG event to publicise a range of educational opportunities. Additionally, a 'flyer' advertising the chance to participate in a self-directed learning group was sent to all GPs. Others were recruited through educational and informal networks. GPs participating were asked to commit themselves to attending six evening meetings once a month over a six-month period. These would be self-directed learning groups, focusing on the application of research evidence to areas of clinical practice selected by the participants themselves. Each of the four groups was facilitated by a GP and all were requested to undertake some clinical audit within their chosen topic area to provide baseline information from which it would be possible to consider any changes in clinical practice achieved.

A project officer was appointed to set up the groups and provide administrative support. This included keeping records of attendance for postgraduate educational allowance and arranging for the payment of incentive payments to participating GPs and pharmacists.* The role also included work to record the experience of the project and the measurement of its impact.

The project officer was closely supported by a consultant in public health medicine and an academic supervisor. These three people, along with the MAAG chairman, a general practice tutor and a research fellow from Royal Free Hospital School of Medicine (now the Royal Free and University College Medical School), constituted the project steering group, whose remit was to oversee the initiative.

---

*The financial incentive to take part in the project was up to £450 (£75 × 6) and 12 hours of approved postgraduate education (from a required annual commitment of 30 hours) for each participating GP, and £240 (£40 × 6) for each pharmacist. (A similar payment had been paid previously to participants in self-directed learning groups in the LIZEI, and was considered to have been an effective aid to recruitment.)

Experience

Four self-directed learning groups met for the first time in September 1997. They were known as Oakwood, Enfield Town, Crouch End 1 and Crouch End 2. These groups were all in the less-deprived west part of Enfield & Haringey, which had not been included in the LIZ. The groups were each facilitated by GPs who had completed half-day training sessions in evidence-based medicine and facilitation skills. The groups themselves decided whether their membership would be restricted solely to GPs or multi-disciplinary. Two groups chose to include pharmacists and practice nurses, while the other two remained exclusively for GPs. The original plan had envisaged that six groups of ten GPs would be convened, covering just over a half of GPs in the area. In fact, only 32 GPs were recruited (about a quarter of those eligible) and it was decided for practical reasons that they should be organised into four groups.

The four groups had the following names, members and GP attendance:

	Membership	GP attendance
Enfield Town	9 GPs + 4 pharmacists	65%
Oakwood	9 GPs + 2 practice nurses	72%
Crouch End 1	8 GPs	75%
Crouch End 2	6 GPs	80%

Payments for attendance were made on the understanding that participants would attend regularly, undertake clinical audit and discuss their experiences individually or in groups with the project officer or individually with the project's external evaluators (the King's Fund). Payments were made to GPs and pharmacists, but not to the practice nurses.

Only three of 18 single-handed GPs eligible participated, one in each of three of the four groups. Some groups included several members from a single practice.

A suggested programme for the six meetings was agreed between the project officer and the MAAG, and was as follows:

1   Introduction and selection of clinical area to study and plan collection of evidence.
2   Review evidence and agree clinical audit methodology.
3   Review clinical audit data, set standards and an action plan for implementation.
4   Select second study topic and review evidence.
5   Review evidence and agree clinical audit method. Evaluation of learning process.
6   Review progress on implementation on topics and project evaluation. Planning for the future.

Meeting 5 included a session facilitated by the project officer who used the group discussion to evaluate the learning processes in each group. He used a set of standard questions to elicit the groups' responses in selected areas (*see* Box 8.1) and tape-recorded the group discussion. This was later transcribed and analysed.

Box 8.1   Questions posed by project officer to evaluate group learning

- What is a self-directed learning group?
- What are the advantages and disadvantages of self-directed learning groups and more formal learning?
- What is evidence-based medicine?
- What is the relevance of evidence-based medicine to general practice?
- Does participation in a self-directed learning group help to consider, discuss and apply evidence-based medicine?
- What is important in bringing about change in clinical practice?
- What do you feel you should have achieved as a group by the last meeting?

The data were analysed by the project officer and consultant in public health medicine and an academic supervisor independently analysed a sample of the data to validate the conclusions of the project officer. The emerging issues from all four groups were coded into categories and themes which emerged from the experiences of the groups.

The data from the four groups were analysed and compared with the views of the GP facilitators, who were interviewed individually. Further data (from field-notes taken by the project officer at the meetings) were also compared with these emerging findings. The initial analysis was discussed with the project steering group and with an academic supervisor. The interpretation of this qualitative data forms the basis of the remainder of this chapter.

All groups started with a discussion to arrive at a range of suggested topics, which entailed a process of suggesting topics of interest, and debate to establish those which had reasonable support and nobody opposed to studying them.

The topics initially chosen by the four groups showed a common interest in lipid management, hypertension, antibiotics for upper respiratory tract infections, back pain, depression, asthma and non-steroidal anti-inflammatory drug prescribing. From this long list, each group negotiated the two topics which it wished to examine in more depth. Two of the original topics (back pain and antibiotics for upper respiratory infections) were not pursued by any of the groups and one topic (lipids) was common to three of the four groups.

The two topics selected by each group were as follows:

	First topic	*Second topic*
Enfield Town	Diagnosis of depression	Osteoporosis
Oakwood	Lipid screening	Lipids in diabetes
Crouch End 1	Lipid management (after myocardial infarction)	Proton pump inhibitors
Crouch End 2	Blood pressure monitoring (subsequently dropped) Non steroidal anti-inflammatory drug prescribing	Lipid management

Evaluation of the group learning process

In meeting 5, the questions posed by the project officer were followed by extensive discussion by each of the groups. The ground covered included the characteristics and dynamics of the group, its identity and cohesion. This was followed by debate about preferred learning styles and techniques for effective learning. The merits of evidence-based medicine were discussed, and overall the main theme to emerge was that the groups preferred to take a questioning approach towards 'evidence'. Once it became clear that the evidence presented could withstand their valid criticism, groups had concluded that clinical practice *should* change in line with the evidence. The extent to which change *could* occur, and the means of achieving it, had been negotiated within each group. The final stage had been to think through plans for the implementation of changes in practice in participants' own workplaces.

Use of clinical audit data

Members of all groups undertook audit around their chosen topics and were happy to share the results of audits from their practices within their groups. Two of the groups were also willing to share their anonymised data with the project officer. The Enfield Town group had initially identified blood pressure monitoring as one of its two topics, however, their audit concluded that blood pressure was being recorded in 80% of patients in a five-year period. They were satisfied with this level of monitoring and decided to look at a different topic, use of anti-inflammatory drugs. The Oakwood group looked at cholesterol management and found that many of their heart attack patients were still smoking, but (rather surprisingly) they decided not to attempt to address this issue. The Crouch End 1 group found a wide variation in the incidence of depression among patients after looking prospectively at consultations over a three-week period. The Crouch End 2 group found higher-than-expected or desirable lipid levels in their diabetic patients. (It is not possible to provide comprehensive details of the audit data because two of the groups had not agreed to share their audit data with the project officer.)

Evidence examined

The groups used various methods to obtain information on clinical effectiveness in their chosen topics of interest. One group searched Medline and looked for relevant information on the Internet. The project officer had obtained material on evidence-based practice where available from the health authority's public health directorate (e.g. the *Effective Health Care* bulletin on cholesterol screening). Several individual group members contacted academic departments for advice. Literature from pharmaceutical company representatives provided further reading (this included papers on key trials of cholesterol-lowering treatments).

Groups also examined summaries of information such as the *Effective Health Care* bulletin on cholesterol and coronary heart disease[4] and looked at major randomised controlled trials such as the WOSCOPS[5] and 4S[6] trials of lipid-lowering treatments in secondary and primary prevention. Published guidelines such as those from Standing Medical Advisory Committee promoting Sheffield tables[7] for assessing overall level of risk were considered. However, two groups felt that they would value external validation of what they had studied and had approached local hospital clinicians. One group sought the advice of a chemical pathologist and another went to a local cardiologist and a rheumatologist for support.

Observation of group processes

An important initial process was taking control and stating their autonomy to decide on educational needs and study topics as well as group membership. Two groups invited other professionals to join and two remained unidisciplinary. Despite these differences in make-up, each group viewed itself as being made up of like-minded individuals with a common purpose. They valued the active learning in groups where participation was expected and they recognised that the group could tolerate their lack of knowledge in a particular area. One of the first tasks, negotiating topics for study, had led to the selection of a set of issues which did not necessarily relate to areas of educational need. They tended to be safe, relatively uncontroversial subjects where it was easy to agree that knowledge was important.

The groups had high expectations of active learning and members expressed disapproval of colleagues who had failed to prepare properly by reading the material circulated in advance of the meetings. All groups were happy to undertake some baseline measurement of their clinical practice for clinical audit and to set criteria on the basis of the evidence they had considered. Clinical audit was well understood and was regarded by group members as a natural activity.

The image and acceptability of evidence-based medicine

Members of the groups were quick to put forward their perception of the special nature of general practice, and the project officer noted that this had the feel of them convincing themselves of this 'fact'. The case was often made that any new approach, such as evidence-based practice, would have to be applied in a special way in order to fit the unique environment in which the GP works. In particular, the breadth of activity of general practice and the practical necessity of tolerating a high level of uncertainty in diagnosis and problem solving were cited as important factors making the application of evidence-based practice different in general practice. The need to meet patients' expectations of treatment in order to sustain the long-term relationship between doctor and patient was seen as a delicate but important issue which could be damaged by the imposition of care which might be clinically appropriate but unacceptable to the patient. The complex process of diagnosis was likened to an art form which was sometimes intuitive rather than analytical. Experience in diagnosis was believed to be very important.

Group members exhibited a highly critical attitude to evidence of clinical effectiveness. They were very suspicious of expert opinion and of pharmaceutical company agendas which they considered likely to show bias. They raised the point that research evidence may only apply to groups of patients in similar states and circumstances to those included in the research, and were thus quick to question the generalisability of a large proportion of studies presented as research evidence. Furthermore, the application of population-based evidence to individual patients was considered to be especially problematic. It was argued that evidence-based medicine could not provide all the answers, and there was strong criticism of the approach (although perhaps less consensus about what is meant by evidence-based medicine). Even when research evidence was accepted, groups were quick to emphasise that when implementation would entail changing clinical practice, it would be likely to be problematic.

In examining the evidence they had found groups were highly critical of the validity and reliability of papers. Nevertheless, when the research evidence was finally accepted, there was agreement in principle that clinical practice ought to change accordingly (e.g. this was highlighted in the work undertaken by the Enfield Town group on the diagnosis of depression). Changes were approached cautiously and the implications considered thoroughly. It was concluded that more time would be needed to consider the practical implications of change, and that it would be essential to have the agreement of partners and other team members before attempts were made to introduce changes within a practice. It was also noted that patients might be surprised by (and possibly opposed to) changes in treatment. It was also predicted that certain team members may resent and may even try to block the implementation of proposed changes.

Negotiating change

The groups discussed the problems of implementing change and how barriers might be overcome. Involvement of practice nurses was suggested several times as a way of initiating changes in clinical behaviour. Another suggestion was to use a computer template which would hold diagnostic questions (this arose in the context of diagnosing depression). It was recognised that some individuals would embrace change easily, while others would be more likely to resist until convinced of its feasibility and benefits.

Facilitation of the groups

The group facilitators felt relatively unprepared for leading a group. In the earlier LIZEI project[2] general practice tutors had been employed with a sessional commitment. They had received more support before taking on the role and had been supported by meeting as a group to reflect on their progress as group leaders. The facilitators of all four groups in our project would all have appreciated that level of support. They felt that their own training had been insufficient and far too superficial to enable them to lead the sessions effectively. With hindsight they thought that they would have been able to make much more of a contribution had they received further training, both in evidence-based practice and facilitation skills.

Attendance

Twenty-three of the 30 GPs recruited missed only one meeting, and 11 attended all of the meetings of their group.* (Data on the attendance of the pharmacists and nurses are unavailable.)

Discussion

We had been informed by local GPs before embarking on the project that the self-directed learning groups used in the earlier LIZEI initiative had been valued by GPs in Enfield & Haringey as a way of examining practice in a supportive environment where each group member was both a teacher and a learner. The groups had respected members' different levels of knowledge and encouraged questions to gain a fuller understanding of the issue. We wanted to test whether this also facilitated consideration, planning and negotiation of changes to their participants' clinical practice. We thought at first that we could measure changed clinical behaviour by clinical audit, but the timescale of the project (which was shortened by the departure from the health authority of the first project lead, and an ensuing period of inactivity, to six months of meetings) proved to be far too short. However, we were able to demonstrate from the evaluation of the group learning that change in clinical behaviour was contemplated and actively planned. We managed to recruit 30 GPs, or one in four, but only reached a sixth of the single-handed practitioners.

The peer group approach seemed important in examining the evidence and in negotiating change and this is in keeping with the theory of decision making in the social influences approach.[8,9] We felt that this method of adult learning was empowering rather than coercive, and provided individual motivation to group members.[10,11]

We thought it surprising that lipid management was such a popular choice and was considered by three of the four groups. This may have been as a result of the Standing Medical Advisory Committee (SMAC) guidance on the use of statins sent to all GPs by the NHS Executive in August 1997. In Enfield & Haringey, the prescription rate for statins is 40% above the national average and the third highest of 14 London health authorities,[12] so from a health authority perspective it is an aspect of care where local performance is good (assuming that the prescriptions are for appropriate patients). Other topics chosen were about prescribing issues, and only one was around diagnosis – of depression (where there is evidence that diagnosis is often overlooked).[13] We

---

*One of the groups, Crouch End 2, met only five times (rather than six).

had wondered whether the clinical topics selected would relate to a health strategy such as Health of the Nation or other national or local priorities. This did not seem to be the case. In fact, it seemed that subjects chosen were likely to be ones which were of interest (but would not be challenging) to practitioners, and where controversy would be minimal. With hindsight, we feel that if groups had stuck with the two topics of interest which were initially proposed but subsequently dropped, antibiotic prescribing for upper respiratory infections and management of back pain, rather more change in their professional practice might have been stimulated.

One group was content with their 80% of patients with blood pressure recorded in five years and did not contemplate change. Despite collecting data on smoking behaviour, which showed very high rates, no further action around smoking was planned, which we regard as very surprising.

Do small groups of clinicians considering evidence-based practice bring about changes in care, and are they likely to select topics where the potential for benefit is great?

The issues chosen by the groups in our project were not ones where there was known to be poor performance or large problems with significant potential for health gain. We are confident that the initiative brought about at least 36 clinicians' contemplation of changing their practice. However, we have not demonstrated that significant change has occurred, nor can we be confident that the topics selected warranted the attention and resources they received. In our experience, left to their own devices, GPs elected to steer a course which avoided rather than confronted challenging issues.

Lessons learned

- Groups valued the learning experience of examining and applying evidence-based medicine to their clinical practice.
- Once recruited, group members attended nearly all the meetings.
- Group members chose to examine areas of clinical practice which were largely uncontentious.
- Group members believed clinical audit was a useful method for examining clinical practice, setting evidence-based standards and implementing change in their practice.

continued opposite

- Group members considered how they would change their professional practice once they had accepted that they had not been providing the best possible clinical care.
- Groups expressed the wish to carry on meeting to examine other areas of clinical practice subject to continued funding.
- Practitioners who have been encouraged by financial incentives may not continue with their preferred method of learning when funding is no longer available.

Things we would do differently if we were starting tomorrow

- link this project more firmly within an academic department of general practice/primary care. We feel that this would provide a firmer foundation in evidence-based practice and facilitate the use of relevant resources such as libraries and access to statistical expertise
- be more proactive in encouraging multi-disciplinary, as opposed to GP-only, groups
- ensure that participants were signed up to a firm commitment to undertake relevant audit and re-audit, and to share audit data with the project steering group
- be keen to influence groups' choice of topics so that the impact of their work in self-directed learning groups might be maximised
- insist on participants' commitment to implementing changes in practice identified as desirable from the work of the self-directed learning groups
- provide a longer induction for facilitators and meet with them as a group during the period of the project
- not provide postgraduate educational allowance (PGEA) recognition at the same time as offering payment to practitioners for their attendance. If it were necessary to offer financial inducements we would offer them for the duration of the project (in our case six months) and thereafter suggest that PGEA allowance might be sought for any further work that groups wished to pursue themselves
- work with the facilitators to demonstrate the groups' successes in changing clinical practice and improving quality of clinical care, and involve the facilitators in writing up the project report.

References

1   Spencer James R (ed) (1998) Self-directed learning for groups. *Education for General Practice.* **9(4)**.

2   Phillips S (1996) *Evaluation of Self-directed Learning Groups in London Implementation Zone Educational Initiative.* Enfield & Haringey MAAG, London.

3   Tomlinson B (1992) *Report into London's Health Services, Medical Education and Research.* HMSO, London.

4   NHS Centre for Reviews and Dissemination (1993) Cholesterol: screening and treatment. *Effective Health Care.* **1(6).**

5   Shepherd J, Cobbe SM, Ford I *et al.* (1995) Prevention of coronary heart disease with pravastatin in men with hypercholesterolaemia. *New England Journal of Medicine.* **333**: 1301–7.

6   Scandinavian Simvastatin Survival Study Group (1994) Randomised trial of cholesterol lowering in 4444 patients with coronary heart disease: the Scandinavian Simvastatin Survival Study (4S). *Lancet.* **344**: 1383–9.

7   Ramsay LE, Haq IU, Jackson PR *et al.* (1996) Targeting lipid lowering drug therapy for primary prevention of coronary disease: an updated Sheffield table. *Lancet.* **348**: 387–8.

8   Robertson N, Baker R and Hearnshaw H (1996) Changing the clinical behaviour of doctors: a psychological framework. *Quality in Health Care.* **5**: 51–4.

9   Grimshaw JM and Russell IT (1994) Achieving health gain through clinical guidelines; II. Ensuring guidelines change medical practice. *Quality in Health Care.* **3**: 45–52.

10 Jacques D (1991) *Learning in Groups* (2e). Kogan Page, London.

11 Grol R (1997) Beliefs and evidence in changing clinical practice. *BMJ.* **315**: 418–21.

12 NHS Executive (1998) *Clinical Effectiveness Indicators.* NHSE, Leeds.

13 Freeling P, Rao RM, Paykel ES, Sireling LI and Burton RH (1985) Unrecognised depression in general practice. *BMJ.* **290**: 1880–3.

Enfield & Haringey commentary

GP learning sets

The key question this project team wanted to answer was: If you give doctors sufficient support, time and money, will they be motivated enough to make necessary changes in their practice *on their own*? Accordingly, the role of this project team was very different from most of the other North Thames projects.

The other North Thames teams worked energetically to convince the people of the usefulness of the evidence-based change. This project team offered administrative support, training in facilitation skills and some evaluation, but they did not have any role in choosing which changes to make or 'selling' them. Several of the survey participants commented that this approach, which meant that the practitioners set their own agenda rather than having it dictated from 'on high', was one of the most positive points of the project. Unfortunately, the agenda they set was largely unchallenging, as one participant himself noted:

'The problem is that the doctors were choosing the topics. You need [it] to be the improvement of healthcare, where the need is maximum.'

Getting the balance right between letting practitioners have complete control over the agenda and imposing a top-down approach can be difficult. Too much in either direction means change won't happen.

One possible reason why the groups chose either areas that didn't need much work or areas that did (smoking) but were then ignored is because they were unidisciplinary. Two were GPs only and two had a minority of members from either practice nursing or pharmacy, but none of them could be described as properly multidisciplinary. Tracey Sweet, in an article on the position of token nurses on Primary Care Boards, wrote:

'The well-documented process of "groupthink", in which a group considers only a limited number of options and does not consider the wider context of its decisions, occurs because groups often come to assume that all members think the same way ... An environment that does not encourage contributions also increases confirmation bias, where the majority seek information consistent with their beliefs and theories.'

[Sweet T (1999) Special brew. *Health Service Journal.* **109**: 5657]

The doctors consistently chose unchallenging topics because there were not enough people from different disciplines to suggest alternatives. At least one group participant that we spoke to knew the uniprofessional composition of the groups was a weakness, saying:

> 'Evidence-based medicine needs to look wider than GPs. We need to do more with primary healthcare teams. But would they be allowed to take it up?'

Working well in a group is a skill which many of the group participants needed to learn. One survey participant remarked:

> 'GPs are very individual. Lots were from small practices and not used to working in a team. [The GPs] were scoring points off of each other ... [Doctors] are used to didactic learning and there was not enough time spent explaining how the system works differently. There was an assumption that people can go into self-directed learning groups without proper training.'

What's more, doctors also need help in applying the research evidence to their own practice. The assumption was that by becoming more familiar with the research evidence and exposing individual practitioners to other doctors' practices through discussion, doctors would then see how the evidence applies to them. But as one survey participant remarked:

> 'They are not sure when it is appropriate for their own practice. We need a step in the middle – how to assess the evidence for their own practice.'

As Wood, Ferlie and Fitzgerald* argue, doctors need skills in translating from research evidence to their own practice. They cannot make that leap on their own.

Payment for GPs for the learning sets was another difficult issue. One project team member commented that the attitude of the GPs was: 'I'm doing this because you want me to do this' not because they themselves were especially committed. One survey participant noted that,

> 'One GP went reluctantly because everyone else was going and the fee finally motivated him to go.'

He thought that money was an inducement, but not the prime motivator. Another survey participant felt that GPs only went because they had £75 more in their pocket. Nurses, who took part in the groups, were not paid anything. It is a long-standing difficulty that many GPs expect payment for postgraduate education and updating their skills, while other professions do not.

Several local participants commented that the groups were very expensive for limited outcomes. Even if a group did get round to thinking about how to make changes in practice, they often cited that others – not themselves – would need to be the ones to implement the change (e.g. practice nurses). This may be because they genuinely did not know how to make change happen. Through the other North Thames projects we've learned that expecting others to make a change for you does not work, especially if they have not been included in the early processes of examining the evidence and seeing how it applies to their practice.

However, the groups were a popular method of learning. All but one of the group participants was keen to participate in a learning group again – if they were paid for their time.

As the shortest North Thames project (effectively 14 months), this project was penalised by running out of time. After five or six sessions, the groups were just beginning to know each other well enough for perhaps some more difficult topics to have been selected. Unfortunately, they had not been around long enough to generate sufficient enthusiasm to continue once the funding had run out. None of the groups is still meeting.

*Wood M, Ferlie E and Fitzgerald L (1998) *Achieving Change in Clinical Practice.* Centre for Corporate Strategy and Change, Warwick Business School, Warwick.

9

Helicobacter pylori eradication, the management of venous leg ulcers and the management of coronary heart disease in Hillingdon

John Aldous and *Chris Deeming*

Introduction

This chapter describes our experience of leading an evidence-based clinical effectiveness initiative in Hillingdon Health Authority, a small district with a population of 244 700.[1] The chapter is divided into two sections, the first outlines the subject areas tackled and the processes used, and the second analyses in more detail some of the key issues arising from the work.

Section 1. The subjects tackled and processes used

A project steering group made up of two local GPs and consultants from the local acute hospital and health authority was established and given the initial task of considering the topic(s) to be selected. Issues such as the strength of evidence, population benefit, extent of inappropriate care, feasibility of achieving change, and the interest and commitment of local professionals were taken into account, and three topics emerged. These were: the management of dyspepsia and *Helicobacter pylori* eradication; the management of venous leg ulcers in the community; and, the management of coronary heart disease within a general practice. Work on each topic was regarded as a subproject of the Health Authority-led Implementation Project and a full-time project officer was appointed for 18 months to support the work. Each sub-project followed a simple methodology:

- establishing that there was an appreciable gap between research findings and current practice
- involving key local players
- defining a local evidence-based message
- developing and implementing a strategy for supporting effective practice and establishing whether practice had changed in the desired way.

Start dates of the subprojects were intentionally staggered, and although the long-term impact of the projects has yet to be assessed, some important findings have emerged in the course of the work. Moreover, the experience of planning, undertaking and evaluating the subprojects has provided some valuable lessons on the *process* of conducting an evidence-based implementation project.

Helicobacter pylori eradication and the management of dyspepsia

The aim of this subproject was to improve the effectiveness of local clinical practice in the management of dyspepsia and the eradication of *Helicobacter pylori*. The objectives were: to offer clinical guidance on the management of patients with dyspepsia; to develop and implement a strategy for the eradication of *H. pylori* on grounds of patient benefit and the cost-effective use of ulcer-healing drugs; and to monitor the impact of this strategy. There were four main factors which set the context for our work. First, dyspepsia is very common. Surveys in Britain suggest a prevalence of around 40% in the community, and around a quarter of sufferers seek medical attention for their symptoms.[2] The prevalence of peptic ulcers in the population is estimated to be 6–13% for men and 2–5% for women between the ages of 15 and 64 years.[3] Second, there was good evidence for the effectiveness of *H. pylori* eradication therapy in curing peptic ulcer and preventing relapses.[4] However, the evidence base for the optimal *management* of patients presenting with dyspepsia is not yet established.[4,5] Third, there was no locally agreed guidance for *H. pylori* eradication. Fourth, the local general hospital did not run a serology testing service for *H. pylori*, therefore GPs in two of our three localities did not have access to a testing service (necessary to establish whether patients have the infection and might therefore benefit from eradication therapy). A working group was established whose members included a GP from each of the three localities; three hospital consultants, including a gastroenterologist and microbiologist; two health authority consultants in public health medicine; and the health authority pharmaceutical advisor. The group agreed that there was an appreciable gap between the research evidence in favour of *H. pylori* eradication in cases of peptic ulcer and local clinical practice, and developed a strategy to support eradication. The strategy included the development and dissemination of local clinical guidance based on the paper in *Effectiveness Matters*, 'Helicobacter pylori and peptic ulcer',[4] and the setting up of a serology testing service for *H. pylori* at the local acute trust. The clinical guidance also suggested management guidelines for the wider topics of dyspepsia and gastro-oesophageal reflux disease in addition to notes on *H. pylori* infection and prescribing information on dyspepsia and *H. pylori* eradication. The guidance was posted to GPs and supported by health authority prescribing advisor's visits to practices* and a lunchtime meeting for GPs and hospital doctors at the local hospital postgraduate centre.

Further dissemination of the guidance was achieved by raising it as a subject and gathering feedback from practitioners at the GP locality commissioning meetings.** A serology testing service was established at the local acute trust and the demand for tests likely to arise from the two localities which had previously been without this service was modelled (estimated at 50 per month, maximum). Incentives for non-fundholding GPs to follow the guidelines on the use of ulcer-healing drugs were incorporated in the health authority's prescribing incentives scheme.***

Our (internal) evaluation attempted to measure the impact on clinical practice of the *H. pylori* project. The local Medical Audit Advisory Group (MAAG) performed an audit shortly after dissemination of the guidance examining the management of patients in primary care following treatment in secondary care. This suggested that hospital doctors had been following an evidence-based approach and that GPs were adhering to their hospital colleagues' recommendations when patients were discharged from secondary care. The audit did *not* examine those patients whose dyspepsia was managed solely by GPs in primary care. The wider evaluation did, however, involve analysis of GP prescribing data at district level which revealed a reduction in the rate of increase in the prescribing of ulcer-healing drugs after dissemination of the guidance and a levelling off in expenditure. It was thought

---

*Visits to GPs were opportunistic. The topic of *H. pylori* eradication was discussed as part of a wider prescribing agenda. Forty percent of GP practices were visited.

**These meetings were held on a monthly basis to ensure that GPs were involved in the process of commissioning local (secondary/tertiary) healthcare.

***This scheme was aimed at non-fundholding GPs who would receive cash payments for practice development if they remained within their prescribing budget and met other prescribing criteria, one of which was introduced for *H. pylori* eradication (confirmed by prescribing data).

unlikely that these changes were simply the result of price changes in ulcer-healing drugs. However, a similar (though less pronounced) downward trend in the total cost of prescribing in this field was seen in the national data.

Although the reduction in the cost of ulcer-healing medicines in Hillingdon was clearly larger than that achieved on average nationally during the same period, we recognise that in the absence of a considerably more elaborate trial design it is not possible to attribute the (desired) changes achieved locally to the impact of our project (*see* Figure 9.1).

Analysis of the hospital serology database showed GP use of the testing service to be approaching our projected 50 tests per month. Qualitative methods were also used to assess impact. A semi-structured interview schedule was used at locality meetings to take collective feedback from GPs on the guidance. The main message, received from about a third of GPs (38:121), was that posting the guidance was only partially successful. Many GPs either could not remember receiving a copy of the guidance or could not remember what the guidance had said. Although a small number had found the guidance useful, many GPs remained unaware of the new serology testing service which had been publicised in the guidance. Our analysis of the hospital serology records also confirmed this. Postal dissemination of the guidance alone had not, therefore, been effective in securing uptake of the service. Further announcement of the service and dissemination of the guidance at a hospital postgraduate lecture for GPs appears to have alerted many more practices,

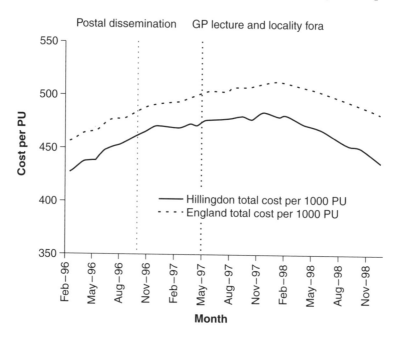

Figure 9.1   GP expenditure on ulcer-healing drugs (moving annual average).

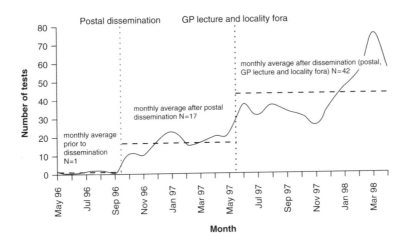

Figure 9.2 Monthly use of hospital serology testing service* following dissemination of local guidance.**

Source: Hospital data set, microbiology.

*This data is for GPs in the two localities who previously did not have access to serology testing. The total number of tests is 598; 462 requested by GPs, 83 requested by hospital doctors and in 53 cases this data was missing.

**Graph excludes HA prescribing advisor visits.

and following the lecture the number of GPs using the service increased by 70% (24:41), with the average number of tests per month more than doubling (17:42, *see* Figure 9.2).

The work to date has clearly achieved significant inroads with regard to the first two objectives. Guidance promoting the eradication of *H. pylori* (as part of a strategy for the management of dyspepsia) was developed and has been disseminated (first objective achieved).

A serology testing service was developed at the district general hospital, enabling the identification of patients with *H. pylori* infection, thereby facilitating the appropriate selection of patients for eradication therapy (an essential prerequisite for the second objective of implementing a strategy for eradication). Progress on the third objective (monitoring the impact of the whole strategy) has certainly been made, however, use of proxy indicators (i.e. use of serology testing and prescribing costs) has limited our ability to assess fully the impact of the strategy.

We also recognise that important, relevant aspects of the subject have not been covered by the work done to date. Most significantly, we currently lack sufficient information on the extent and appropriateness of the clinical management of *H. pylori* in patients with confirmed peptic ulcer disease who are managed *solely* in the general practice setting, and further work is planned in this regard.

The management of venous leg ulcers in the community

The aim of this subproject was to improve the effectiveness of local clinical practice in the management of venous leg ulcers in the community. The objectives were: to offer guidance on the effective management of patients with venous leg ulcers; to support the organisation and development of effective management in the community; and to evaluate the impact of our project interventions. There were five main factors which set the context of the project. First, about 1.5–3.0 per 1000 of the population have leg ulcers and prevalence increases with age up to around 20 per 1000 in people over 80 years[6] and most people with leg ulcers are managed in the community by GPs and community nurses (both practice and district nurses).

Second, there was good evidence of clinically effective management of venous leg ulcers, particularly with regard to the use of Doppler ultrasound in assessment, high-compression bandages for treatment and compression hosiery for prevention of recurrence.[6]

Third, an audit initiated by MAAG had reported that local clinical practice in this field did not match the best evidence-based care. It had also found that community nurses were having problems accessing the materials necessary for effective practice, particularly orthopaedic wool, which was not available on the community Drug Tariff (FP10).[7]

Fourth, the local community trust had not promoted the use of local clinical guidance for the management of venous leg ulcers by district nurses. Fifth, there was minimal co-ordination of community leg ulcer services across the district, and a recognised shortfall in support and training for leg ulcer management. A project group was formed to develop a strategy to improve the effectiveness of leg ulcer management in the community. Table 9.1 shows the membership of this group.

The strategy included: the appointment of a part-time 'H-grade' nurse to co-ordinate leg ulcer care across the district for a one-year period; the

Table 9.1   Membership of the venous leg ulcer group

Primary care/MAAG	*Community hospital trust*
MAAG chair	District nurse development specialist
MAAG practice nurse	District nurse
	Locality manager
Acute hospital trust	*Health authority*
Consultant surgeon	Consultant in public health medicine
Tissue viability nurse	Practice nurse professional advisor
Leg ulcer nurse	Prescribing advisor
	Project manager

development and dissemination of local guidance to GPs and community nurses; education and training for both practice and district nurses; and the supply of orthopaedic wool. The overall cost for this subproject was calculated to be £29 000 for a one-year period, which would have taken the overall cost of the three subprojects to well in excess of the total (£50 000) of the Health Authority-led Implementation Project (from the Regional R&D Implementation Programme). Fortunately, the health authority management and a GP policy group approved this necessary additional resourcing.

The project group produced local guidance for GPs to facilitate the care of patients with leg ulcers by providing information on the principles of managing the condition. This was largely based on the *Effective Health Care* bulletin on compression therapy for venous leg ulcers,[6] and covered initial assessment and diagnosis, treatment and the prevention of recurrence. The guidance was posted to all GPs and supported by further active dissemination, including two GP postgraduate lectures at local hospitals in both the north and south of the borough. The guidance recommended to GPs the use of the three types of high-compression bandage which were available on the community Drug Tariff (some high-compression bandages were unavailable on the Drug Tariff, however, Setopress, Surepress and Tensopress could be obtained). As noted, orthopaedic wool padding, a component of high-compression bandage systems (in simple terms, it goes *under* the bandage), was not available on prescription at the time so funding was made available for the community trust to procure wool at seven health centres across the district for the use of community nurses. (NB: in December 1998, orthopaedic wool became available on FP10, enabling GPs to prescribe it, and making this method of acquisition no longer necessary.)

The project nurse organised a training programme for community nurses on the management of venous leg ulcers. The training was provided over three sessions, each session lasting three hours, and its impact is being evaluated by an audit of nurses' knowledge both before and after. By January 1999, two training programmes had been run, reaching 51 nurses, 42 district nurses and nine practice nurses. Four more training programmes have been planned. The programme is outlined in Table 9.2.

Table 9.2 Community nurse training programme on the management of venous leg ulcers

Session 1	Session 2	Session 3
Epidemiology and aetiology	Doppler training	Bandaging
Assessment and diagnosis	Wound management	Pain control
Use of assessment charts	Nutrition	Aftercare
Diabetic leg ulcer		
Surgical treatment for arterial ulceration		

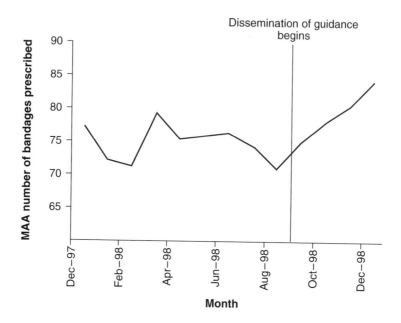

Figure 9.3   Moving annual average (MAA) number of Drug Tariff high-compression bandages prescribed by GPs in Hillingdon (Setopress, Surepress, Tensopress).

The project nurse also led the development of venous leg ulcer guidelines for the community trust. These guidelines were disseminated to community nurses attending the training programme.

In this subproject clinical audit was used to provide a baseline before project intervention. The audit found that a Doppler ultrasound had been taken in only 66% of assessments and that high-compression bandaging had been applied in only 29% of venous leg ulcers treated. GP prescribing data have also been used to monitor the impact of the project interventions (*see* Figure 9.3).

The work has been successful in meeting the first two of our objectives: first, guidance on the management of patients with venous leg ulcers has been produced and disseminated; second, the organisation and development of leg ulcer management in the community has been enhanced by the appointment of the project nurse and the establishment of the training programme. The third objective, evaluation with the aim of establishing the impact of our intervention, is continuing, and a district wide audit in the summer of 1999 found that, in the practices involved in the original audit, 95% of venous leg ulcers had been assessed with a Doppler ultrasound and 52% were being treated with high compression bandaging. For the district as a whole the figures were 92% and 55% respectively. The main reason why compression therapy was not being used was patient preference and compliance.

The management of coronary heart disease within general practice

This subproject was undertaken by five GP practices with a practice population of approximately 20 000. The aim of the project was to improve the effectiveness of local clinical practice in the management of coronary heart disease (CHD). The project objectives were: to improve the medium-term and long-term care of patients after myocardial infarction (MI) within the primary care setting; to improve the management of angina within the primary care setting (particularly the interface between primary and secondary care); and to evaluate the impact of the project.

There were four main factors that set the context of the project. First, the management of CHD is a significant part of the workload of GPs: the prevalence of clinically diagnosed angina is estimated to be 1750 people in a population of 100 000; and at least 255 people could be expected to present with an acute MI per year.[8] For the practices, the prevalence of clinically diagnosed angina is estimated to be 350 cases, with 51 cases of acute MI per year. Second, there was generally accepted research evidence for the secondary prevention of CHD, with powerful trial evidence existing for the preventative power of a number of drug types when prescribed to appropriate groups of patients.[9–16] Specifically, these are aspirin, which has a *number needed to treat* (NNT)* of 12 post MI, angiotensin-converting enzyme (ACE) inhibitors for left ventricular dysfunction post-MI (NNT = 10) and HMG-CoA reductase inhibitors or statins (NNT = 6).[17] Third, there had been no systematic approach to the management of CHD across the practice. Fourth, the practices were keen to look at the boundary between primary and secondary care in the management of CHD.

A project group was formed, the core of which consisted of two TPP GPs and a project nurse, a health authority consultant in public health medicine and a project officer. Other GPs and cardiologists attended evening project meetings. Local guidance for the management of post-MI and the management of angina was developed using a review of the literature by Moher[12] and the *Effective Health Care* bulletin on the management of stable angina.[14] This guidance was disseminated to GPs at an evening cardiology meeting, attended

---

*Number needed to treat (NNT) is a measure of the clinical significance of an intervention. Technically, it is derived by taking the reciprocal of the Absolute Risk Reduction in patients who have the intervention. A comprehensive explanation of NNT can be found in Sackett *et al.* (1991),[18] but for the purpose of reading this chapter, it is sufficient to understand that NNT means exactly what it says, in other words the NNT is the *number* of people (with the target condition) you would *need to treat* in order to avoid one adverse event (in this case over a five-year period).

Table 9.3   Secondary prevention baseline audit (selected indicators*, proportion of patients receiving treatment)

	Aspirin** %	Beta blockers*** %	ACE inhibitors*** %
Practice A	77	45	66
Practice B	44	39	36
Practice C	57	15	33
Totals	**59**	**33**	**45**

*The proportion of patients receiving statins according to the SMAC guidance[11] was also included in this audit.

**Post-MI, post-revascularisation, angina.

***Post-MI.

by eight out of the 13. Analysis of computerised practice data provided a first crude baseline audit to start discussions with the practices. This merely examined the treatment being prescribed to various diagnostic groups and took no account of indications and contraindications for treatment in individual patients (*see* Table 9.3).

Project evaluation is not yet complete and it is not known whether we have met our objectives of improving the care of patients post-MI and the management of angina within the practices. Nevertheless, the project group considers that some objectives have been achieved, notably the development of clinical guidance and GP participation in the baseline clinical audit in the practices. Currently the health authority is building on the work of this project and is developing comprehensive district wide care pathways for coronary heart disease. Helping to encourage that initiative was a substantial impact of the project. However, judgement on the impact of this initiative in terms of its effect on prescribing must be reserved until there is a re-audit. We are optimistic that the results will show that the proportion of patients receiving secondary prevention treatment has risen substantially, as has been the case in a number of other initiatives.[19] It should be recorded that in the work concerning patients with angina we experienced major difficulty. Specifically, our work on referral criteria to secondary care was limited by the fact that neither clear research evidence nor strong professional consensus was apparent in the literature.[14,20]

Section 2. Our experience of implementation

This section describes the experience and challenges of the Health Authority-led Implementation Project in Hillingdon, and summarises the lessons learned.

Creating an evidence-based message at the start of the project

Despite the significant health impact of the three topics considered (*H. pylori* and dyspepsia, venous leg ulcers and CHD), and the presence in each case of a reasonable evidence base, local, district-wide clinical policies had not been established. The development of a clear evidence-based message was therefore seen as one of the key tasks that faced the subproject groups. Reviews of primary research and guidance documents from national organisations and professional bodies were critical in achieving this and gaining agreement within the project groups.

However, perhaps not surprisingly, we found areas where clear research evidence appeared to be lacking. There were knowledge gaps in the professional literature and we sometimes experienced different interpretations from our local experts, several of which we were unable to resolve. For example, in the CHD project we found a lack of clear evidence in the literature for how long medical treatment for secondary prevention should be *continued*, and whether the effects of medical treatment (aspirin, beta blockers and ACE inhibitors) are *additive* in the management of patients post-MI.[9] One of the local cardiologists questioned the applicability of evidence for beta blockers in the management of patients post-MI on the grounds that despite being classified as A1[12] the evidence used was based on trials undertaken in the pre-thrombolytic era. Another cardiologist questioned whether there was conclusive evidence for aspirin in the management of chronic stable angina. (This question was subsequently settled as a result of the systematic review by Eccles *et al.*,[21] confirming the value of the therapy in patients with this condition.) We also found neither clear evidence nor consensus on the subject of secondary care referral for chest pain presenting in general practice[15,21] (a question currently being investigated under the Health Technology Assessment (HTA) programme).[20]

In our feedback from local GPs on the dyspepsia guidance we were also reminded that health professionals are exposed to a variety of different and sometimes competing clinical management strategies. Although firm evidence is present for some aspects of care, the optimal strategy for the management of patients presenting with dyspepsia has not been firmly established. Our project group was able to reach a consensus and agree a local strategy. However, this strategy is somewhat at variance with the national guidelines subsequently produced by the British Society of Gastroenterologists (BSG).[22] Specifically, the local guidance recommends that patients under 45 years with no alarm symptoms should be considered for *H. pylori* testing and should be treated if tests indicate infection. The BSG guidelines recommend the treatment of *H. pylori* infection only for duodenal and gastric ulcer after confirmation by endoscopy.*

Effectiveness Matters on *H. pylori* and peptic ulcer[4] reports four options for the management of patients presenting with dyspepsia, one of which is similar to our own strategy and one to the BSG strategy. This source, which was distributed by the NHS to all GPs, acknowledges that it is uncertain from present research which of these options or combination of options is best, and in what circumstances. Moore, in a systematic review of the evidence on *Helicobacter* and peptic ulcer disease,[3] explores the possible policy consequences of these options and argues that for practical reasons the strategy we recommended is most appropriate where waiting times for endoscopy are long, while the strategy recommended by BSG is most appropriate where there is rapid open access to endoscopy. Moore concludes that our strategy would save costs, whereas the BSG strategy would add to costs, but stresses that local strategies should be congruent with the local provision of necessary services.

Changing practice

In each of our projects, we found many barriers or impediments to implementing effective clinical practice. These included: gaps in the research evidence and lack of professional consensus; lack of district-wide organisation and co-ordination; lack of district-wide training and education initiatives; and lack of local support services and/or supplies.

Our strategies were developed to overcome these barriers, and required considerable time and effort by health professionals to develop and implement. They included: the establishment of local evidence-based messages; local service development; local education and training initiatives; staff appointments; and evaluation and clinical audit. Needless to say these projects were costly, both in time and resources. They required project management skills such as co-ordinating relationships between organisations and healthcare professionals and managers, planning activity and managing time.

Evaluating our work

Monitoring implementation and evaluating the project interventions were important aspects of each of the subprojects. No attempt was made to monitor

---

*The national guidance is based on the consensus statement made by the (US) National Institutes for Health on *H. pylori* in peptic ulcer disease in 1994. This recommends that patients with dyspepsia who test positively for *H. pylori* and are symptomatic should have an endoscopy (primarily to rule out the possibility of cancer) prior to receiving *H. pylori* eradication therapy.

health outcomes as this would have been difficult, costly and, we would argue, inappropriate, given that the selection criteria for topics included the requirement for robust research evidence of clinical effectiveness. The aim of each subproject was to close the gap between the research evidence and actual care in practice and to monitor any improvements. Each used clinical audit data and routine quantitative data (such as GP prescription data and hospital data) for evaluation, and, where possible, routine data were analysed both before the project intervention to establish a baseline, and after to measure impact. In one topic, qualitative methods were also used to help to understand the effect of our intervention. In our experience a period of at least 18 months is essential to complete an evaluation cycle in a project of this nature.

The evaluations have also confirmed the importance of co-ordinating implementation. In the *H. pylori* project we attempted to establish the impact of our staged implementation strategy by using GP uptake of the serology testing service as a proxy indicator for compliance with the local guidance. Figure 9.2 (*see* p 197) showed that the postal dissemination of the clinical guidance was not, by itself, effective. Further dissemination of the guidance eight months later through the postgraduate lecture, and then at GP locality forums, ensured greater GP awareness and use of the service.

Conclusion

The common process followed for each of the subprojects worked well (i.e. forming a project group to establish a gap between research evidence and local practice; defining the appropriate message; and identifying barriers to change and strategies to overcome them). It is clear that any policy to encourage the adoption of effective clinical care needs to take a wide view so that a whole range of potential organisational, financial and professional barriers are taken into account. Research on changing professional behaviour in healthcare suggests that there are a wide range of interventions that all work to some extent in some settings, but there is little knowledge of their relative effectiveness in particular circumstances.[23,24] These include: clinical audit and feedback; using guidelines and opinion leaders; education and training conferences and seminars; clinical prompts and support systems; individual discussion and outreach education ('academic detailing'); and patient education and awareness. The experience of our project, in a small district in London, appears to conform with the systematic review by Oxman,[23] in that no single intervention applied on its own is likely to achieve significant change, and that the most effective approach is to use an appropriate *combination* of interventions in a co-ordinated fashion.

Acknowledgements

We would like to acknowledge the following people for their support in this work: Dr Mitch Garsin and the members of Hillingdon Medical Audit Advisory Group; Dr Ian Goodman and colleagues, Mr Trevor Paes, Dr Greg Holdstock, Dr Diana Rimmer at Hillingdon Hospital Trust; Betty Bowden and Karen Hume at Harrow & Hillingdon Community Trust; Dr Bill Gutteridge, John Peattie and Jan Pearcey at Hillingdon Health Authority.

Lessons learned

- Despite choosing areas for work that are well researched, important gaps still remained in the evidence about clinical care and the organisation of services.
- Local disagreement on research evidence came to light *during* the project.
- It was essential to identify all barriers or impediments to effective practice.
- Considerable time and effort was needed by health professionals to undertake this work.
- Additional financial resources for training and service developments were often required.
- Benefits were obtained from co-ordinating clinical audit programmes and postgraduate education with the project objectives.
- It was necessary to establish project-specific data collection systems. However, routine data systems could sometimes support the evaluation of the project by providing an indication of the *direction* of change.

Things we would do differently if we were starting tomorrow

- in the *H. pylori* project we would concentrate the clinical audit on the management of known peptic ulcer *within* primary care
- ensure a tighter timescale between the postal dissemination of our guidance to GPs and dissemination at the local hospital postgraduate lecture (there had been eight months between these events in our project)
- in the CHD project we would concentrate our efforts into work on the management of patients *within* primary care and put less effort into the management of patients at the interface with secondary care (where the paucity of conclusive evidence has reduced the momentum of our work).

References

1   Office of Population Census & Surveys (OPCS) (1995) *1993-based Population Projections for Health Authority Areas in England.* OPCS, London.

2   Medical Resource Centre (1997) Dyspepsia, peptic ulcer and *Helicobacter pylori. MeReC Bulletin.* **8(2).**

3   Moore RA (1995) Helicobacter pylori *and Peptic Ulcer. A systematic review of the effectiveness and an overview of the economic benefits of implementing what is known to be effective.* Health Technology Evaluation Association, Oxford.

4   Effectiveness Matters (1995) *Helicobacter pylori* and peptic ulcer. *Effectiveness Matters.* **1(2).**

5   Logan R (1997) *A Randomised Trial of Early Endoscopy,* Helicobacter pylori *Testing or Empirical Treatment for Dyspepsia.* (Cited in the National R&D Programme in the area of the primary secondary care interface, three-year programme report.) NHS Executive, London.

6   Effective Health Care (1997) Compression therapy for venous leg ulcers. *Effective Health Care.* **3(4).**

7   Department of Health (1998) *Drug Tariff* (July). The Stationery Office, London.

8   Langham S, Normand C, Piercy J and Rose G (1994) Coronary heart disease. In: A Stevens and J Raftery (eds) *Health Care Needs Assessment, Vol 1.* Radcliffe Medical Press, Oxford.

9   Royal College of Physicians (1994) *Guidelines: the management of acute myocardial infarction.* RCP Publications, London.

10 Royal College of Physicians (1994) *Guidelines: investigation and management of stable angina.* RCP Publications, London.

11 De Bono D and Hopkins A (1994) *Management of Stable Angina.* Royal College of Physicians Publications, London.

12 Moher M (1995) *Evidence of Effectiveness of Interventions for Secondary Prevention and Treatment of Coronary Heart Disease in Primary Care. A review of the literature.* NHS Executive, Anglia and Oxford.

13 Effectiveness Matters (1995) Aspirin and myocardial infarction. *Effectiveness Matters.* **1(1).**

14 Effective Health Care (1997) Management of stable angina. *Effective Health Care.* **3(5).**

15 NHS Executive (1997) *SMAC statement on use of statins.* EL(97)41. NHSE, Leeds.

16 British Heart Foundation (1997) Bypass surgery or angioplasty for angina. *Factfile.* **10.**

17 Cardiology 2000 (1996) *Evidence-based Strategies for Secondary Prevention of Coronary Heart Disease.* Merck, Sharp & Dohme Ltd. [This is a booklet containing

numbers needed to treat which the Clinical Effectiveness Project Manager considered to be derived from apparently credible sources.]

18 Sackett DL, Haynes RB, Guyatt GH and Tugwell P (1991) *Clinical Epidemiology: a basic science for clinical medicine* (2e). Little, Brown and Company, London.

19 Health Education Authority (1997) An aspirin a day ... *Health Gain News.* Issue 5.

20 NHS R&D Health Technology Assessment Programme (1997) *Call for Proposals: Investigation of chest pain presenting in general practice.* National Co-ordinating Centre for Health Technology Assessment, University of Southampton, Southampton.

21 Eccles M, Freemantle N and Mason J (1998) North of England evidence-based guideline development project: guideline on the use of aspirin as secondary prophylaxis for vascular disease in primary care. *BMJ.* **316**: 1303–9. (NB published erratum appears in *BMJ* (1998) **316**: 1733.)

22 British Society of Gastroenterology (1996) *Guidelines in Gastroenterology: 1 Dyspepsia.* BSG, London.

23 Oxman AD, Thomson MA, Davies DA and Haynes RB (1995) No magic bullets: a systematic review of 102 trials of interventions to improve professional practice. *Canadian Medical Association Journal.* **153**(10): 1423–31.

24 Effective Health Care (1994) Implementing clinical guidelines: can guidelines be used to improve clinical practice? *Effective Health Care.* **1(8)**.

Hillingdon commentary

Helicobacter pylori, leg ulcer and coronary heart disease (CHD) within general practice

The Hillingdon projects are notable for two key characteristics. The first is the continuing commitment of the project team to evaluation, and the second is their informal approach to involving others.

When we asked this team in June 1997 about their plans for evaluation, they gave us a number of possible sources of information that could be used to measure change. When pressed further, the public health consultant said that part of their work was to look at which ones really would be feasible.

Although this was a concern for all of the North Thames projects, very few did much about it. The Hillingdon team has. They have established a baseline for all three topics. They have also completed the evaluation cycle for the *H. pylori* work and have concrete plans for the 'after' audit for the leg ulcers and CHD work. Discovering whether their work has made a difference is important to them.

What's more, they have taken their commitment to evaluation one step further. First, they used PACT data to show that the direction of change for the *H. pylori* work is in accordance to guidelines.

But they wanted to learn more, specifically how exactly GPs are managing dyspepsia patients in their daily practice. One primary care group (PCG) is particularly keen on *H. pylori* work, and so their pharmaceutical advisor is carrying out an audit adapted from a model suggested by the project team. If this is successful, then the two other Hillingdon PCGs will have a headstart in carrying out their own audit, should they choose to.

From the start, the project team worked hard in finding the right people. They got them involved by finding out how these people viewed the problem rather than coming in with a pre-determined set of solutions. The team then kept up interest by regular updates. When meeting resistance, they listened to the concerns of key people and genuinely tried to work out the best way to resolve difficulties. They consistently looked for incentives, such as a new serology testing service or a nurse-led leg-ulcer training programme. Consequently, they have not received the same degree of suspicion by GPs and community nurses as some of the other North Thames Health Authority-based projects.

The *H. pylori* project reaffirms that a message needs to be broadcast more than once before it makes enough of an impact for practitioners to consider adopting it.[24] With the dyspepsia guidelines, the first notice was when the announcement about the new serology service went out and only a few people took up the invitation to send their patients along for testing.

The second attempt was much bigger and stronger, with the postgraduate lectures and three GP locality forums. This led to GPs using the service, but they still weren't hearing the whole message, since a large proportion of referrals were for the over-45s, which is not in accordance with the guidelines. Now, presumably after the PCG dyspepsia management audit, they will think through the feasibility of making a third attempt to find out how to help GPs refer the most appropriate patients.

10

The diagnosis and management of heart failure in primary care and the introduction of an open-access echocardiography service in Kensington, Chelsea & Westminster

Sonja Hood and *Stephanie Taylor*

Introduction

Primary care is characterised by large caseloads and a wide variety of disease, and offers an almost overwhelming opportunity for projects seeking to apply research evidence to everyday clinical practice. Ideally, an evidence-based approach in primary care would target a common condition with a poor prognosis, amenable to effective, yet underused, treatment. Heart failure fulfils these criteria, and on that basis was selected by Kensington, Chelsea & Westminster as its Health Authority-led Implementation Project under the Regional Research & Development (R&D) Implementation Programme. This chapter describes our project to influence the diagnosis and management of heart failure in primary care.

The problem

Heart failure is a relatively common, life-threatening condition affecting 0.4–1.5% of the total population and up to 8% of those aged over 65.[1-4] Every year nearly two thirds of the most severely affected will die and half of those with mild heart failure will be dead within five years.[5]

Despite the gravity of the condition, evidenced by its poor prognosis, heart failure can be difficult to diagnose clinically. Studies suggest that up to half of all diagnoses may be incorrect.[6,7] In the UK, much of the management of heart failure is carried out in the community.[3,6,8,9]

Echocardiography is generally regarded as the 'gold standard' for the diagnosis of heart failure, and its use is widely recommended.[10,11] This is a non-invasive investigation, which must be performed and interpreted by a trained technician; until recently, therefore, it has remained the preserve of secondary care. In recent years, however, echocardiography services to which GPs have direct access (i.e. do not require a referral to a consultant) have become increasingly popular.[12]

The accurate diagnosis of heart failure has been confirmed by strong evidence from randomised controlled trials which have shown that relatively new drugs, angiotensin-converting enzyme (ACE) inhibitors, prolongs life, improves symptoms and reduces hospitalisations in patients with heart failure.[5,13,14] Despite this, it has been shown that ACE inhibitors are under-prescribed in heart failure.[1,3] For example, a Nottingham-based study found that only 17% of heart failure patients receiving symptomatic treatment with loop diuretics (or 'water tablets', which are conventionally used as the mainstay of treatment for patients with heart failure) were also being prescribed an ACE inhibitor.[15]

Our project evolved from a combination of the health authority's awareness of the powerful research evidence, the opportunity provided by the regional R&D Implementation Programme and local opportunities. There was pressure from both GPs and cardiologists to establish open-access echocardiography: GPs felt that this would improve their ability to diagnose heart failure, and cardiologists argued that open access to tests would reduce the length of their waiting lists by enabling patients requiring only tests to have direct access at the request of their GP, rather than needing to have a consultation with a cardiologist first. Furthermore, preliminary analysis of general practice prescribing data in our health authority revealed wide variations in ACE inhibitor prescribing, but, beyond this, we knew little about the way in which heart failure was being managed locally.

When our project commenced there were no nationally approved guidelines for the diagnosis and management of heart failure in primary care, although local guidelines had been developed in several other parts of the country. The European Society of Cardiology had produced heart failure guidelines,[10,16] but the extent to which these were applicable to primary care in the UK was unclear. The overall aim of the project was to improve the effectiveness of the diagnosis and management of heart failure in primary care locally. The objectives of the project were:

• to describe current local practice around diagnosis and management of heart failure, based on an audit of patient notes and a survey of GPs

- to develop guidelines for the diagnosis and management of heart failure in general practice, and for the use of an open-access echocardiography service
- to determine the effect of the guidelines a year after their introduction by audit of the open-access service, a survey of GP views and re-audit of practice notes.

Our approach

We decided to pilot the project in one of the four geographic 'localities' that made up our health authority. The chosen locality included nine practices with between one and three partners, and with varying levels of computerisation. The project was conducted by a research officer who was allocated to the project full time (initially a part-time post was considered, but it became apparent at an early stage that the role required full-time commitment). Throughout the duration of the project, our approach has been characterised by the following key features:

- a multidisciplinary project team
- recognition of the importance of local ownership
- pragmatism (e.g. amending *existing* guidelines to be locally relevant)
- continual involvement of *all* the practices in the locality
- efforts to involve the entire primary care team – not only the GPs
- recognition that time is a precious resource in primary care – wherever possible the project was taken to the individual practices and all the audit work was carried out on behalf of the practices.

The methods used to meet our objectives are summarised in Table 10.1.

Experience: describing current practice

The baseline audit

This was based on a review of relevant literature and discussions with local cardiologists and members of the primary care team. The audit was designed around two standards:

- Any diagnosis of heart failure should be supported by an investigation (chest X-ray, ECG or, preferably, echocardiography).[10]
- All patients with a diagnosis of heart failure should be considered for ACE inhibitors.[16]

Table 10.1 Summary of methods

Objective	Element	Method
1 Description of current local practice around the diagnosis and management of heart failure	Baseline audit of primary care notes*	Identification of patients being treated for heart failure in primary care through repeat prescribing registers, computer codes and GP memory. Approach tailored to each practice. Demographic, diagnostic and management data were extracted from each set of notes identified
	Survey of GP opinions	Informal, semi-structured interviews with GPs about heart failure in primary care; followed up with a short, structured postal questionnaire
2 Guidelines development	Develop guidelines for the diagnosis and management of heart failure in primary care	Results of Phase 1 of the project were fed back in writing, and in person, to each practice. Summaries of the relevant literature, including the European Cardiology Society's guidelines, were prepared to stimulate discussion
	Develop guidelines for the use of the open-access echocardiography service	All local GPs, echocardiography technicians, cardiologists and pharmacy advisors were invited to one of two discussion sessions. In total, 15 GPs, one technician, three practice nurses, three cardiologists, two pharmacy advisers and two public health doctors attended the sessions. The project officer drafted guidelines based on these meetings and disseminated these to all the participants for comment; the guidelines were revised accordingly and re-disseminated
3 Assessment of effect of project	Audit of the open-access service Survey of GP opinion Re-audit of practice notes	

*Copies of the original Microsoft Access audit tool developed for this project are available from S Hood, via Kensington, Chelsea & Westminster Health Authority, 50 Eastbourne Terrace, London W2 3QR.

We wanted to know how primary care teams reached a diagnosis of heart failure, and how they managed the patients they believed to have the condition. Therefore, our audit included any patient with a diagnosis of heart failure *anywhere* in their notes (and a list of the signs, symptoms and tests on which this diagnosis was based).

A disadvantage of our approach was that we undoubtedly missed patients who did have heart failure but who had not been diagnosed as such; and included patients who might have been diagnosed with heart failure in error. Other studies have attempted to address this problem by searching patient notes for a minimum set of signs or symptoms or test results, rather than for an actual mention of heart failure. We tested this alternative method but found it to be extremely time-consuming and lacking in rigour as it effectively meant re-diagnosing patients simply on the basis of their notes. Our approach was simpler and more transparent, and made it easier to remain consistent, however, we are mindful of its shortcomings.

Seven out of the nine practices in the locality took part in the audit. Information from patient notes was extracted directly into a database written in Microsoft Access. As practices used a variety of computerised and written notes, and computer systems had widely different roles within practices (some were used only for repeat prescribing, others contained entire patient histories), a different approach to data collection was adopted for almost every practice. We underestimated the time it would take to conduct the audit for the following reasons:

- We tried to identify heart failure patients by looking through the notes of all patients with a prescription for a loop diuretic: this was very time-consuming as only about half of these patients had a recorded diagnosis of heart failure.
- When patient records were held both on computer and in *Lloyd George* (the standard UK medical record cards used in general practice) paper format, the time taken to review notes was effectively doubled.
- Notes were often incomplete and time was spent searching for data to plug the gaps in information.

The audit gave us a clear picture of primary care patients with diagnosed heart failure in our locality. In all, 286 patients were identified, the average age at the time of the audit was 78 years, and 58% (167) of the patients were female. The average age of these patients at the time of diagnosis was 75 years. Over half (55%) of the heart failure diagnoses appeared to have been made in the community and almost one third of patients had been managed entirely in primary care. Thus the audit confirmed that heart failure was an important issue for primary care. The audit also identified several areas of concern about the diagnosis and management of heart failure in the locality:

- 37% of diagnoses had not been supported by an investigation
- 37% of patients had not been considered for an ACE inhibitor
- only 31% of patients had undergone echocardiography
- one fifth of diagnoses were made with no record of signs or symptoms in the patient's notes

- information about the underlying aetiology of the heart failure was rarely provided.

The survey of GPs

At the start of the project every GP in the locality (21 in total) was sent a brief survey about their current practice and views around the diagnosis and management of heart failure. The survey was returned by 17 (81%). The results appeared to highlight inconsistencies between the way the GPs believed heart failure should be managed and their own perception of the way they actually managed it. Key findings from the survey included:

- GPs felt that their diagnoses of heart failure were almost always based on patients' symptoms and signs and only sometimes based on investigations (chest X-rays, ECGs or echocardiograms).
- Fewer than half of the GPs completing the survey reported that they used ACE inhibitors routinely in the treatment of heart failure.

These findings contrast strongly with the GPs' opinions of 'best practice', summarised in Table 10.2.

Overall, the survey suggested that GPs supported the use of ACE inhibitors for the treatment of heart failure, and give no clue as to why the prescribing of ACE inhibitors in general practice for heart failure was generally low. The GPs also appeared to support the use of echocardiography and ECG. Fourteen of the 17 respondents said they would definitely be interested in using an open-access echocardiography service.

Experience: guidelines development

The second phase of the project was to develop guidelines for the diagnosis and management of heart failure in the community, which would coincide with the introduction of a new open-access echocardiography service. Building on discussions held in the first phase, and influenced by workshops we attended for people involved in several of the North Thames Health Authority-led R&D Implementation Projects, we developed the following criteria for the guidelines development phase:

- guidelines must be evidence-based
- guidelines must be applicable to current practice in primary care (i.e. they should build on the evidence gathered in the first phase of the project)

Table 10.2 GPs' opinions of 'best practice' (survey results)

In your opinion, do you agree or disagree with the following statements?	GP responses (n)			Summary of evidence
	Agree	Disagree	No opinion	
Patients with suspected heart failure should always have an ECG	12	4	1	Patients with heart failure are very unlikely to have a normal ECG – this is therefore a good, inexpensive, first-line test
Patients with suspected heart failure should always be referred for echocardiography	11	4	2	Echocardiography is widely recommended for routine use in the diagnosis of heart failure – notably, though, there are no randomised trials supporting the use of echocardiography
Patients with suspected heart failure should always be considered for ACE inhibitors	16	1	0	Guidelines recommend that ACE inhibitors be considered for all patients with heart failure due to systolic dysfunction, unless contra-indicated (e.g. by renal artery stenosis)
There are usually difficulties in administering ACE inhibitors to patients for the first time	4	12	1	Studies show that first-dose effects from ACE inhibitors are actually quite rare[17]
ACE inhibitors improve quality of life in patients with heart failure	12	2	3	Randomised trials of ACE inhibitors have shown these drugs improve quality of life compared with placebo[18]
ACE inhibitors improve length of life in patients with heart failure	11	3	2 (+1 n/a)	Randomised trials of ACE inhibitors have shown these drugs improve length of life compared with placebo[5,13]

- as far as possible, guideline development should be led by the users (i.e. GPs and other members of the primary care team), in consultation with cardiologists
- once agreed, guidelines should be brief and to the point.

Initial discussions in primary and secondary care

Throughout the project, the project officer had regular formal and informal contacts with the participating practices. All members of the primary care team were invited to discuss the audit results for their practice with the researcher, and to make suggestions about the progress achieved. Discussions also covered the diagnosis and treatment of heart failure, relationships with acute units and preferences for the open-access echocardiography service. The available evidence around heart failure management was summarised for the practices and each was given a copy of the European guidelines on the diagnosis and management of heart failure.[10,16] The project officer also met local cardiologists to talk about the process with them. Questions and concerns raised by GPs were fed back to the cardiologists, and these discussions subsequently formed the basis for the guideline development sessions.

Guideline development sessions

Two guideline development sessions were held at the trust where the new open-access service was to be based. Both sessions were chaired by a local GP and were attended by GPs, practice nurses, cardiologists, echocardiography technicians, the pharmaceutical advisor and other representatives from the health authority. Six of the eight general practices in the locality were represented at the sessions.

Each session included the following:

- an overview of the audit findings
- a talk by a cardiologist about heart failure and the use of ACE inhibitors
- a chance to view the echocardiography service in practice
- open discussion about the diagnosis and management of heart failure.

At the end of these sessions, it was agreed that the project officer would prepare draft guidelines, a patient information leaflet and an echocardiography referral form, and would circulate these to all participants for comment. It was also agreed that the new open-access echocardiography service would be experimental and that the results of the final phase of this project (re-audit of heart failure management in primary care, audit of use of the echo service by GPs from the locality) would help to determine whether the new service should become permanent and should be extended to primary care throughout the health authority.

Agreeing guidelines

A draft guideline flow chart was prepared, which attempted to synthesise these local discussions together with the published evidence around the diagnosis and management of heart failure in a clear and simple format. The referral form for the open-access service was also disseminated and amended in line with the feedback received. This form was designed to serve as a 'prompt' for management of patients along the lines indicated by the flow chart.[19] Finally, a patient information leaflet was drafted, circulated to each participant and piloted with patients attending for echocardiography at the hospital. (The guidelines chart, referral form and patient information leaflet are all included in Appendix 1 at the end of this chapter.)

Re-audit of patient notes

Two years after the original audit, we re-visited the notes of all the patients, to determine what changes – if any – had occurred. On average, follow up time for each patient was 26 months (SD, two months). We were able to locate notes for 249 of the original 286 patients. Of the remainder, 26 patients had moved, and notes for the remaining 11 patients were missing (nine of these patients had died). At the time this book went to press, we had only begun to analyse the follow up data, so only present preliminary results here.*

Of the 249 patients we followed up:

- 74 (30%) had died
- 71% of diagnoses were supported by an investigation (compared with 63% in the first audit)
- 63% of patients had been considered for an ACE inhibitor (the same proportion as in the first audit)
- 43% of patients had undergone echocardiography (compared with 31% in the first audit).

Further analysis is required before we can say how much of the improvement in diagnosis can be attributed to the project. However, we can report on two further sources of information which provide an *indication* of the value of the project: a survey of GPs about the open access echocardiography service and the guideline; and a completed audit of the open access service.

---

*We are happy to provide interested readers with further details of the re-audit data via the London Regional Office web site http://www.doh.gov.uk/ntrd/rd.htm

GPs' views of the open-access service and the guidelines

Just over a year after the open-access service commenced, all GPs were sent a survey about the service and the guidelines. Eighteen of the 23 GPs* returned the survey. Ten of these 18 GPs had used the service; of the remaining eight, five said they rarely saw a patient with heart failure, and two stated that they preferred to refer straight to cardiology (one did not give a reason).

The ten GPs who had used the open-access service felt that the diagnostic information given with the results of the echocardiogram was useful, and all but two felt that the management advice was also helpful. The timeliness of the service was highlighted as a problem: five said their patients had to wait at least three weeks to be seen, although most said that results came back within two weeks.

Ten of the 18 GPs had a copy of the guidelines that had been developed, which they found either 'very' or 'somewhat' useful. No changes were suggested for the guidelines. The remaining eight GPs requested copies of the guidelines.

GPs' use of the open-access service

By the end of its first year, the open-access service had seen 131 patients referred from GPs across the health authority. Thirty-four referrals were from GPs who participated in this study. Of these 34 referrals:

- 18 (53%) were related to heart failure
- one was for a patient referred for left ventricular hypertrophy, and two for other reasons
- 13 were for patients referred for assessment of a murmur.

Ten of the 18 patients referred for heart failure were female (average age for women 76, average age for men 70). Echocardiograms were within normal limits for seven of the 18 patients.

Information from the open-access service was consistent with the GPs' perception that access to the service was too slow. The 131 patients referred to the service had waited an average of 34 days (range 0–69 days) for their test. Attempts to prioritise access to the service had been hampered by the continued use by certain practices of an old referral form, rather than the new one

---

*The total number of GPs working in the locality had increased from 21 when the project started to 23 when the survey was conducted.

developed specifically for the purpose. Perhaps predictably, service technicians commented that some referrals to the service have been inappropriate.

The service features on the local PCG agenda, and the model used in the project has already been applied in another locality (at the request of local practitioners). The future of the open-access echocardiography service is currently being reviewed jointly by GPs and cardiologists (a debate which will be informed by the forthcoming results of the re-audit). The review will decide whether the service should be maintained, extended or withdrawn. Whatever the decision, we regard the fact that local GPs and the hospital-based cardiology consultants are now engaged in a constructive and informed dialogue about testing as an important achievement. We consider the fact that these groups are now working together with mutual respect and heightened awareness of each others' perspective confirms the value that the project has had as a catalyst and a stimulus for improving patient care across the interface between primary and secondary healthcare.

Lessons learned

Primary care notes provide a valuable source of 'real' data but they can be difficult to access and are often incomplete

- The results of our baseline audit were encouragingly similar to those in previously published research into heart failure in primary care. However, extracting the data was often extremely time-consuming and some data items which we originally wanted to collect, such as details of ethnicity, smoking status, and blood urea and electrolyte levels, were poorly completed in the primary care notes.

Projects like this can be conducted by people without a medical or nursing background

- When the project was first planned many of the clinicians involved felt that it would be essential for the project officer to have a medical or nursing background. In fact, our project officer had a social science and health services research background, and rather than being a hindrance, our experience was that this worked to our advantage. We think that this was at least partly because by informing the GPs at the outset that the project officer was a 'lay' person who would have no judgemental view of their work, the clinicians felt more relaxed about the audit than they might otherwise have done.

Even a comparatively simple project like this can be expensive

- The project required the time of a full-time researcher for a year. As stated above, in our case a social scientist was employed; projects which really do require staff with a nursing or medical background may prove more expensive.

continued overleaf

Local politics are important

- Relations between individual GPs; between practices; between GPs and the hospital; among consultants; and between hospital departments all impact on success and must be taken into account. We found that diplomacy worked much better than autocracy, and learned that it was more effective to *involve* rather than (try to) *command*.

Published literature can be valuable but does not always contain all the answers

- Much of the literature about heart failure is based on hospital patients. Our general practice population with heart failure proved to be quite different from people in these trials. In particular, our population was predominantly female and very elderly. This contrasts with published randomised trials of ACE inhibitors: for example, patients in the SOLVD trial had an average age of 60, and 88% were male[13]; in the CONSENSUS trial the average age was 71, and 70% of patients were male.[5]

GPs are not as uninformed as some literature might suggest

- Some published papers which have found that ACE inhibitors are under-prescribed in general practice have suggested that GPs may not be aware of the benefits of this treatment. We did not find this to be the case, but we are not able to offer an alternative explanation for the under-prescribing of ACE inhibitors in general practice. Suggestions would be that GPs observe more side effects of ACE inhibitors in elderly patients, or that they are not always certain that a patient has heart failure, or that they do not see the quality of life benefits shown in the trials. However, we remain unclear, and look forward to the emergence of explanations. Finally, we noted with interest that many of the patients in our study who had heart failure had also been treated in hospital, but still were not being prescribed ACE inhibitors. We took this as an indication that a reluctance to prescribe ACE inhibitors may not be solely a characteristic of doctors in general practice.

Things we would do differently if we were starting tomorrow

- **allocate more time and resources to the audit.** The audit phase of the project was originally intended to be quite short, however, we seriously underestimated the amount of time it would take to extract data from notes in primary care
- **involve *care of the elderly* physicians as well as cardiologists.** Initially, we involved GPs and cardiologists in the design and conduct of the project. As we progressed, we identified other key players, including geriatricians, who are responsible for the management of heart failure in many patients. Within the hospital setting, different specialities had quite

continued opposite

different approaches to the care of the condition, which caused some confusion. This could be avoided by identifying and involving *all* stakeholders from the outset

- **allow more time in the project for qualitative work with GPs**. A central question raised by the project concerned the reasons why GPs do not prescribe ACE inhibitors to all patients with heart failure. We did not have time or resources to address this interesting aspect of the work. Building into the project plan a capacity for qualitative research would be a way of capitalising on opportunities which arise in the course of an implementation project

- **extend the scope of the project to include 'roll out' to other practices**. Once the project was complete in our chosen locality, rolling out to other practices happened in a reasonably ad hoc fashion, led by local GPs, while the project officer moved on to another role. In many ways it would be better to involve the main driving force behind the pilot in the subsequent roll-out (in our case the project officer) in the roll-out phase. This would help to achieve continuity of service development across the whole health authority

- **not assume that the published literature holds all the answers!** Despite choosing a project where the evidence was regarded as very good, we found that there were, in fact, very few community-based studies of the diagnosis and management of heart failure, and that those which have been published are quite small. Our early confidence that the evidence was clear-cut became tempered over time by the realisation that *some* was, but *all* of it certainly was not. It may be better to start an implementation project with more realistic expectations of the degree to which available research evidence can answer questions in the target environment.

References

1   Parameshwar J, Shackell MM, Richardson A, Poole-Wilson PA and Sutton GC (1992) Prevalence of heart failure in three general practices in north-west London. *British Journal of General Practice*. **42**: 287–9.

2   Sutton GC (1990) Epidemiologic aspects of heart failure. *American Heart Journal*. **6**: 1538–40.

3   Mair FS, Crowley TS and Bundred PE (1996) Prevalence, aetiology and management of heart failure in general practice. *British Journal of General Practice*. **46**: 77–9.

4   Clarke KW, Gray D and Hampton JR (1995) How common is heart failure? Evidence from PACT (prescribing analysis and cost) data in Nottingham. *Journal of Public Health Medicine* **17**: 459–64.

5   Swedberg K (1987) Effects of enalapril on mortality in severe congestive heart failure: results of three co-operative North Scandinavian Enalapril Survival Study (CONSENSUS). *N Engl J Med*. **316**: 1429–35.

6 Wheeldon NM, MacDonald TM, Flucker CJ, McKendrik AD, McDevitt DG and Struthers AD (1993) Echocardiography in chronic heart failure in the community. *Quarterly Journal of Medicine.* **86**: 17–23.

7 Remes J, Meittinen H, Reunanen A and Pyorala K (1991) Validity of clinical diagnosis of heart failure in primary care. *Eur Heart J.* **12**: 315–21.

8 Francis CM, Caruana L, Kearney P *et al.* (1995) Open-access echocardiography in management of heart failure in the community. *BMJ.* **310**: 634–6.

9 Hillis GS, Al-Mohammad A, Wood M and Jennings KP (1996) Changing patterns of investigation and treatment of cardiac failure in hospital. *Heart.* **76**: 427–9.

10 Task force on heart failure of the European Society of Cardiology (1995) Guidelines for the diagnosis of heart failure. *European Heart Journal.* **16**: 741–51.

11 Morgan R and King D (1995) An audit of echocardiograms in acute left ventricular failure. *Postgrad Med J.* **71**: 738–40.

12 Askenasy OM, Dawson D, Gill M, Haines A and Patterson DLH (1994) Audit of direct access cardiac investigations: experience in an inner London Health District. *J Roy Soc Med.* **87**: 588–90.

13 SOLVD Investigators (1992) Effect of enalapril on mortality and the development of heart failure in asymptomatic patients with reduced left ventricular ejection fractions. *N Engl J Med.* **327**: 685–91.

14 Borghi C, Ambrosioni E and Magnani B (1996) Effects of the early administration of zofenopril on onset and progression of congestive heart failure in patients with anterior wall myocardial infarction. *American Journal of Cardiology.* **78**: 317–22.

15 Clarke KW, Gray D and Hampton JR (1994) Evidence of inadequate investigation and treatment of patients with heart failure. *British Heart Journal.* **71**: 584–7.

16 Task force on heart failure of the European Society of Cardiology and Remme WJ (1997) The treatment of heart failure; the task force of the working group on heart failure of the European society of cardiology. *European Heart Journal.* **18**: 736–53.

17 Dargie HJ, McMurray JJV and Poole-Wilson PA (1996) *Managing Heart Failure in Primary Care.* Blackwell Healthcare Communications, London.

18 Rogers WJ, Johnstone DE, Yusuf S, Weiner DH, Gallagher P *et al.* (1994) Quality of life among 5,025 patients with left ventricular dysfunction randomised between placebo and enalapril: the studies of left ventricular dysfunction. *JACC.* **23(2)**: 393–400.

19 Buntinx F, Winkens R, Grol R *et al.* (1993) Influencing diagnostic and preventative performance in ambulatory care by feedback and reminders. A review. *Fam Pract.* **110**: 219–28.

Appendix 1

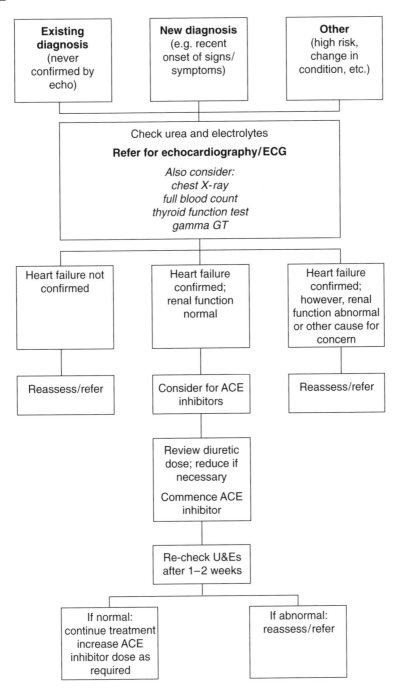

Figure 10.1   Management of heart failure in primary care: guidelines for GPs.

REQUEST FOR OPEN ACCESS ECHOCARDIOGRAPHY
(HEART FAILURE)

Patient details

Name   ....
Date of birth ....
Address   ....
              ....
              ....
Telephone   ....
NHS number   ....

General Practitioner details (or stamp)

Name   ....
Surgery ....
Address ....
         ....
         ....
Telephone ....
Fax   ....

Service requested (please tick one):
❒ Echocardiography only
❒ Echocardiography and ECG

Priority of referral (please tick one):
❒ High priority (to be seen ASAP)
❒ Medium priority (within the next few weeks)
❒ Low priority (within the next month)

Clinical symptoms/signs
❒ Unexplained breathlessness
❒ Unexplained oedema
❒ Heart murmur
❒ Raised JVP

❒ Pulmonary crepitations
❒ Other (please specify):

Relevant patient history
❒ MI (year: _____)
❒ Hypertension
❒ Atrial fibrillation
❒ Heart surgery
❒ Murmurs
❒ Diabetic
❒ Family history of heart disease

Smoker: ❒ Current ❒ Past ❒ Never
Number of units of alcohol
per week: ....
Other relevant condition
(please specify):

Medication (tick as applicable)   Name   Dose
❒ ACE inhibitor
❒ Diuretic
❒ Other:

Results of previous tests and investigations

Has the patient had an **ECG:**   Yes / No If YES, were results: Normal / abnormal

Has the patient had a **chest X-ray:** Yes / No If YES, were results: Normal / abnormal

Any other relevant information:

(Extract from patient information leaflet)
What is an echocardiogram?
An echocardiogram uses ultrasound to take a moving picture of your heart. This shows how well your heart is working.

- It is completely safe, and should not cause you any pain.

What happens?
You will be asked to lie down on your side for about 20 minutes. A technician will move a small probe over the surface of your chest, which will produce images of your heart on a screen.

Why do I need to have an echocardiogram?
The echocardiogram will help your doctor to find out more about how well your heart is working. Some patients develop a condition called 'heart failure', which means the heart is no longer pumping as efficiently as it used to. (This might cause symptoms such as swollen ankles or difficulty with breathing.) If the echocardiogram confirms that you have heart failure, some very effective treatments are available.

Will I need any other tests?
When you visit the cardiology department for your echocardiography, you may also have an ECG (electrocardiogram). This measures the electricity produced by your heart. Once again, you will be asked to lie down, this time for about ten minutes. A number of sticky pads will be attached to your chest and arms, and a machine will record your heart beat.

- ECG is completely safe, and should not cause you any pain.

What happens next?
The results from the echocardiography and ECG (if you have had one) will be sent back to your GP. If you have heart failure, your doctor will discuss the best types of medication available with you. If you do not have heart failure, your doctor will consider other possible causes for your condition.

For your echocardiogram, you will need to go to:

> The Cardiology Department
> First Floor
> Hospital address

Getting to the hospital:

- **A Hoppa Bus Service** runs between the hospital and the South West-minster Clinic. For details, ring General Services on (0181) 746 8128.
- Ask at your surgery for details of other buses and tubes to the hospital.
- **Car parking** is available in the underground car park or in metered spaces in nearby streets.

Diagnosis

The European Society of Cardiology Guidelines[10] for the diagnosis of heart failure specify three criteria to diagnose heart failure.

1   Symptoms of heart failure (at rest or during exercise).
2   Objective evidence of cardiac dysfunction.
3   Response to treatment for heart failure (where the diagnosis is in doubt).

This document provides a brief summary of the European guidelines, and some recommendations for implementation in Kensington, Chelsea & Westminster.

1 Symptoms and signs of heart failure (at rest or during exercise)

Table 10.3 summarises the main symptoms and signs of heart failure. It is important to bear in mind that most of these are, on their own, non-specific

Table 10.3   Main symptoms and signs of heart failure

Symptom/sign	Comments
• Breathlessness • Ankle swelling (dependent oedema) • Fatigue	These are the three classic symptoms of heart failure; however, it is important to note that: • they can be difficult to interpret • in isolation, none of these is specific for CHF
Hepatomegaly	Non-specific to CHF
Raised venous pressure	Characteristic sign of congestion of systemic veins. Determination of a raised JVP can be difficult, and may not be present in many patients with even severe heart failure (if, for example, predominantly left-sided)
Tachycardia	Non-specific to CHF; may be absent in even severe heart failure
Apex beat	Often difficult to palpate, not an accurate measure of cardiomegaly
Third heart sound	Difficult to hear; low inter-observer agreement. However, in patients aged over 25, this is indicative of ventricular dysfunction
Pulmonary crepitations	Non-specific to heart failure; low inter-observer agreement. Measure is also insensitive – a patient can have pulmonary oedema without crackles

to heart failure; and that furthermore, many are difficult to measure accurately.

2 Objective evidence of heart failure – non-invasive investigations

ECG

A normal ECG is rare in heart failure patients and, if present, suggests that the diagnosis should be carefully reviewed. The ECG is crucial in determining the heart rhythm, however, abnormalities on the ECG may not suggest an underlying cause. The presence of Q waves suggests a myocardial infarction, but in the absence of an appropriate history this should be confirmed by other investigations.

Chest X-ray

There is a poor relationship between heart size on X-ray and left ventricular function. Cardiomegaly is frequently absent in acute heart failure, but the presence of cardiomegaly lends support to a diagnosis of heart failure, especially when accompanied by upper lobe diversion. A chest X-ray is also useful in excluding pulmonary disease as a cause of symptoms.

Echocardiography

Echocardiography should be used routinely for the optimal diagnosis of heart failure, enabling assessment of the functional integrity of the valves, chamber dimensions, ventricular hypertrophy systolic and diastolic function, and regional wall motion abnormalities. This is not yet a useful instrument for measuring diastolic heart failure, and measures may be less reliable if the patient has atrial fibrillation.

3 Response to treatment for heart failure

Response to treatment for heart failure is not, on its own, sufficient evidence to make a diagnosis; although a patient should generally experience some improvement from a diuretic, ACE inhibitor or digoxin. It is important to note that treatment may obscure a diagnosis of heart failure by relieving a patient's symptoms.

Treatment

The European Society of Cardiology's guidelines on the management of heart failure[16] provide information about a variety of aspects of treatment. This summary concentrates on guidelines for pharmacological therapy.

DIURETICS

Thiazide and loop diuretics

Diuretics are essential for symptomatic treatment when fluid overload (peripheral oedema or lung congestion) is present. Symptoms may be treated with a thiazide diuretic or, if symptoms are more severe, with a loop diuretic. Combinations of loop and thiazide diuretics may also be used in cases of severe heart failure, or where symptoms have failed to respond to a loop diuretic alone.

Potassium-sparing diuretics

In cases of hypokalaemia, a potassium-sparing diuretic may be prescribed. These can be prescribed in combination with a loop diuretic. However, it is important to note that if the patient is being treated with ACE inhibitors, potassium-sparing diuretics should generally be avoided. If potassium-sparing diuretics are prescribed, particular attention should be paid to serum creatinine and potassium. Levels should be monitored: during initial treatment, every 5–7 days until levels are stable and thereafter every three months (and eventually every six months).

ACE INHIBITORS

ACE inhibitors are indicated in all stages of symptomatic systolic heart failure.

ACE inhibitors have been shown to improve symptoms, survival and functional status, and reduce mortality and hospitalisation in patients with moderate to severe heart failure.

In addition, evidence suggests that patients with asymptomatic left ventricular dysfunction also benefit from ACE inhibitors.

Adverse effects and contraindications

Major adverse effects:	Hypotension, syncope, renal insufficiency, hyperkalaemia, angio-oedema (otolaryngeal) and dry cough (note that cough can be difficult to distinguish from that due to pulmonary congestion).
Minor adverse effects:	Rash, taste disturbance.
Absolute contraindications:	Bilateral renal artery stenosis and angio-oedema during previous ACE inhibitor therapy.

Initiating ACE inhibitors

Briefly, the recommended procedure for initiation of ACE inhibitors is as follows:

1   Stop diuretics 24 hours before treatment.
2   Initiate treatment in the evening (as this may minimise the potential negative effect on blood pressure), or in the morning under observation.
3   Start with a low dose, build up to a maintenance dose.
4   Renal function should be regularly monitored: before initiation of treatment, at 3–5 days during drug titration, at three months and at six-monthly intervals (more often if the patient has a history of renal dysfunction or electrolyte disturbances). It should also be checked whenever treatment is changed. *If renal function deteriorates, stop treatment.*
5   Avoid potassium-sparing diuretics and NSAIDs.
6   Check blood pressure 1–2 weeks after each dose increment. Patients with low systolic blood pressure (less than 100 mmHg) should have ACE inhibitors initiated under observation. Low blood pressure (≤90 mmHg) during treatment with ACE inhibitors is acceptable if the patient is asymptomatic.

Recommendations for implementation of guidelines in Kensington, Chelsea & Westminster

The flow chart in Appendix One provides a simple template for diagnosing and treating heart failure. It builds on the following conclusions:

1   In the absence of a credible alternative diagnosis, all patients presenting with signs or symptoms of heart failure should be referred for an ECG, chest X-ray and echocardiogram. Urea and electrolytes should also be checked.
2   Where diagnosis is confirmed, patients with fluid overload should be started on either a loop or a thiazide diuretic.
3   In the absence of any absolute contraindications, patients should be started on an ACE inhibitor. Initially a low dose should be used, building up to the recommended maintenance dose. In certain cases (see above) the ACE inhibitor should be initiated under observation.
4   Urea and electrolytes should be checked 3–5 days after starting ACE inhibitors, and at regular intervals thereafter.

Kensington, Chelsea & Westminster commentary

Heart failure and open-access echocardiography

Three of the 17 North Thames projects looked at the management of heart failure, each one from a different point. The Barking & Havering project is community-based; the Brent & Harrow project was designed and managed by a local hospital; and the Kensington, Chelsea & Westminster (KCW) project falls between the two.

We do not know much about the Brent & Harrow project as they dropped out of the evaluation. But we can make a few comparisons between the Barking & Havering and KCW projects. The Barking & Havering team emphasised an educational approach through developing guidelines and auditing practice. They were unable to do much more from their purely community base.

The KCW team incorporated both guideline development and audit and added a big incentive – a new open-access echocardiography service. In looking at changing practice, the question the KCW project throws up is: how useful is the incentive of a much-valued service in giving clinicians a push towards changing their behaviour?

Keeping in mind that 30% of the sample population died, results from the follow up audit seem to suggest that the new service has had some impact on increasing the number of diagnoses supported with an investigation (up 8%) and numbers of patients undergoing an echocardiography (up 12%). But there has been no change in the consideration of prescribing ACE inhibitors. We assume that this means that the impact on actual prescribing is weak.

Although this project may still have some way to go in changing prescribing behaviour, it has been useful in providing excellent evaluative data. A key message from that work is what people say they do and what they actually do can be very different.

For example, before setting up the echo service, 82% of surveyed GPs (14/17) said they would use the service. One year later, 43% (10/23), half as many as expected, have made a referral. Even more importantly, the survey on how GPs think they would treat heart failure patients varies considerably from the evidence brought to light in the two audits of GP notes. This project is rich in data on just how complex changing behaviour can be.

In the process of getting that data, this team has learned that obtaining robust, accurate evaluation information is very time consuming. So time consuming, in fact, that many other North Thames project teams have understandably been put off trying. However, having collected that data, this team is making very good use of it, both at a local level and nationally.

A key factor to making the project work, mentioned by many local participants in our survey, was the 'personable' personality of the project worker. Using the approach of 'we're here to develop the service for you', the project worker was able to gain access to the practices and, even more importantly, the practice notes. To get an idea of how difficult that was, as external evaluators we were unable to get anyone to talk to us for the first survey and only got access to local clinicians for the second survey after the project worker wrote a note to all concerned.

In terms of sustainability, the outlook for this project is good. At one workshop, the project manager commented that since they were taking a discrete project approach, she feared that their work might not spread. Instead, the success of the project has been such that GPs from a neighbouring patch actually asked if they could do the audit as well. What's more, a chair of one of the PCGs told us that on the basis of the referral audit, the PCG has taken up the issue of refining and improving the quality of the service with the local hospital. The health authority may have set the service up; but in at least one patch, local practitioners now value it sufficiently that they are taking over the responsibility for how it should run.

11

Implementing clinical guidelines in primary care in Redbridge & Waltham Forest

Sue Collett and *Peter Elliot*

'LET'S SEE, HOW SHALL WE MONITOR YOUR BLOOD PRESSURE THIS TIME?'

Introduction and outline

Redbridge & Waltham Forest is situated on the north-east edge of London. It has a population of around 450 000, and ranges from an 'inner-city' environment (south), to suburban Epping Forest (north). It has 125 general practices with 240 GPs which, during the period of the project, were divided into ten commissioning groups which were being piloted. These have subsequently been reconfigured as three PCGs.

In Redbridge & Waltham Forest, as elsewhere, we realised some time ago that there is no shortage of guidelines in the NHS! Though most genuinely attempt to inform practitioners of the best course of action to take in a given context, quality is infinitely variable, and many recommendations lack evidence and sometimes conflict with other guidelines. Even when we have confidence in a guideline, to assume that dissemination will result in its uptake, and consequent changes in clinical practice, would be very naïve indeed. Influencing practitioner behaviour is a complex process, fraught with problems, and simple production and dissemination has usually been ineffective.[1]

Nevertheless, it has been shown that if sufficient effort is put into developing, discussing and promoting a guideline, and introduction is co-ordinated with other supportive activities (such as educational events), guideline implementation is possible and can lead to improved care.[2] It was with this understanding (i.e. that guidelines *could* help to improve clinical practice, but only with appropriate preconditions and supporting activity) that we chose a guideline implementation programme as our Health Authority-led Implementation Project. It was both 'down to earth' and ambitious because the initiative aimed not only to produce and promote several sets of usable guidelines, but to develop a local *model* for facilitated implementation of changes in care based on research evidence.

Establishing a framework for the dissemination and implementation of locally developed guidelines (or local adaptations of national clinical guidelines) was at the core of the project. We based our model on successful elements from other initiatives,[3–5] and our own learning. The 'Clinical Guideline Steering Group' was set up as the engine for our project, with a remit to prioritise and co-ordinate activity across the district, promoting effective healthcare, and attempting to reduce morbidity and mortality in major disease areas. A guideline facilitator was appointed to co-ordinate the work and drive the project.

At the time of writing, guidelines have been developed for antibiotic prescribing, paediatric shared care and diabetes, and these have been disseminated and implemented within primary care across the district. A locally developed draft hypertension guideline is currently being piloted by several practices. An asthma guideline was also planned, for implementation in summer 1999. The original timescale of the project was 18 months, but an organisational structure has been developed and local resources identified, which has ensured that the work is continuing beyond the period initially funded through the Regional R&D Implementation Programme. This chapter provides details of the experience of the guideline initiative over the past two years, discusses the factors which have influenced its impact and sustainability, and draws out the lessons from our work.

Aims and objectives

The main, visible aim of the project was to set up a mechanism whereby locally developed or adapted guidelines could be disseminated, assimilated and applied by practitioners. This was to be achieved within 18 months (dictated by the terms of Regional R&D funding for the project). A central element of the plan was to employ a guideline facilitator who would work in a variety of ways with GPs to promote the uptake and implementation of guidelines (such as using of computer-prompted guidelines as a tool for the improvement of diabetic care). Parallel to this process of guideline implementation we considered that it would be vital to develop ways of auditing the use and impact of guidelines.

Within the context of the overall aims, we had more specific objectives for the project, which were congruent with the broader service and organisational priorities of the health authority. These were:

- to clarify the referral criteria for GPs and specialists, which we thought would help with the successful integration of primary and secondary care services
- to develop the commissioning of services from the perspective of diseases and care groups (in preference to commissioning by 'block contract')
- to improve local standards of chronic disease management in primary care and monitor them
- to reduce unplanned admissions for the selected conditions
- to reduce the rate of disease complications (in diabetes).*

Getting started

A guideline facilitator was recruited and located within the local Multi-professional Audit Advisory Group (MAAG). The facilitator was responsible for the day-to-day running of the project, reported to the MAAG Chair (a local GP),** and was managerially accountable to the medical advisor at the health authority.

The first stage in designing a model for implementing evidence-based practice locally was to undertake a simple search of national and local research on the subject. This involved discussions with interested local clinicians and a hand-search of the local library for relevant literature. The intention was to avoid unnecessary duplication of effort, to assess local knowledge and forge

---

*Although reducing the rate of disease complications was a long-term objective, it was hoped that some progress could be made within the lifetime of the project. The objective was stimulated by a report showing that diabetics in Redbridge & Waltham Forest had a high level of amputation as a result of complications.[6]

**The MAAG Chair was a major local player, and a key ally for our project. He also chaired the local Education Board and was Clinical Director of a group, the Inner City Lecturer Team, which had the aims of improving clinical practice locally and involving local primary care clinicians in teaching and research at St Bartholomew's & The Royal London Medical College.

strategic links with existing structures and key players, and to prepare the ground locally.

The next step was establishing an Educational Outreach Team which would support practice-based educational updating. The team comprised: the guideline facilitator, three GPs (clinical/research fellows), a nurse practitioner and an audit facilitator (from the MAAG). It was agreed that practice-based sessions to promote guideline use and associated audits would be offered as informal, one-hour, lunchtime meetings. These were multiprofessional, approved for PGEA (i.e. counting towards doctors' postgraduate educational allowance) and offered certificates (enabling nurses to demonstrate attendance as part of PREP portfolios).

These, and all subsequent steps in the development of the projects are set out in Figure 11.1.

Topics

The original project proposal, which was largely a response to local need and demand from practitioners, identified diabetes, hypertension and asthma as the disease areas to be tackled within the district. Independently of our project, two further sets of local guidelines had been generated by the health authority, which had not been disseminated at the time our project began. These were a guideline on antibiotic prescribing, which was considered to be complete and ready to be printed, and a guideline on paediatric shared care, divided into four component parts: urinary tract infections; upper respiratory tract infections; febrile convulsions; and diarrhoea and vomiting, which was in the final stage of development. It was decided that dissemination of these additional guidelines should be delayed to enable their 'marketing' to form part of a cohesive process.

In total, therefore, there was potential for up to five sets of guidelines to be promoted as part of the initiative: two sets where work was under way or complete, and three where development on guidelines had not started but where local clinicians had expressed a wish to see them produced. This would clearly be a large agenda, however, we were mindful of the research evidence that implementation of any more than two guidelines per year is unlikely to be successful,[7] and were therefore keen to phase implementation sequentially.

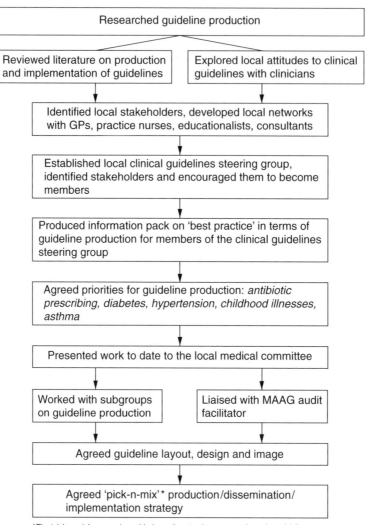

Figure 11.1 The steps followed in the project (from the perspective of the guideline facilitator).

Development, style and the implementation process

Each set of guidelines was developing by a group comprising local GPs, hospital consultants and other healthcare professionals, as appropriate. The groups used nationally developed guidelines as a starting point, and made adaptations to ensure that they would fit in with the local circumstances (being sensitive to both local need and service provision). The resulting local guidelines have been produced in a standard style and format, with an easily recognisable bright-yellow cover bearing a trademark blue 'tick' to signify approval. An audit data collection pro forma is incorporated into each guideline.

The guideline implementation process was based on a pragmatic combination of research evidence[4] and local opportunities, which often became apparent during practice visits by the the guidelines facilitator. The strategy is predominantly educational and relies heavily on practice-based updating sessions. These are designed to encourage primary healthcare team members to reflect on:

- their current clinical practice and how it compares with the guideline recommendations
- the relevant roles and responsibilities within the primary healthcare team
- any necessary amendment or updating of relevant practice nurse protocols
- the introduction or maintenance of chronic disease registers and recall systems (with the objective of reaching agreement on one member of the team taking responsibility)
- the IT skills and the consistency and quality of data entry
- the benefits of auditing processes of care
- the value of local guidelines, and the resources available to help implementation.

Experience

The guidelines were launched at scheduled educational meetings. In the case of the paediatric shared care and hypertension guidelines these were regular GP lunchtime meetings and MAAG workshops. For the antibiotic and diabetes guidelines, district-wide 'launches' were held in a local hotel. A system whereby practices could choose to work on implementation of the guideline of most relevance to their practice population ('pick-n-mix') was used.

All launches were followed up by individual practice visits, intended to help practices embed the use of the guidelines into their working routines. These visits were usually undertaken by the guideline facilitator and one of the three GPs from the educational outreach team. Other members of the team, such as the nurse lecturer or audit facilitator, were involved as appropriate. Locality workshops, attended by several practices, were also held for most guidelines. These workshops were convened by a local GP tutor, with GPs from the locality invited to participate. GP members of the guideline team and local consultants co-presented the guidelines and discussed the development process, evidence base, recommendations and local relevance.

Several important issues emerged relative to developing a successful programme of practice visits.

- **Targeting.** Initially, only 'friendly' practices (i.e. where contact with the audit team had already been established) were interested in visits. Discretion, and the promise of confidentiality, were of paramount importance in persuading other practices that they should take advantage of the offer of visits.
- **Access.** Networking with GPs, practice nurses and practice managers was vital. We learned that winning the support of practice managers was particularly important, as they frequently acted as 'gatekeepers' to the practice. Practice nurses could also be very effective at instigating visits, if they were involved and interested. As a consequence we realised that time and effort invested in establishing a good relationship with practice managers and nurses was very worthwhile, and we worked hard to cultivate these relationships. Not only were they frequently the gateway into the practice, but they were often enthusiastic about contributing to 'best practice', and could keep up the momentum of guideline use or an audit after a visit. The guideline facilitator attended as many meetings and seminars involving local practices as possible, in order to become 'recognised'. This visibility was important, even after the work had begun to take off. Initially, face-to-face requests for visits appeared to work best, and attempts at telephone recruitment usually failed. At the time of writing, however, two years into the project, this has changed, and it is now possible for the team to arrange visits over the telephone.

  On several occasions the facilitator found that the GP she was visiting would not be present at the surgery, having left to make house calls. An attempt was made to prevent this situation by telephoning the practice two days prior to the visit to confirm the appointment. However, we found that these confirmation calls were often used by practices as an opportunity to cancel visits (invariably because they were 'so busy'), so the policy was discontinued and a certain level of cases where GPs were missing was accepted as unavoidable.
- **Engagement of team members.** We learned that on the first visit it was vital to pitch the session in such a way as to build a supportive relationship with the team members. It was important to recognise that no two teams were the same, and essential to avoid having preconceptions about the team dynamics. This first visit mainly aimed at identifying training needs. Our sessions were informal, flexible and non-judgemental. The facilitator listened and worked at building up trust. Practice team members often reported that they felt overwhelmed with their current workload and were too busy to take on 'another task'. Many considered

that for a variety of reasons it would be difficult to make changes within the practice. We learned to use this response as an opportunity to share the strategies which other 'busy practices' had used. On the initial visit, the primary healthcare team was encouraged to audit the topic area and support was provided as required. We suggested that a relatively small number of patients (about 50)* should be used for the audit. Audit data were analysed, often by the audit facilitator, although sometimes by members of the practice. 'Reluctant' practices found it helpful if the guideline facilitator went through the audit process with a member of the practice staff, helping them to complete the audit data form. Results were further analysed by the MAAG, and feedback was provided to the team by the guideline facilitator at a subsequent visit, normally within a period of 4–6 weeks. We found that this timescale allowed for data collection and analysis, but was not so long as to allow enthusiasm to evaporate!

- **Feedback.** We were aware that this needs to be sensitive, and found that non-judgemental prompts such as 'Were the results in line with what you expected?' were effective in avoiding embarrassed silences and encouraging positive discussion. Depending on the audit results, practice teams usually decided to instigate changes either to clinical or organisational processes. In some cases, training and educational needs were also identified. The guideline team provided information and/or support wherever possible. Practices were then contacted within 6–9 months and encouraged to re-audit changes, the idea being that this would be a sufficiently lengthy period for the results of the changes implemented to be picked up in the repeat audit (*see* Table 11.1).

- **Changing the *organisation* of care.** Our experience confirmed that audit can also be used to stimulate important changes in the organisation of care. For example, the following action was taken by practice staff in one practice, with very encouraging results:
  - a search for patients on diabetic drugs was conducted and a computerised disease register was set up
  - patients seen regularly at the diabetic clinic were identified (about a third of the total on diabetic drugs)

---

*We had included various recommended numbers for audits in the guidelines. However, it soon became apparent that for practices for whom audit was a new experience, working with large numbers was too daunting. We took the view that it would be better to get practices involved, albeit with a smaller-than-ideal audit, rather than risk losing them altogether. Thus the use of audits of 50 records, selected randomly from the relevant disease register, was based on pragmatism rather than methodological rigour.

Table 11.1   Results of re-audited changes: comparison 1997/1998

	Number 1997	Percentage	Number 1998	Percentage	Percentage improvement	95% confidence interval
HBA1c levels checked	12	23.0	48	96.0	73.0	(60, 86) p < 0.0001
BP checked	47	90.4	48	96.0	5.6	(−4.1, 15.3), p < 0.23
Feet checked	8	15.4	30	60.0	44.6	(27.9, 61.4), p < 0.0001
Urine checked	–	–	44	88.0	–	
Eyes checked	10	19.2	38	76.0	56.8	(40.8, 72.7), p < 0.0001
Diet checked	–	–	47	94.0	–	
BMI checked	–	–	48	96.0	–	

HBA1c levels		1997	1998	Change
Good control		0%	49%	50% (95% CI 36, 64), p < 0.001
Moderate control	(7.0–9.0%)	60%	30%	−30% (95% CI −48, −11), p = 0.003
Poor Control	(>9.0%)	40%	21%	−18% (95% CI −36, −1), p = 0.05

NB: There were 52 patients included in the 1997 audit. There were 50 patients included in the 1998 audit.

- a method of recall for *all* patients on the diabetic register was devised. This entailed:
  - colour-coding notes according to the month of each patient's birthday
  - working with a patient-participation group to design a birthday card to be used as a prompt
  - sending birthday cards with appointments for a review and blood test form
  - arranging for the blood test to be carried out ten days prior to a clinic appointment (so that results would be available)
  - arranging for the practice nurse to have a one-day update with the local diabetic nurse specialist
  - arranging for the practice nurse to have one extra diabetic clinic session per week.

As a result of these innovations in the *organisation* of care, patients have been attending (following receipt of the reminders), and feedback on the 'birthday card' format has been very positive!

Evaluation

The evaluation of the local guideline initiative was intended to cover two dimensions:

- evaluation of the impact of each guideline on clinical practice
- evaluation of the impact of the initiative itself and the degree of local acceptance of the *process* of guideline implementation.

The original evaluation criteria focused very much on the impact of each guideline. These included changes in A&E department attendances, usage of diagnostic tests and referral patterns for the chosen conditions. During the first year of the project, it became apparent that these original evaluation criteria had been far too ambitious. For example, we found it very difficult to collect the data on blood glucose control that would have been necessary in order to measure the effect of the guidelines in practices that had received an educational intervention. Even when it was possible to gather these statistics we were unsure of their value, given that we had no feel for the length of time it would take for 'real' changes to become apparent. We recognised that our initial evaluation objectives, which had sought to measure the outcomes of guideline use, were in reality unworkable, and that despite having appeal (because they focused on patient care rather than our own activity) they were in fact of questionable value.

As a consequence we set aside the original criteria and refocused on indicators of *likely* success which we could realistically expect to be able to gather. We came to realise as the project evolved that greater flexibility was a virtue and would be a strength rather than a weakness. It is in this respect that the contrast between the rigorous, *inflexible* approach, which gives rise to the highest quality *research evidence*, and the *flexible*, pragmatic approach necessary for *research implementation*, is most marked. Our view is that this difference should not be seen as contradictory, but recognised as logical in that different activities require different ways of working.

At the time of writing, with the exception of two things, all of the original project objectives had been achieved. The two things which had *not* been done were the piloting of the asthma guidelines (which was partly delayed as a result of focusing effort on the other guidelines and partly deferred in the interest of avoiding overload) and the piloting of computerised diabetes guidelines.

The aim of producing and piloting computer-prompted diabetic guidelines unfortunately had to be abandoned due to a combination of adverse circumstances. The clinical lead for the computerised guidelines left the district and the departure of key personnel from the computer company (which had originally been signed up as a partner in the project) led to the withdrawal of its support. The increasing national controversy around the issue of confidentiality (which has brought into question the ethical status of computerised disease registers) was another factor which weighed against this aspect of the project.

With hindsight we think that setting up a computerised guideline was too big a project to be achievable within one health authority. Our view is that larger-scale developments, perhaps shared around the service via the NHS Net, might provide a cost-effective solution to the widespread current lack of computerised tools, assuming that outstanding issues about patient confidentiality can be resolved.

Notes on each set of guidelines

Paediatric shared care guidelines for urinary tract infection, febrile convulsions, upper respiratory tract infections and diarrhoea and vomiting were disseminated to all GPs in the district, together with a small quantity of paediatric urine collection bags ('tiddler bags') which attracted added attention. Active implementation was confined to lunchtime presentations to GPs, because no practices selected this as a their first choice for implementation when choosing their 'pick-n-mix' priority.

The **antibiotic prescribing** guideline was disseminated to all GPs and community pharmacists (for information). Practice-based education was offered, however, most GPs declined to participate. Although some GPs acknowledged that the guideline was useful, many questioned the motives of the health authority in promoting the guideline (suggesting that it might be a 'top-down, cost-cutting' measure). The involvement of a group of local GPs and microbiologists from local trusts had not allayed these fears. This cynicism and resistance, which we found difficult to counter, led to our decision not to expend too much energy on the promotion of this guideline, but to focus *active implementation* on the guidelines for chronic diseases (i.e. diabetes, hypertension and asthma).*

The **diabetes** guideline was developed locally, by a multidisciplinary group comprising GPs, nurses (including diabetes nurse specialists), diabetologists, dieticians, chiropodists and ophthalmologists. The group looked for evidence of best practice in published work on the effectiveness of treatments, using searches of Medline and the Cochrane Database of Systematic Reviews. A

---

*We felt that there would be less cynicism about the motives of the health authority in the context of the chronic condition guidelines because GPs themselves had expressed a need for guidelines on these topics. Additionally, practice nurses had made it known that they were keen to participate in multidisciplinary education within the practice setting, and we wanted to capitalise on their enthusiasm.

guideline was produced and disseminated to all GPs, practice nurses, community nurses and community pharmacists across the district, as well as other interested parties, such as each of the local trusts and ophthalmologists. Practice visits were undertaken to promote the guideline, which was generally well received except for criticism of one recommendation which was considered by GPs to be unrealistic. (This was the recommendation for annual ECGs, which had been included at the request of a local diabetologist. In fact, following challenges from several GPs, it proved impossible to find evidence of the value of this investigation from the literature. With hindsight we can see that in this case our aim of maintaining *evidence* as the underpinning principle had been to some extent compromised by the guideline development process.)

A **draft hypertension** guideline has been developed by local cardiologists working with a GP lead, again using the Cochrane Database of Systematic Reviews and Medline searches. Hypertension was a priority for local GPs, and eight practices were recruited to pilot the draft guideline across the district for a minimum of three months. A prospective audit was included and at the time of writing, data are currently being analysed and fed back to participating practice teams. The draft guideline is also being amended as appropriate. This guideline has been welcomed enthusiastically by the practices involved in the pilot. It is planned that as a promotion, large size blood pressure cuffs (provided by two pharmaceutical companies working in partnership with the health authority) will be distributed with the finalised guideline.

Asthma. It was hoped that these would be available by summer 1999.

Coverage

Piloting the guidelines had the benefit of ironing out difficulties before the final draft, and demonstrating to practices that they had been tried and tested. As shown in Table 11.2, over 25% of practices across the district have

Table 11.2 Number of practices participating

Total number of practices in Redbridge & Waltham Forest	125
Total number of GPs in Redbridge & Waltham Forest	240
Total number of practice nurses in Redbridge & Waltham Forest	140
Total number of practice visits to introduce topic	35
Total number of GPs participating	59
Total number of practice nurses participating	48
Total number of associated baseline audits	29
(own computerised diabetes/hypertension audits completed)	3
Total number of follow-up practice visits	33

participated in practice-based education for one or more guidelines to date. This corresponds to approximately 30% of GPs and practice nurses. The original target of 50% of practices was unrealistic within the timescale. Practice visits average two per week (usually during lunchtimes), and we have found that Tuesdays and Wednesdays are the best days for local primary healthcare teams. Visits have been undertaken by the guideline facilitator, accompanied by a GP member of the guideline steering group.

Practice-based education

Practice-based education was a new 'venture' for the health authority and initially recruitment of practices was a slow process. However, as the project has progressed we have found it easier to involve practices. We think that this is probably attributable to our own experience and growing confidence, and practices' increased familiarity with the process, which has increased the acceptability of educational visits.

Understandably, practices were keen to avoid being visited during (or immediately before and after) holiday periods. This limited the amount of activity possible at certain times of the year, and it was important that this was taken into account when planning.

In our experience, group practices were more inclined to participate than single-handed GPs, and to compensate we put extra effort into the recruitment of single-handed GPs. We considered this important because the majority of single-handed GPs are concentrated in parts of the district where social deprivation is greatest and support for practitioners may be most effective.

Most guideline presentations involved audiences from ten to 50 health professionals. Over 100 attended the diabetes guideline launch and the majority of GPs and practice nurses in Redbridge & Waltham Forest have now been introduced to the guidelines in one way or another.

Two key observations from our experience were first, that the implementation process was unavoidably slow, and second, that practices were much more likely to take up an offer of support in introducing a guideline when it related to one of their *own* priority areas. (In our case this resulted in the favourable reaction to the hypertension guideline and the generally negative response to the antibiotic prescribing guideline, which was perceived to be 'outside imposition'.)

The practice-based educational sessions have been evaluated regularly by the guideline team, and primary healthcare team members attending sessions have been asked to complete a brief evaluation questionnaire. We found that this constant monitoring enabled us to remain responsive to users' needs. Of the 35 practice visits, all except two have received 'excellent' evaluations (on a scale from 'poor' to 'excellent'). Interestingly, in both cases where 'excellent' had not been the verdict, the GPs had used the sessions primarily as a forum to voice their general concerns regarding the pressure of an increasing workload.

Ninety percent of practice visits resulted in practices undertaking baseline audits, and in many cases this was being done for the first time. All practices have requested further visits to work on other topics. Using MAAG for detailed analysis of the audit data enabled the guideline facilitator to remain engaged with the primary care team and to offer support as necessary (i.e. the guideline facilitator was perceived as the *relayer* of messages rather than the source. This distancing was particularly important in protecting the relationship of the guideline facilitator with practices where the feedback given was critical).

Although at the time of writing we do not yet have audit data over a lengthy period, the repeat audit material which is available does contain some striking results, as is shown in the audit/re-audit of patients with diabetes (*see* Table 11.1). We recognise that the small numbers involved limits the power of the results, and we accept that for methodological reasons we cannot claim that the results are solely attributable to our intervention. Nevertheless, we consider that the positive direction of travel observed in the results, and the logical connection between the messages in the guidelines and the changes in care achieved, gives reasonable reassurance that the project has been a beneficial influence.

Feedback from the evaluation forms completed by practice staff highlighted the following further advantages of practice visits:

- increased awareness of the condition(s) involved. The visits brought about a 'whole team' focus to patient management
- improved communications, both *within* the primary care teams and with secondary care colleagues, raising awareness of the range of local services available
- identified and acknowledged the skill mix needed for best care
- raised the profile of the work of the clinical guideline steering group, clarified its aims and objectives, and helped to define the meaning of 'clinical effectiveness'.

Organisational issues addressed by the project

Our view is that improved standards in primary care can be achieved not only through increased clinical effectiveness, but also through improving the effectiveness of the way care is organised. From our experience we found that the following organisational changes or innovations were effective in facilitating the implementation of guidelines, thereby improving patient care.

- **Chronic disease registers.** These were initiated or updated by a person with dedicated responsibility. Surprisingly, when we started our project only a third of practices had a chronic disease register.
- **Patient recall systems** were initiated or reviewed. Again, when we started our project few practices had a recall system.
- **Practice nurse protocols** were agreed or reviewed. When we looked at existing protocols we found that 50% of these protocols were out of date or inconsistent with the new guidelines.
- **Dedicated clinics** were considered for appropriate topics, such as diabetes and hypertension.
- **Audit skills** were developed. In our case before the project started two thirds of the practices had *never* undertaken an audit.
- **IT quality.** The consistency and quality of data entry were reviewed within practices (i.e. across team members). This revealed wide differences in the coding of data and use of systems.
- **Manual records.** These were reviewed and we found that before our project four out of five practices were not using a template or record card for diabetes (a simple way of prompting appropriate routine testing and ensuring completeness of patient data).
- **Ethnicity data.** When we started, 98% of practices were not recording ethnicity data. (Ethnicity is important in the context of chronic diseases, such as diabetes, which are considerably more prevalent in certain ethnic groups.) We encouraged practices to start gathering this data, *routinely* for new patients, and *opportunistically* for existing patients.

The project has raised awareness of considerable IT skills gaps in primary care. There was a clear lack of consistency and quality of data entry *within* and *across* practices. For example, raised blood pressure can have at least five different Read codes, and in many practices all had been used! (This particular problem will hopefully be addressed by a MAAG training initiative on Read coding.) The extent of computer usage varied greatly, ranging from one extreme, where computerised records were only being used for repeat prescriptions, to paperless practices where all records were computerised. The proliferation of different systems was a further complication (more than 12 different practice systems were being used across the district).

On the positive side, we found that by increasing practices' awareness of the value of a disease register, and by teaching them the skills necessary to set one up, we had given them an incentive and capability which they were keen to apply in other contexts. For example, several practices had set up disease registers for *other* chronic conditions in the time between the guideline facilitator's first and second visits.

Culture change and acceptance?

We know from the literature and from our own local experience that changing clinical practice is a lengthy and complicated process. Disseminating guidelines alone has little effect on clinical practice and there is now growing evidence that comprehensive, multifaceted implementation programmes are much more effective than single interventions in influencing clinician behaviour.[2,3]

Our local implementation process was overtly educational and we tried hard to integrate it within existing local educational structures. We believe that approach was important because it reduced the scope for the project to be dismissed as a 'yet another new demand on time', and exploited sensible connections with respected individuals and credible programmes. We were very pleased that in addition to addressing issues of quality and consistency in specific clinical areas, the guidelines project has provided a focus for multi-professional education and tested a new style of educational provision across the district (practice-based education). We regard the following observations as indicators of the likely success of the project.

- It is now much easier to recruit practices than it was when the project began. New practices have recently approached the guideline team *requesting* a visit. Previously, it had taken a long time, considerable patience and many contacts before a visit could be agreed.
- The guideline team has been invited to revisit practices to witness the progress made and to discuss other chronic disease topics.
- The wide acceptance of recent guidelines (e.g. the *hypertension* guideline) and the generally higher positive profile that the guideline work now has within the district.
- The incorporation, by each of the ten local pilot GP commissioning groups, of the guidelines into their commissioning, prescribing, training, and education and IT strategies (now subsumed into the PCGs).
- The commitment of all three of the new PCGs to the continued use of the existing guidelines and future use of the process for implementation established in the course of the project.
- The commitment of the health authority to funding the guideline initiative beyond the point when Regional R&D funding of the Health Authority-led Implementation Project expired. Arrangements have been agreed with the local PCGs to enable the work to continue, and further suggestions for topics have been made. It is envisaged that the process is likely to fall within the clinical governance agenda.

Although the guideline implementation process is now much more widely accepted, it is by no means perfect. Some GPs have criticised the guidelines on the grounds that they represent 'gold standard' care which is unattainable given current levels of resources. We took the view that it would be impossible to please all GPs all the time, and we were reasonably content that for the most part our guidelines have achieved an acceptable and pragmatic balance between quality of care and available, affordable, local services. We look forward to the development of the debate over guidelines which will undoubtedly flow from the work of the new National Institute for Clinical Excellence (NICE). With hindsight, we consider that the following factors have been most important to the impact of the project.

- Although the health authority was the instigator of the project, and funds were received on that basis, care was taken to avoid creating the impression that the project was health authority *dominated*. Locating the facilitator and guidelines within MAAG was one way in which this message was conveyed.
- Strategic links were forged with local educationalists and existing educational events were used.
- Care was taken to ensure that the guideline team included motivated, skilled and credible individuals.
- We were (for the most part) responsive to national and local priorities, and adopted a sensitive, flexible and supportive approach. We felt that this approach was important as we had no power to enforce guideline use. As we put it, we carried only carrots and no stick!
- We understood and respected issues of confidentiality, which was critical in earning the trust of practices.
- We worked hard at gathering information and were grateful for advice and support from other guideline initiatives, e.g. East Riding and East London & the City Health Authority, whose team willingly shared their expertise.[5]

Lessons learned
- Allow twice as much time as you first think you will need for implementation.
- Do not place too much reliance on technology, it may let you down!
- Concentrate on a small number of topics initially; expand only when you have gained experience (yourself) and the confidence of others.
- Start from where local work is already happening.
- Do not waste time on guidelines that clinicians do not want.
- Use an educational approach and plug into credible existing frameworks.
- Maintain a degree of independence from the health authority.
- Use locally respected GPs as part of the implementation team.
- Take every opportunity to raise the profile of guidelines.

> **Things we would do differently if we were starting tomorrow**
> - include practice managers in the process from the outset
> - not be seduced by the prospect of linking into a grandiose computer project
> - be cautious that unreasonable 'wants' are not slipped into guidelines
> - incorporate economic evaluations into the guideline recommendations
> - start off with more reasonable success criteria.

References

1 Newton J, Knight D and Woolhead G (1996) General practitioners and clinical guidelines: a survey of knowledge, use and beliefs. *BJGP.* **46**: 513–7.

2 Anon (1994) Implementing clinical practice guidelines. *Effective Health Care.* **8**.

3 Grimshaw J and Russell I (1993) Effect of clinical guidelines on medical practice: a systematic review of rigorous evaluations. *Lancet.* **342**: 1317–22.

4 Grol R (1992) Implementing guidelines in general practice care. *Quality in Health Care.* **1**: 184–91.

5 Feder G, Griffiths C, Highton C, Eldridge S, Spence M and Southgate L (1995) Do clinical guidelines introduced with practice-based education improve care of asthmatic and diabetic patients? A randomised control trial in general practices in East London. *BMJ.* **311**: 1473–8.

6 Clarke A (1994) *Population Outcome Indicators – diabetes.* North Thames Regional Health Authority.

7 Grimshaw J, Freemantle N, Wallace S, Russell I, Hurwitz B, Watt I, Long A and Sheldon T (1995) Developing and implementing clinical practice guidelines. *Quality in Healthcare.* **4**: 55–64.

8 Dawes M (1996) On the need for evidence-based general and family practice. *Evidence Based Medicine.* **1**: 68–9.

9 Johnson M, Langton K, Haynes R and Mathieu A (1994) Effects of computer-based clinical decision support systems on clinical performance and patient outcome: a critical appraisal of research. *Ann Int Med.* **120**: 135–42.

Redbridge & Waltham Forest commentary

Primary care guidelines

This project team had a very ambitious agenda. In principle, they had 125 practices with over 350 different practitioners (GPs and nurses) to work with. As has been shown with the other North Thames projects, even reaching just a fraction of that number is daunting.

They also had a large number of guidelines to implement (five). Other North Thames projects had a maximum of three, but usually only one fell within the confines of this external evaluation.

As a multi-organisational project, the health authority, MAAG and GP educationalists were all equally active in this project team. In other North Thames projects, one organisation tended to lead with the assistance of other organisations, if other organisations were involved at all.

Despite these major hurdles, this project has done remarkably well. One survey participant, who is now a PCG Chair, commented:

'They got into practices and got them talking and that is a success in itself.'

In several other North Thames projects, the project worker came in, audited notes and then went away again, leaving the practice unaffected. This project team saw their role differently. They used the guidelines as a vehicle to get in and provide needs' assessment and education to practices. A major component of their work was team building.

As a result, one of the most important outcomes is that some practices have actually been motivated enough to go through the pain of making changes, in some cases for more than one condition. This team seems to have got the approach just right in that they make it clear that it is up to the practices to take responsibility for making any necessary changes. But they will offer any support they can in helping practices to develop the necessary skills. With many of the other North Thames projects, the onus was on the project team to do the hard work of comparing actual with best practice and coming up with corrective action. If outsiders, like the project team, are doing all the work, long-term sustained change on the part of the practices is patchy.

Another indication of their success is that they have managed to reach some small practices. One of our survey respondents was an Asian GP working in a two-partner practice, who we met opportunistically at an outside event. Even though he was not on the list of contact names given to us by the project team, when asked what difference the project had made to his clinical practice, he said enthusiastically:

'[It's made an] enormous difference. I didn't have a sense of direction before ... We've done a first proper audit of diabetes and have a second one coming up.'

A further indicator of their success is that practices are cautious about using guidelines that come from other sources. One local consultant sent out his own guidelines, without going through the guidelines group. Several GPs rang the project team to complain.

But there are drawbacks. Several survey participants, including one from the health authority, commented that the project was not properly resourced, especially as it is so labour-intensive. Identifying exactly who should pay for this service is difficult, especially with the arrival of PCGs. Because the financial future is so uncertain, all the members on the project team have had short, fixed-term contracts. This means that the key to their approach, building up relationships to gain the trust of practices, is constantly undermined, as at any time project staff could go. This is not the only project to suffer from this 'short-termism' of outlook.

The future for this project at this moment is not clear. Both the project worker and the project manager within the health authority have recently left. This may not mean that the work will stop. In its short life, this project has had many 'leads' including a director of public health, public health senior registrar, a MAAG and education board chair, and a medical advisor. So they have learned how to respond to rapid NHS turnover. The project worker and GP facilitator posts have also been made more attractive as they are now two-year rolling contracts, a clear signal that the health authority is committed to this work.

If any project has learned how to create a genuine team approach and keep on going, even in the face of major challenges such as losing a much-valued project worker and an enthusiastic project manager, then this is it.

12

Improving the management of older people with hypertension in South Essex

Lizzi Shires, Anna Hansell and Mike Gogarty

Background
Treating hypertension in older people

Raised blood pressure is a major reversible risk factor for stroke.[1] Evidence-based guidelines for the management of hypertension have been produced by the British Hypertension Society (BHS)[2] as well as internationally.[3,4]

Evidence from trials treating hypertension in the elderly[5,6] shows that treating this group is particularly effective at reducing strokes and cardio-vascular events (*see* Box 12.1).

Box 12.1   Comparison of five-year numbers needed to treat (NNT) in patients aged 60–79 and in patients under 60

Five-year numbers needed to treat in patients aged 60–79

To prevent one cerebrovascular event ~43	To prevent one cerebrovascular death ~183
To prevent one coronary event ~61	To prevent one coronary death ~78

Five-year numbers needed to treat in patients aged under 60

To prevent one cerebrovascular event ~168	To prevent one cerebrovascular death ~365
To prevent one coronary event ~184	No data on coronary deaths

Derived from high-quality randomised trials.[6]

GPs' beliefs about treating older people with hypertension

A recent survey in East Anglia[7] showed that many GPs remain unconvinced that older people with hypertension should be treated as vigorously as younger patients. In many cases, treatment would only be considered in older patients when their blood pressure was at higher levels than those which would lead to treatment being initiated in younger people. In the survey, the lowest level of systolic and diastolic blood pressure at which GPs initiated treatment in people aged over 65 was over 175/100. This was despite growing evidence around the importance of treatment, particularly of a raised systolic level,[8] and is contrary to the BHS recommendation that proposes a threshold for treatment of 160/90 in this age group.

The South Essex stroke strategy

Approximately 1100 people are admitted to hospitals in South Essex each year following a stroke, many of whom suffer considerable long-term disability. The Health of the Nation[9] Strategy (1992) set national targets to reduce strokes, and in South Essex a stroke strategy group comprising local stake-holders was established by the health authority. The remit of the group was to examine ways of reducing the mortality and morbidity associated with stroke, and to produce a wide range of recommendations in support of the objective of reducing the incidence of stroke in South Essex.

One of the recommendations of the group was that the management of hypertension in the elderly across South Essex should be improved. In the light of the findings of the East Anglian survey,[7] and to gain fuller knowledge of local practice, GPs in South Essex were sent (in 1995) a questionnaire to elicit their views on local stroke services. This included a specific question asking at what level of blood pressure they would treat a 65-year-old for hypertension.

The survey results echoed the pattern of the published work in East Anglia insofar as many of the South Essex GPs who responded reported that they would consider initiating treatment in older people only at *higher* levels of blood pressure than those recommended. Although the response rate to this survey was poor (15%), our feeling was that any resultant bias would be likely to be causing *understatement* rather than overstatement of the problem because we considered it probable that it had been the *more motivated* practices that had responded.[10] As a result of this finding it was agreed that the stroke strategy would specifically aim to address the misconception that older people should be treated for raised blood pressure at higher threshold levels than younger people.

The project to improve management of older people with hypertension consisted of four elements:

* developing local guidelines and circulating them to all practices
* finding a way of increasing the time available to practices to participate in the project
* offering a range of academic seminars to support the implementation of the guidelines
* evaluating the project.

Changing clinician behaviour

It is recognised that there are often delays in getting important research findings into practice.[11] Influencing clinicians' behaviour is complex and difficult, and evidence from trials of numerous methods and combinations of interventions suggests that a multifaceted approach may be the most effective.[12,13]

Evidence-based guidelines, developed locally and implemented with active educational interventions,[14] have been advocated as a method to change management and improve patient care.[15] This was the method South Essex Health Authority sought to use in its Research Implementation Project.

Locally developed guidelines

Evidence-based guidelines on the management of blood pressure in the elderly were developed by a local consultant cardiologist, a GP and a public health consultant, based on the BHS guidelines.[2] The main message was of the clear benefits of treating older people with hypertension (consistent with the meta analysis by Sanderson – personal communication). The document was produced as one of a series promoted by the health authority called the *'Really useful Guidelines'*.[16] These have become widely recognised and well received by local practitioners (*see* Appendix 1 at the end of this chapter).

The guidelines were circulated to local GP advisory forums and the LMC for discussion prior to dissemination. GPs at these meetings endorsed the guidelines, but highlighted the increased workload which their implementation would create, and pointed out that this would be problematic given the prevailing degree of pressure on GPs' time. It was suggested that allowing them to relax the stipulation that all patients over 75 should have an annual review* (the 'over-75s' check) would be a pragmatic means of managing the impact of increased work generated by following the guideline. This idea was accepted and is discussed further below.

A local contract for the elderly

Effective management of hypertension as an alternative to routine 'over-75' checks

Although the over-75s check was a national requirement, its implementation is open to some local interpretation. The project team discussed with local stakeholders the relative merits and opportunity costs of treating older people with hypertension, and routine over-75s checks. This discussion was followed by consultation with the health authority, local consultants, the LMC, the community health councils (CHCs) and a local pensioners' action group. The result was agreement that GPs would not be compelled to offer routine checks to all patients over the age of 75, provided that they would undertake to participate in the project by managing older hypertensive patients (aged 60–79) in line with the BHS recommended guidance. It was also agreed that GPs would continue to provide over-75 checks to any patient *requesting* one, and that any problems or complaints arising from this arrangement would be referred to the health authority. A letter, with the guidelines, had been sent to all GPs asking them to participate in the project.

Educational seminars for GPs

A supporting educational programme was produced by a health authority consultant in public health in collaboration with local hospital consultants, GP tutors and audit facilitators. The programme consisted of a series of PGEA-accredited seminars across the district. The seminars were part of the existing education and audit programme and therefore GPs were not required to attend any *additional* meetings.

GPs were presented with evidence on the effectiveness of treating older people with hypertension, and estimates were given of the likely workload

---

*The 1990 GP contract,[17] made it mandatory for all practices to offer a health check to all patients over 75 years old. There has been debate about the value of these checks. Many practitioners argue that the scheme has little merit[18] because most older patients consult GPs regularly and those who do not tend to be healthier.[19-21] Patients over 75 years old consult their GP an average of 6.5 times a year and over 90% of this age group see their GP at least once a year. There is only limited evidence of the likely benefit of the programme.[21]

implications for a practice implementing the guideline (numbers that re-quiring screening, numbers likely to be hypertensive and numbers requiring treatment). The likely health benefit for a practice population was also outlined, together with the likely prescribing costs (*see* Box 12.2).

During the seminars several GPs voiced the opinion that aggressive treat-ment to lower blood pressure in the elderly was not always appropriate due to co-morbidity and iatrogenic side effects.[22]

Box 12.2   Illustrative workload in a practice list of 2000 from managing patients aged 60–79 in line with BHS guidelines

Number of patients aged 60–79	=300
Number of patients who would 'screen' hypertensive	=100
Number of patients who after confirmatory checks would be diagnosed as hypertensive	$\simeq$33
5 year NNT to prevent a vascular event (stroke or coronary)	=18
$\therefore$ in list of 2000 could prevent	$\simeq$2
Cost per patient per year of 1st line treatment (thiazide)	$\simeq$£4

Evaluation of the project

The project was evaluated in four stages:

- change in knowledge after the seminars
- the uptake of the project
- change in GPs' self-reported treatment threshold in 60–79-year-old patients
- actual changes in hypertension treatment.

Change in knowledge after the seminars

Prior to the seminar, attendees were given a questionnaire which asked the level of systolic and diastolic pressure at which they would treat older people with raised blood pressure. The questionnaire was repeated at the end of the session. Results from questionnaires relating to one of the seminars showed that while opinion on treatment had shifted, some GPs remained reluctant to treat blood pressure as aggressively in the elderly as they would in younger patients.

Participation

All 344 GPs in the health authority received a copy of the guidelines and were invited to participate in the project. Sixty percent of the 147 practices in the district participated in the project (it was assumed that those who did would continue to offer over-75 health checks). The health authority and CHC received no complaints about GPs not offering over-75 checks.

Five seminars were held, which 242 GPs attended, and two seminars were held for practice nurses, which 67 attended.

Questionnaire on GPs' management of hypertension

A questionnaire (*see* Box 12.3) was sent to all GPs six months after the project had started. All GPs were surveyed, whether or not they had officially joined the project. (We thought this important because the guidelines and educational interventions had reached all GPs even if they had not taken the opportunity to drop the over-75 health checks.)

Box 12.3

1 Did you agree to take part in the initiative and not offer routine over-75 checks?
2 Did you have any problems with either implementing the hypertension initiative or with not offering the over-75 checks?
3 At what level of blood pressure would you treat a patient aged 65 as a hypertensive?

Results of questionnaire

The response rate to this survey was 50% (172 GPs). A number of respondents answered on behalf of their practices, which had the effect of reducing the overall response rate. No problems were identified in not offering over 75 checks. The results of Question 3 are shown in Figures 12.1 and 12.2.

Respondents stated that they would now treat patients at levels of blood pressure closer to those recommended by the BHS than had been suggested by the previous survey. This applied equally to practices that had taken part in the project and those that had not been involved. Although the response

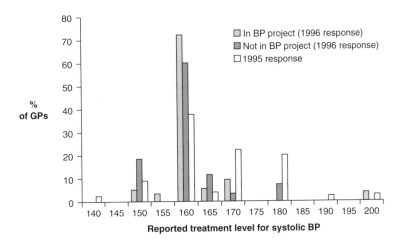

Figure 12.1   South Essex 1996 survey: A comparison of systolic levels at which GPs said they would initiate treatment in a 75-year-old with hypertension before and after the project.

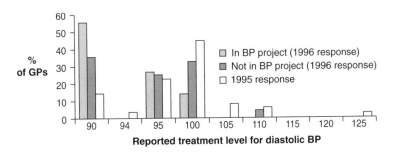

Figure 12.2   South Essex 1996 survey: A comparison of diastolic levels at which GPs said they would initiate treatment in a 75-year-old with hypertension before and after the project.

rate was lower than we would have hoped, the results did suggest a shift in the views of GPs with regard to this issue, which is consistent with the message of the project, and may, at least in part, have been influenced by our initiative.*

---

*We acknowledge that without a considerably more robust study design (which would have been beyond our capacity to resource) it is impossible to attribute this change to the impact of our project.

Were self-reported changes in GPs' views of the appropriate level of blood pressure at which to begin treatment in elderly patients indicative of changes in practice?

The questionnaire results showed that the respondents were more aware of the levels of blood pressure at which it is appropriate to treat older people with hypertension, but we were mindful that this *expressed behaviour* among general practitioners may not be translated into practice.[23] We wanted to know if the project had *really* had an effect on patient management across South Essex.

We set about conducting a detailed retrospective study of casenotes to address this question. We considered that to be of value, the study would need to examine the actual management of older people with hypertension and avoid criticism on the grounds of generalisability (which would be a danger if participants/respondents were self-selected).

The population

The Castle Point locality of South Essex which has a population of 86 000 was recruited for an audit. The 42 GPs were recruited by a public health consultant via their locality forum meeting and *all* agreed to take part. All patients aged between 70 and 75 (a group near the middle of the range of ages targeted by the project, 60–79) were identified using the health authority's computerised register of patients.

Pilot study

A pilot study of 79 patients was undertaken at one, single-handed, practice. Following the pilot, the data collection form was modified to allow the forms to be scanned automatically to extract the data (*see* Appendix 2 at the end of this chapter).

Data collection

All general practices were sent data collection sheets, project instructions and the names of the patients whose notes were to be audited. Advice and practical support was given to the practices by an audit facilitator. The data were collected by a practice nurse within the practice.

Results of the data analysis

In the target age group in 17 practices (42 GPs) in the locality, 6208 patients were identified (from Family Health Services Agency records). Sixteen of the practices returned data forms on *all* patients and one practice returned forms for half of its relevant patients. A total of 5234 patients' data was returned (which represented 84% of the total). (The difference between the total number of patients and the number of forms returned is attributed to incomplete data from one large practice and the inflation of patient numbers in the health authority records.)

Ninety-nine patients were excluded from the analysis because data entry was inadequate. Of these, 53 had died or moved away. Data for the remaining 5135 patients were analysed. Most measurements of blood pressure were recorded in multiples of ten (only 17% of initial records contained blood pressure readings between these multiples).[24]

DID MORE PATIENTS HAVE THEIR BP RECORDED AFTER THE INTERVENTION?

	Before intervention	After intervention
BP recorded	3322 (64.7%)	3383 (65.9%)

McNemar's test showed no statistically significant difference.

HOW MANY PATIENTS HAD TREATMENT INITIATED AFTER THE INTERVENTION?

Patients started on treatment prior to project	1123
Patients started on treatment after project	273
Total number of patients on treatment	1396

HAD THE PROJECT REDUCED THE NUMBER OF PATIENTS WITH HIGH SYSTOLICS?

2523 patients had systolic readings before and after the project launch. Prior to the project 240 (9.5%) had a systolic > 160. After the project 230 (9.1%) had a systolic > 160.

799 patients only had systolic readings before the project launch and 73 (9.1%) of these had a systolic above 160. 860 patients only had systolic readings after the project launch and 111 of these (12.9%) had a systolic above 160.

Combining the paired and unpaired readings (statistical method: personal communication from Professor M Bland and Dr Barbara Butland, St George's Hospital Medical School) the weighted average difference showed 1.0% fewer patients with a systolic BP above 160 after the project launch, but this was not statistically significant at the 5% level.

DID THE PROJECT REDUCE THE NUMBER OF PATIENTS WITH HIGH DIASTOLICS?

2522 patients had diastolic readings before and after the project launch. Prior to the project 147 (5.8%) had a diastolic > 90. After the project 123 (4.9%) had a diastolic > 90.

799 patients only had a diastolic reading before the project launch and 54 (6.8%) of these had a diastolic > 90. 861 patients only had a diastolic reading after the project launch and 61 (7.1%) of these had a diastolic > 90.

Combining the paired and unpaired readings (statistical method: personal communication from Professor M Bland and Dr Barbara Butland, St George's Hospital Medical School) the weighted average difference showed 0.7% fewer patients with a diastolic BP above 90 after the project launch, but this was not statistically significant at the 5% level.

DID GPS INITIATE BLOOD PRESSURE TREATMENT AT LOWER PRESSURES AFTER THE PROJECT LAUNCH THAN THEY HAD BEFORE?

Mean level of systolic blood pressure when therapy commenced: prior to the project launch = 181.0 (sd 21.67); after the project launch = 180.7 (sd 19.34). There was no statistically significant difference before and after the project began.

Mean level of diastolic blood pressure when therapy commenced: prior to the project launch = 102.9 (sd 11.22); after the project launch = 99.3 (sd 10.35). There was a small, but statistically significant, reduction in the mean diastolic blood pressure of 3.6 mmHg (95% confidence intervals 2.0 to 5.3).

Summary

The project was well received by GPs who, for the most part, were supportive of the health authority in promoting an evidence-based approach as an alternative to 'policing' adherence to the letter of the National GP Contract. We consider that recognition by the health authority that increasing the level of interventions to prevent stroke in the elderly would have resource implications for primary healthcare teams was critical in ensuring that the project would have credibility with GPs. Furthermore, by making a positive, pragmatic suggestion, clearly designed to ensure best use of limited resources, we believe the health authority sent an important message to primary care about its own role as a responsible and flexible component of the health service. We also have limited evidence from the survey that GPs' views had changed (over the time of the project) in relation to the level of raised blood pressure that they regard as being a threshold for intervention.

Notwithstanding these positive aspects we must concede that in terms of the *effect on clinical practice*, our attempt at measurement would suggest that the project has not been successful.

Acknowledgements

The authors thank all at Castle Point general practices who participated in the project, Chris Joyce and Barbara Butland for advice on the design and conduct of the research, PM Ali, A Azulay, Magie Luck and Lynda Brindley for their help in carrying out the project, Pamela Milnes, Pamela Burton, Dawn Bolingbroke and Liz Halls for assisting with the compilation and graphical illustration of data, Graham Butland and the South Essex Stroke Strategy Group for their support, and Mala Rao for her help with the planning of the project and preparation of this chapter.

Lessons learned

- **Evidence-based guidelines can be developed at district level.** National guidelines can be modified easily to meet local needs. Specific areas of practice where research evidence may not be being applied (such as treatment of older people with hypertension) can be candidates for local guideline development.

- **Improved relationships.** The process of guideline development, dissemination and educational seminars brought many interested parties together and led to the forging of lasting relationships. GPs appreciated the 'concession' with regard to offering 'over-75 checks' and the recognition of time constraints in primary care, and were happy to participate in the evaluation by submitting practice data to the health authority for analysis. Involvement with the LMC led to a closer partnership and a more positive working relationship with the health authority.

  The project was useful in developing community links with the local pensioners' action group, which gave its support to the project and joined the stroke strategy group. No respondents identified any problems by not routinely offering checks to people over 75, but several suggested that their workload had increased as a consequence of doing more hypertension management.

- **Participation in research implementation projects in primary care can be increased by recognising and addressing resource constraints.** We are certain that the high degree of participation in this project was directly attributable to allowing practices to modify their commitment to the 'over-75' checks.

- **Evaluating research implementation initiatives in the NHS is difficult.** Projects to implement changes in practice at health authority level (which by their nature are neither randomised nor controlled) can be easy targets for criticism if the criteria which would be used to evaluate *trials* are applied.[25] We would argue that to apply these criteria would in

continued overleaf

any case be inappropriate. We used several alternative approaches to evaluate the effectiveness of the intervention.

- **Questionnaires are a mixed blessing.** Questionnaires are easy and relatively cheap to undertake and are a convenient method of evaluating local implementation district initiatives. However, the very low response rate to the questionnaires we used (in common with many other studies[26]), which may be a consequence of the other pressures on GPs,[27] makes reliance on them problematic, especially as GPs who respond may not be representative of the whole population of GPs.[10]
- **Changes in GPs' self-reported *views* may not be reflected by commensurate changes in *practice*.** Although the questionnaire suggested that GPs' views on the level of blood pressure at which intervention was appropriate in elderly patients, this was not manifest in the majority of findings from the audit. Although there had been a small change in the level of diastolic blood pressure at which GPs initiated treatment, changes in practice relative to treating at lower levels of systolic blood pressure were not significant.
- **Participation in evaluation needs mutual trust.** In our project all practices in one locality were invited and agreed to participate in the evaluation. This high level of participation reflected the positive light in which GPs viewed the scheme. Data collection represented a considerable amount of work for practices, and their willingness to undertake this work and to submit data to the health authority for analysis reflected the level of co-operation that had been built up over the duration of the project.

Things we would do differently if we were starting tomorrow

- **involve the whole practice team.** The project was primarily aimed at GPs because of our assumption that GPs initiate treatment for hypertension. Although the educational programme was open to nurses, few attended and the guidelines were sent only to GPs. With hindsight we should have made a much greater effort to involve practice nurses as well as GPs. Practice nurses have become increasingly responsible for the screening and management of hypertension in the elderly, and we are aware that practices' organisation plays an important role in recording cardiovascular risk factors.[28] We feel that the impact of our project may have been greater had we involved the whole of the practice team
- **keep up the momentum.** The project launch in 1996 was high profile and intensive, however, we were unable to sustain the focus and identity of the project. Similar initiatives on secondary prevention of ischaemic heart disease and management of dyspepsia may have overloaded practitioners with similar messages and diluted the message about blood pressure and

continued opposite

stroke in the elderly. With hindsight it may have been better to have pushed longer and harder on one target condition before moving on to other issues

- **support practices in developing their skills in using their computer systems for prompts and audits.** At the time of the project most practices in South Essex had computerised records. There was an ongoing training programme on using practice systems for audit. However, we failed to link into this to ensure that practices had the necessary training and resources to use their computer systems to identify older patients who needed to have their blood pressure measured. Had this been done, and subsequent management been recorded on computerised records, audit would have been much easier. With hindsight we would therefore ensure that appropriate computer training was available and that systems were being used effectively in day-to-day practice, facilitating both effective prompting and simple audit[29]
- **pilot after every change.** We changed the data collection forms after the initial pilot from a manual system to one that enabled automatic scanning on to a computer. This caused a number of problems during the analysis because the new forms had not been piloted and were actually quite difficult to use, and omitted key details which had to be added manually.* Many hours were spent cleaning the data to rectify these design errors in the new data collection form which might have been avoided had we re-piloted the system.

*For example we had not included boxes for 'died' or 'moved away' on the form, so these details had to be counted manually.

References

1 Simin JA (1996) Treating hypertension: the evidence from clinical trials. *BMJ.* **313**: 437–40.

2 Sener P, Beevers G, Bulpitt CJ *et al.* (1993) Management guidelines in essential hypertension: report of the second working party of the British Hypertension Society. *BMJ.* **306**: 983–7.

3 Jackson R, Barham P, Bills J *et al.* (1993) Management of raised blood pressure in New Zealand: a discussion document. *BMJ.* **307**: 107–10.

4 Sub-committee of WHO/ISH Mild Hypertension Liaison Committee (1993) Summary of 1993 World Health Organisation–International Society of Hypertension guidelines for the management of mild hypertension. *BMJ.* **307**: 1541–6.

5 Beard K, Bulpitt CJ, Mascie-Taylor H *et al.* (1991) Management of elderly people with sustained hypertension. *BMJ.* **304**: 412–16.

6   Mulrow CD, Cornell JA, Herrora CR *et al.* (1994) Hypertension in the elderly; implications and generalisability of randomised trials. *JAMA.* **272**: 1932–8.

7   Dickerson JEC and Brown MJ (1995) Influence of age on general practitioners' definition and treatment of hypertension. *BMJ.* **310**: 574.

8   SHEP Co-operative Research Group (1991) Prevention of stroke by antihypertensive drug treatment in older persons with isolated systolic hypertension. *JAMA.* **265**: 3255–61.

9   Health of the Nation (1992) *A Strategy for Health in England.* HMSO, London.

10 Cartwright A (1978) Professional as responders: variation in effect of response rate to questionnaires. *BMJ.* **ii**: 1419–21.

11 Haines A and Jones R (1994) Implementing findings of research. *BMJ.* **308**: 1488–92.

12 Oxman A (1995) No magic bullets. A systematic review of 102 trials of interventions to help healthcare professionals deliver services more effectively or efficiently. *Can Med Assoc J.* **153**: 1423–3.

13 Davis D, Thompson MA *et al.* (1995) Changing physician performance. A systematic review of the effect of continuing medical education strategies. *JAMA.* **274**: 700–4.

14 Anon (1994) Implementing clinical practice guidelines. *Effective Health Care.* **8**.

15 NHSE (1996) *Promoting Clinical Effectiveness. A framework for action in and through the NHS.* NHS Executive.

16 *'Really useful guidelines' for South Essex in angina, IHD, dyspepsia.* Public Health Department SEHA, Brentwood.

17 Department of Health and the Welsh Office (1989) *General Practice in the National Health Service. A new contract.* HMSO, London.

18 Tremellen J (1992) Assessment of patients aged over 75 in general practice. *BMJ.* **305**: 621–4.

19 Williams E (1984) Characteristics of patients over 75 not seen during one year in general practice. *BMJ.* **188**: 119–21.

20 Ebrahim S, Hedley R and Sheldon M (1984) Low levels of ill health among elderly non-consulters in general practice. *BMJ.* **289**: 1273–5.

21 Williams ES and Barley NH (1985) Old people not known to the general practitioner: low risk group. *BMJ.* **291**: 251–5.

22 Fahey T (1998) Applying the results of clinical trials to patients in general practice: perceived problems, strengths and assumptions and challenges for the future. *British J Gen Prac.* **48**: 1173–8.

23 Putnam RW and Curry L (1989) Physicians' participation in establishing criteria for hypertension management in the office: will patients' outcomes be improved? *CMAJ.* **140(7)**: 806–9.

24 Wen SR, Kramer MS *et al.* (1993) Terminal digit preference, random error and bias in routine clinical measurement of BP. *J Clin Epidemiol.* **46**: 1187–93.

25 Crombie I (1996) Research in health care. In: *Why Health Service Research is Difficult.* John Wiley & Sons, Chichester.

26 McAvoy BR and Koner EFS (1996) General practice postal surveys: a question too far. *BMJ.* **313**: 732–3.

27 Koner E *et al.* (1998) So much post, so busy with practice, so no time. *B J Gen Pract.* **48**: 1067–9.

28 Drenth B *et al.* (1998) Relationship between practice organisation and cardio-vascular risk factor recording in general practice. *Br J Gen Prac.* **48**: 1054–8.

29 Pearson N, O'Brian J, Thomas H *et al.* (1995) Collecting morbidity data in general practice: Somerset Morbidity Project. *BMJ.* **312**: 1517–20.

Appendix 1

The Really Useful
Information Service

Bulletin No 5

Treating Hypertension and Preventing Strokes
in Older Patients

SOUTH ESSEX HEALTH AUTHORITY
The Really Useful Information Service

Treating hypertension and preventing strokes in older patients

A Stroke is a Tragedy

**You can prevent more strokes by making sure that you treat
hypertension in the elderly**

- in young patients (<60) you have to treat 170 patients for 5 years to save one stroke
- in patients who are in the 60 to 79 age group you only have to treat 43 patients for 5 years to save one stroke

**Older patients who are treated for hypertension also have a
reduction in the incidence of subsequent coronary heart disease**

Small-dose thiazide diuretics are the treatment of choice.
The incidence of side effects is very low and there is **proof** that they work!

Fact File
Hypertension and Stroke Prevention

Why bother to treat mild to moderate hypertension in older patients?
- Treating *mild to moderate* hypertension reduces stroke risk by 35%.
- The older the patient, the greater the risk of stroke, so you will actually save more strokes and lives by treating the elderly.
- In young patients you need 850 treatment years (170 patients for five years) to save one stroke.
  BUT – in older patients you only need 215 treatment years (43 for five years) to save one stroke.
- Relatively small reductions in pressure yield results – 15 mm systolic and 7 mm diastolic reduction in blood pressure will produce the effects detailed above.

How is hypertension defined?
- Most of the trials have been done in patients with blood pressures greater than 160 systolic or 90 diastolic and this is the level for treatment recommended by the British Hypertension Society.
- However, blood pressure levels are normally distributed and there is a linear relationship with the incidence of stroke. It is reasonable therefore to state that there is no abrupt threshold when treatment becomes mandatory. A patient with a pressure of 160 /90 will be at significantly less risk than a person with a pressure of, say, 170/100. There is a greater weight of evidence for treating systolic hypertension than for treating mild to moderately raised diastolic pressures.
- Trials are mainly based on sitting blood pressures. Sphygmomanometer cuffs must be of an adequate size. A small cuff on a big arm will give an erroneously high reading.

Who should we treat?
- Each patient should be assessed as an individual!
- There are other risk factors for stroke (and disease associated with an increased risk), apart from hypertension. The principal ones are: ischaemic heart disease; diabetes; previous history of TIA or CVA; peripheral vascular disease; smoking is an independent risk factor.

And: the older the patient the greater the risk of stroke. In statistical terms, the older the patient, the greater the potential benefit from treatment.* However, this has to be balanced against the social and psychological effects of starting any long-term treatment.

Editors' note: although this may not apply in the very elderly.

So: a 60-year-old patient with a blood pressure of 160/90 and **no other risk factors** might be a candidate for watchful waiting and lifestyle advice

the presence of one or more of the above risk factors makes active treatment more worthwhile

any *sustained* pressure of 170/100 or greater should be considered for treatment. Greater importance should be attached to raised systolic readings as there is still some uncertainty about the aetiological effect of moderately raised diastolic pressures (90/105).

What should our first line of treatment be?
Based on many trials, most authorities agree that small-dose thiazides (2.5 mg bendrofluazide) are the first choice. We know that this dose is effective and significant adverse effects are less than 1 per 100 treatment years.

BUT always be willing to move on to other treatment if control is not good.

Other drugs may lower blood pressure but there may not be any proof that they reduce the incidence of strokes. For instance, beta-blockers are effective antihypertensive agents, but in trials they have not been as effective as the diuretics in reducing incidence of stroke.

What about those patients over the age of 80?
- As yet, there is little evidence on which to base opinions.
- For those already on treatment, it might be reasonable to leave well alone.
- For those not on treatment, decisions should perhaps be based on overall physical and mental status (biological age) rather than on chronological age.
- Severe hypertension should be treated at any age.

SOME FURTHER POINTS TO CONSIDER

1   About a third of your patients over the age of 60 will have a blood pressure of 160/90 or above.

Always take at least three readings before labelling a person hypertensive. Two thirds of the patients found to have borderline pressures on screening will revert to normal levels if followed up for three months.

A survey of training practices in Oxfordshire showed that half the patients on treatment had only one BP reading recorded before treatment was started!

Unless you have an emergency on your hands, i.e. you suspect malignant hypertension, never ever start treatment without further checks. Some alarmingly high BPs will settle when the patient becomes less anxious.

2   A selective approach, based on risk factors, should be taken for those who are at the lower end of the range. The benefits of treating those at low risk have to be balanced against the bad effects of labelling someone as 'ill' and the side effects of any drug therapy.

3   Where practical, involving your patient in the decision-making process eases the burden on you. They need to know what sort of risks they are running so that they can make an informed choice.

4   Many elderly patients have regular medication for other reasons. Some of these drugs may interact with antihypertensives. NSAIDs will oppose the antihypertensive action of thiazides. These should not be given together unless absolutely necessary.

5   A number of surveys have shown that the control of many hypertensives is not good. About half of all treated patients have pressures well above the 160/90 level. Should you audit your results?

6   Other ways of reducing the risk of stroke are:
    •   getting patients to give up smoking. *More effective than treating BP!*
    •   give aspirin to those with a history of TIA / CVA / MI
    •   give aspirin or anticoagulate those with atrial fibrillation.

Where is the evidence for this?

THE REFERENCE FILE – HYPERTENSION IN THE ELDERLY

1 MacMahon S, Collins R, Peto R *et al.* (1990) Blood pressure, stroke and coronary heart disease. *Lancet.* **335**: 765–74, 827–37.

This was an overview of prospective observational studies, covering all ages. Clear evidence of direct relationship of increased stroke incidence with higher diastolic blood pressure and that reducing diastolic pressures with treatment produced a 42% reduction in stroke incidence.

2 SHEP Co-operative Research Group (1991) Prevention of stroke by antihypertensive drug treatment in older persons with isolated systolic hypertension. *JAMA.* **265**: 3255–61.

Isolated systolic hypertension (>160) was treated in patients over the age of 60 years. This reduced the incidence of stroke by 36%. From 8.2 to 5.2%. over five years. The effect was still evident in patients over the age of 80 years.

3 Beard K, Bulpitt C *et al.* (1991) Management of elderly patients with sustained hypertension. *BMJ.* **304**: 412–16.

Analysis of six randomised trials. Clear evidence of reduction in incidence of stroke and of cardiac events in treating patients with blood pressures above 160 / 90. Diuretics very effective. Beta blockers not effective.

4 MRC (1992) MRC trial of treatment of hypertension in older adults. *BMJ.* **304**: 405.

The target group was patients with systolic hypertension of >160, aged 65 to 74 years of age. There were three groups – placebo, diuretic treatment and beta blocker treatment. Diuretics produced a reduction of stroke of 31%, of coronary events of 44% and of all cardiovascular events of 35%. Beta blockers had no effect. It is interesting to note that smokers did not benefit from diuretics either.

5 Mulrow C, Cornell J *et al.* (1994) Hypertension in the elderly. Implications and generalisability of randomised trials. *JAMA.* **272**: 1932–8.

A review of all the trials to date. The six best trials showed: you need to treat 43 patients for five years to prevent one stroke; 61 patients for five years to prevent one coronary event; 18 patients for five years to prevent any vascular event (cerebral or cardiac). The evidence to date for treating mild to moderate hypertension in the over 80s is not as yet clear.

Appendix 2

Data collection pro forma
Great Warley, Brentwood, ESSEX CM13 3BE

Patient's Name / ID

Date of Birth   Sex

M ☐   F ☐

BP recorded 1/1/93–31/3/96
(Note: If more than one BP reading
was recorded please enter the lowest)

BP recorded 1/4/96–31/3/98
(Note: If more than one BP reading
was recorded please enter the lowest)

If not recorded please tick ☐

If not recorded please tick ☐

On BP treatment   Y ☐ N ☐

Date treatment started:

Level of BP when treatment started:

If prior 1/1/93 please tick ☐

If not recorded please tick ☐

South Essex commentary

Hypertension in elderly people

This project team had an excellent starting point in terms of the relationship between themselves and the people they hoped to influence, in this case primary care practices.

Attendence at the seminars was very high, with over 300 GPs and practice nurses taking part (most project teams were pleased if they managed to reach over 50 practitioners). For the evaluation, they managed to get *all* 16 GP practices in one locality to send in their data. What's more, the practice nurses themselves, not an outside project worker or audit facilitator, carried out the enormous task of accessing over 5000 patients' notes. Even with this degree of enthusiasm, they still faced difficulties.

One of the most confusing findings from our South Essex survey is that all of the participants said that the project had been successful in getting GPs to treat elderly hypertensives earlier, when clearly their evaluation has shown that it has not. Educational interventions can shift practitioners *beliefs* about what makes good practice, which is a substantial achievement in itself. But getting them to *act* in accordance with their new beliefs means considerably more effort. As one of the project team said:

> 'The difficulty is not so much getting clinicians to agree, but getting them to apply it on a consistent basis. Clinicians often say that they are using guidelines, but in reality may only be using them for every third patient.'

Practitioners know what they should do, and genuinely think they are doing it. So the challenge for project teams becomes twofold: showing them, in an unthreatening way, that they are not acting *systematically* in accordance with their beliefs and working with them so that they can start to apply best practice.

This project is fascinating as this team carried out the most comprehensive evaluation of all the North Thames projects. While most of the other projects divided their funding between intervention and evaluation (not necessarily in equal parts), this team carried out the intervention *before* North Thames money was available. They then spent all of their £50 000 on the evaluation, which gives an idea of how expensive and time-consuming a well-conducted evaluation can be.

Other North Thames project teams looked at process measures (numbers of GPs requesting guidelines and so forth) and proxy measures, such as prescription rates. These give general indications on trends which indicate that something is happening, but are not specific enough to let us know whether the project has had any effect on real-life practice.

This evaluation does. And as such, it really calls into question the impact that any of the implementation projects have had in changing *actual* practice as opposed to *expressed* practice. Without good evaluation data, we just don't know what difference these implementation projects have made in the privacy of the consultation room.

Even though this team has not been successful in changing practice, this project has had many other unexpected, beneficial outcomes. One survey participant said:

> *'One of the by-products [is that] ... the relationships are now permanent between (Public Health Consultant), GPs, GP tutors – and that bodes well for clinical governance. Perhaps, that's the most important thing.'*

Because of their experience with this project, Public Health have learned a great deal about the practicalities of clinical governance. They realise that if clinical governance is going to work, resources need to be spent on finding out exactly what is actually happening in the practices. Systems need to be set up. Just how these systems can be resourced and who exactly will be responsible for the considerable workload are two issues still under consideration.

They have also learned that in implementation projects there needs to be one clear operational lead, someone who organises the meetings and takes the work forward. Because they had three, very little happened between our first meeting with them in June 1997 and our second in February 1998 as no one was quite sure who was responsible. They deliberately chose not to have a project worker as they felt it would be harder to transfer lessons or have something sustainable if the lessons resided primarily with one person. The team still feels that this was a good decision, but they do recognise that momentum was harder to sustain.

So in the end, although this team did not change clinical practice, they and we have benefited a great deal. They have even better relationships with their GPs, which has smoothed the way for PCGs. And we have learned that educational approaches incorporating seminars, guidelines and audit along with widespread enthusiasm are not enough *on their own* to get evidence into practice.

Further reading

Primary Care R&D Resources and Training Initiative: picking list

1 Kirkwood BR (1988) *Essentials of Medical Statistics*. Blackwell Science.

2 Tarling M and Crofts L (1997) *The Essential Researcher's Handbook for Nurses and Health Care Professionals*. Bailliere Tindall and RCN.

3 Holloway I and Wheeler S (1996) *Qualitative Research for Nurses*. Blackwell Science.

4 Bowling A (1997) *Research Methods in Health: investigating health and health services*. Open University Press.

5 Silagy C and Haines A (1998) *Evidence-based Medicine in Primary Care*. BMJ Books.

6 Holloway I (1997) *Basic Concepts for Qualitative Research*. Blackwell Science.

7 Greenhalgh T and Weatherall D (1997) *How to Read a Paper: the basics of evidence-based medicine*. BMJ Books.

8 Coggan D (ed) (1997) *Epidemiology for the Uninitiated*. BMJ Books.

9 Sackett D, Richardson WS, Rosenberg W and Haynes B (1997) *Evidence-based Medicine: how to practice and teach EMB*. Churchill Livingstone.

10 Carter Y and Falshaw M (eds) (1998) Workbook 1: Introduction to Evidence-based Primary Care and its Application in Commissioning. In: *Evidence-based Primary Care: an open learning programme*. Radcliffe Medical Press.

11 Carter Y and Falshaw M (eds) (1998) Workbook 2: Finding the Papers: a guide to Medline searching. In: *Evidence-based Primary Care: an open learning programme*. Radcliffe Medical Press.

12 Carter Y and Falshaw M (eds) (1998) Workbook 3: What the Papers Say. In: *Evidence-based Primary Care: an open learning programme*. Radcliffe Medical Press.

13 Carter Y and Falshaw M (eds) (1998) Workbook 4: Decision to Treat. In: *Evidence-based Primary Care: an open learning programme*. Radcliffe Medical Press.

14   Carter Y and Falshaw M (eds) (1998) Workbook 5: Judging Clinical Effectiveness. In: *Evidence-based Primary Care: an open learning programme*. Radcliffe Medical Press.

15   Carter Y and Falshaw M (eds) (1998) Workbook 6: Resources and Continuing Education. In: *Evidence-based Primary Care: an open learning programme*. Radcliffe Medical Press.

16   Haines A and Donald A (1998) *Getting Research Findings into Practice*. BMJ Books.

17   Altman DG (1990) *Practical Statistics for Medical Research*. Chapman & Hall.

18   Bowling A (1997) *Research Methods in Health* (hardback version). Open University Press.

19   Carter Y and Thomas C (1997) *Research Methods in Primary Care*. Radcliffe Medical Press.

20   Carter Y and Thomas C (1999) *Research Opportunities in Primary Care*. Radcliffe Medical Press.

21   Burns N and Grove S (1997) *The Practice of Nursing Research: conduct, critique and utilisation*. WB Saunders.

22   Cormack D (1996) *The Research Process in Nursing* (3e). Blackwell Science.

23   Denzin NK and Lincoln NS (1994) *Handbook of Qualitative Research*. Sage Publications.

24   Field P and Morse J (1996) *Nursing Research: the application of qualitative approaches* (2e). Stanley Thornes.

25   Miles MB and Huberman AM (1994) *Qualitative Data Analysis: an expanded sourcebook* (2e). Sage Publications.

26   Polit-O'Hara D and Hungler B (1998) *Nursing Research: principles and methods* (6e). Lippincott.

27   Robson C (1993) *Real World Research: a resourcebook for social scientists and practitioner researchers*. Blackwell Science.

28   Silverman D (1993) *Interpreting Qualitative Data: methods for analysing talk, text and interaction*. Sage Publications.

29   Strauss A and Corbin J (1998) *Basics of Qualitative Research: techniques and procedures for developing grounded theory*. Sage Publications.

30   Yin RK (1994) *Case Study Research: design and method*. Sage Publications.

31   Chalmers I and Altman DG (1995) *Systematic Reviews*. BMJ Books.

32 Swinscow TDV (1996) *Statistics at Square One* (revised by M Campbell). BMJ Books.

33 Li Wan Po A (1998) *Dictionary of Evidence-based Medicine*. Radcliffe Medical Press.

34 Sackett DL (1991) *Clinical Epidemiology: a basic science for clinical medicine*. Little, Brown & Co.

35 Streiner DL and Norman GR (1996) *PDQ Epidemiology*. Mosby.

36 Ridsdale L (ed) (1998) *EBP in Primary Care*. Churchill Livingstone.

37 Tarling M and Crofts L (1998) *The Essential Research Handbook for Nurses and Health Care Professionals*. Bailliere Tindall.

38 Greenhalgh T and Hurwitz B (1998) *Narrative Based Medicine*. BMJ Books.

39 Blaster L, Hughes C and Tight M (1996) *How to Research*. Open University Press.

40 Mays N and Pope C (eds) (1999) *Qualitative Research in Health Care*. BMJ Books.

41 Rowntree D (1982) *Statistics Without Tears*. Macmillan.

42 Gordis L (1996) *Epidemiology*. WB Saunders.

Other Radcliffe Medical Press titles

Chambers R (1998) *Clinical Effectiveness Made Easy*

Eccles M and Grimshaw J (eds) (2000) *Clinical Guidelines From Conception to Use*

Humphris D and Littlejohns P (eds) (1999) *Implementing Clinical Guidelines: a practical guide*

Hutchinson A and Baker R (eds) (1999) *Making Use of Guidelines in Clinical Practice*

Mathers N, Williams M and Hancock B (eds) (2000) *Statistical Analysis in Primary Care* PRIMARY CARE RESEARCH SERIES

Roberts R (1999) *Information for Evidence-based Care* HARNESSING HEALTH INFORMATION SERIES

Saks M, Williams M and Hancock B (eds) (2000) *Developing Research in Primary Care* PRIMARY CARE RESEARCH SERIES

Wilson A, Williams M and Hancock B (eds) (2000) *Research Approaches in Primary Care* PRIMARY CARE RESEARCH SERIES

Index